DOUBLE EXPOSURE

Cultural Memory

in

the

Present

Mieke Bal and Hent de Vries, Editors

DOUBLE EXPOSURE

Cutting Across Buddhist and Western Discourses

Bernard Faure

Translated by Janet Lloyd

STANFORD UNIVERSITY PRESS

STANFORD CALIFORNIA

2004

Stanford University Press
Stanford, California

This book has been published with the assistance of the
French Ministry of Culture—National Center for the Book.

Double Exposure was originally published in French
in 2000 under the title *Bouddhismes, Philosophies et Religions,*
© 2000, Flammarion.

English translation © 2004 by the Board of Trustees
of the Leland Stanford Junior University

Printed in the United States of America
On acid-free, archival-quality paper

Library of Congress Cataloging-in-Publication Data

Faure, Bernard.
[Bouddhismes, philosophies et religions. English]
Double exposure : cutting across Buddhist and western discourses /
Bernard Faure ; translated by Janet Lloyd.
    p.   cm. — (Cultural memory in the present)
  English and French.
  ISBN 0-8047-4347-9 (cloth)—
  ISBN 0-8047-4348-7 (paper)
    1. Buddhism and philosophy.   2. Buddhism—Relations.
3. Buddhism—China.   I. Lloyd, Janet.   II. Title.
III. Series.
BQ4600.F3713 2003
181'.043—DC21

                                              2003005749

Original Printing 2004

Last figure below indicates year of this printing:
13   12   11   10   09   08   07   06   05   04

Typeset by Tim Roberts in 11/13.5 Adobe Garamond

Contents

Prologue ix

1 Do We Know What Buddhism Is? 1
2 Buddhism and Rationalities 18
3 Buddhism and Chinese Thought 49
4 A Hybrid Teaching 64
5 The Major Schools 86
6 "Transcendental" Concepts 101
7 Twofold Truth 125
8 External Thought 142
  Epilogue: After All ... 173

Pronunciation of Sanskrit, Chinese,
  and Japanese Sounds 175
Notes 177
Bibliography 183
Index 191

Prologue

Buddhism, it is said, is in fashion. So much the better, or perhaps the worse. The present interest in Buddhist "spirituality" results from a misunderstanding. The attraction of Buddhism probably stems from the fact that it seems strangely familiar to us: familiar because, like Western thought, it stems from an Indo-European ideology; strange because it is misunderstood. Buddhism, as a historical tradition, needs to be distinguished from the various versions of Neobuddhism, which relate to Buddhism much as the *Reader's Digest* relates to literature.

Buddhism, lofty philosophical thought that, however, manages to keep its feet on the ground, provides us with a way of overall thinking about what, to us Westerners, is characterized by an antinomy (that of "faith or reason," "idealism or materialism"), for, as we will soon see, in the realm of Buddhist double truth, there is no excluded middle; the old choices are wide of the mark. In the first place, Buddhism is not only a philosophy, but also a religion, and not just the kind of purified and unpindownable religion, cut off from all context and all true transcendence, that is known as spirituality. No: a real religion, with its myths and its rites, its cosmology and its mysteries. And, as if that were not enough, it is also—indeed, some would say above all—a psychosomatic discipline, a technique both physical and mental that is in some respects close to psychoanalysis, but in others distant from it.

All in all, Western philosophy is closely circumscribed. The ancient paths along which it used to be possible to roam freely have become obligatory routes leading to the mausoleums of Plato, Kant, Hegel, and Heidegger and now constitute superhighways of thought, complete with toll booths and fast-food stops along the way. We find our way in thought by making for these reassuring landmarks, forgetting that the primary requirement for all true thought should be to call our mental habits into question and thereby disorient us.

Our culture seeks to slough off a transcendence in which it no longer believes, but that nevertheless remains buried deep in our language games, constantly reasserting itself in our ethical demands. We have shifted from a vertical transcendence to a horizontal one, the transcendence of great ethical principles, but basically our mental reflexes remain unchanged. Buddhism lends itself rather better to thought that is decentered, disseminated, pagan, or polytheistic, thought that some might call "postmodern." Taking an interest in Buddhist thought does not mean "becoming Buddhist" through a conversion that would still imply belief in some "transcendent" truth. All that it means is seeing that our questions could—in many cases quite easily—be posed differently. It means realizing that we are, in some respects, already Buddhist, or rather that Buddhism is one of the cultural manifestations of virtualities that we possess, but have too long repressed in the name of certain Greek and/or Christian concepts of our identity. Certainly we speak more and more of an identity crisis, but nativist ideology lags behind the reality against which it claims to be reacting. Despite all our protestations, our thought is by now already truly hybrid—probably always has been. Philosophical attempts to make clean-cut epistemological breaks and to purge formal discourse change nothing: Beneath the paving stones of logical discourse stretch the sands of imaginary representations, with all their associations, which are "as numerous as the grains of sand of the Ganges." If, moving on from the Greeks to the Romans, the Jews, and the Arabs, Western thought has been contaminated, this has generally been to its advantage. The violence of racist reactions reveals (or rather attests) the amplitude of the sociological, psychological, and intellectual mutations currently pervading our societies.

Buddhism is itself double, hybrid, bastardized. On the one hand, it is a powerful intellectual system with tendencies both rationalist and abstract, almost structuralist and universalist. On the other, it is a form of local, pagan, quasi-shamanistic thought. By the same token, it is irreducibly plural. As the eminent Indianist Paul Mus has remarked, there are not just two, but at least half a dozen Buddhisms. It is purely to simplify the language and, as it were, "in quotes," that I use the singular and the "ethnographic present" (in expressions such as "Buddhism thinks that"), where I should really each time use a clearer formulation such as "the Buddhists of such or such a school, such or such a tendency, such or such a period, such or such a place, thought that . . . " But I will leave the reader to supply the plurals where necessary.

The epistemological reasons that favor a rediscovery of Buddhism are supported by others of a geopolitical nature. The economic and political factors that, in the eyes of some and in the past, may have justified the arrogance of colonial Europe and its sense of intellectual superiority have now disappeared. The Westernization of the world is, in return, opening up the West to external influences on an unprecedented scale. The encounter with other cultures and the discovery—joyful or horrified—that they, too, think and have put up with Western pretensions for far too long lead one to reconsider the privileges up until now granted to certain dominant forms of rationality. Such a revision is also encouraged by the tragic "dialectic of enlightenment" that, from the eighteenth century to the black suns of Auschwitz and Hiroshima, have led us to call into question our naïve belief in scientific progress.

In the pages that follow, I would like to examine the possible relations between Western rationality and Buddhism in its twofold philosophical and religious aspect. In no way do I recommend a kind of "concordism" between Western and Buddhist thought. My aim is simply, on the one hand, to pick out from our Western thought certain more or less concealed elements that might render this or that aspect of Buddhism more accessible and, on the other hand, to see whether certain Buddhist notions, through the slight shift that they may prompt in our own habitual ways of thinking, might not lead us to reformulate a number of the classical problems of Western thought.

Some of the questions that arise (for me) are the following: Can Buddhism be introduced, on an equal footing, without condescension or fetishism, into Western philosophical discourse? Is it possible to establish a real philosophical dialogue (with no confessional connotations)? How can we integrate or at least open ourselves up to certain Buddhist notions without overadulterating them? Can such a graft be effected without slipping back into the myths of an "Oriental Renaissance" and without repeating all the old Orientalist scenarios? How far can we follow the reasoning of Buddhism without becoming trapped in it? And, from the contrary point of view, are there grounds for submitting Buddhism to external critiques, without—however—seeking to reduce it to extrinsic norms? In other words, can we, here and now, embark on thinking with Buddhism as our point of departure?

I will not dwell upon the debates that bewitched the early years of the twentieth century, in particular those outdated efforts to distinguish between science, magic, and religion. If I return to the unimaginative question "Is Buddhism a philosophy or a religion?" it is not in order to plunge through a door that is already ajar, but to underline the implications of such a question that are usually ignored. First of all, I would like to show that Buddhism not only thinks, but is "good to think with." There is a kind of Buddhist philosophy that has managed to pose some of the same questions as Western philosophy (and a number of others, too) and to produce answers to them that are different, but just as pertinent, or that has proceeded along certain paths that we did not even know existed. But I must also emphasize that Buddhism also acts. It is thought in action (in particular, ritual action).

After doing away with a few old Orientalist clichés, I will try to claim a space of its own for Buddhism, equidistant from a purely philosophical understanding (which, despite the best of intentions, is often reductionist) and from a naïve faith frequently manipulated by ideologues of the New Age type.

As we will see, Buddhism, as a system of philosophical thought, is founded upon the two-truths theory: conventional, worldly truth, and also ultimate, supramundane truth. That may seem strange to us, accustomed as we are to thought founded upon the dogmatic intransigence of Jewish or Christian monotheism and the Greek logic of the excluded middle, according to which if one of two contradictory propositions is true, the other is necessarily false. Nevertheless, Buddhist thought is perfectly systematic, and its ontological and epistemological findings deserve our attention.

As a religion advocating a relationship with the absolute that is sometimes direct, sometimes mediated, Buddhism is not the variant of "Eastern mysticism" with which it is all too frequently identified. It is not simply a return to the "oceanic feeling" of a natural mysticism, but a consequential attempt to acquire a deeper understanding of reality, making the most of all our human faculties, both physical and mental.

As a moral doctrine, Buddhism has developed certain virtues, such as compassion. Buddhist compassion includes not only the human race, but all living creatures. Despite an initial tendency to condemn the world of the senses, Buddhism has, in this way and thanks to its contacts with the cultures of China and Japan, managed to produce an system of ecological thought in advance of its time.

As a symbolic system, Buddhism reveals to us an *imaginaire* of remarkable richness. One of the tasks that face us is that of opening up Buddhist mythology to questions relating to cultural anthropology, bypassing the traditional kind of symbolic analysis.

Finally, we must not ignore the fact that, as an ideology, Buddhism (like most religions and many philosophies) has frequently led to thinking and practices associated with power—and also with counterpower. Depending on the circumstances, it has been linked sometimes with the various forms of sacred royalty that have prevailed in Asia (for instance, the Japanese imperial system), sometimes with millenarianist utopias and popular revolts. As we demystify such ideological themes, we must therefore draw attention to some of the social, political, and economic principles than underpin the Buddhist doctrine.

In this book, I mean to give not so much an objective and erudite account of Buddhism, but a personal reflection prompted by the confrontation of the two poles of my research (the one Western, the other Asian). I aim to review certain classic themes of Western thought in the light of Buddhist thought. My starting point could well be the advice proffered by the sociologist Marcel Mauss: "First, we must draw up the fullest possible list of categories, starting with all those that men are known to have used. We will then see that there have been and still are plenty of dead, pale, or dark moons in the firmament of reason." I will be suggesting that some of the stars rising in our firmament are Buddhist. However, as will soon become clear, I am not proposing to write an apology for Buddhism. Some readers may even judge my critique of certain of its aspects to be somewhat iconoclastic, but it is inspired, I hope, by an iconoclasm of a truly Buddhist nature. Furthermore, it seems to me that a digression by way of Buddhist thought offers a means of reintegrating large swaths of our own philosophical heritage. Not only is this thought, like our own, of Indo-European origin, but the pure philosophy in the name of which people tend to exclude the thinking of Asia itself also relegates to the shadows a considerable proportion of our Western heritage.

When all is said and done, no one is beyond criticism, as the following anecdote suggests:

At a mountain temple there were four monks who wished to experience the Reality which is beyond words and practice the silence of Vimalakīrti.

Vowing their intention, the four adorned the practice hall, and, cutting off the myriad worldly attachments and quieting the activities of body, word, and thought, they entered the hall to begin seven days of silence. A single attendant had access to the room.

It had grown late and the night was dark. Seeing that the lamp was about to go out, the monk in the lowest seat called out: "Attendant. Raise the taper!"

"In the hall of silence there is to be no talking," said the monk seated next to him.

The monk in the third rank was extremely annoyed at hearing the two speaking. "You have lost your senses!" he cried.

The old monk in the senior seat thought it shameful and irritating that the others had spoken out, though each had done so for different reasons. "I alone have said nothing!" he remarked, nodding his head. With his superior air he looked especially foolish.

When we consider this incident, we are reminded that for everyone it is difficult to avoid such attitudes.[1]

DOUBLE EXPOSURE

Do We Know What Buddhism Is?

The Indian: "What can you expect? He has the prejudices of his country,
those of his party, and his own, too."
The Japanese: "Oh! That is altogether too many prejudices."
—Voltaire, *Philosophical Dictionary*

As early as 1925, the Belgian scholar Louis de la Vallée Poussin dismissed out of hand both "right-wing apologetic preoccupations," which sought to prove the superiority of Christian virtue and Aristotle's logic, and likewise "left-wing prejudices," which turned Buddhism into a rough draft of atheism, agnosticism, and pragmatism.[1] That Buddhist-like rejection of extremes is still very much to the point today. La Vallée Poussin concluded, "To plunge Buddhism into the waters of Lake Geneva, the Spree, or the Thames is to do it a great injustice." Despite that warning, and no doubt encouraged by the implantation of a Tibetan community in my own neighborhood of Périgord, I was seized by a desire to plunge Buddhism into the waters of the Dordogne, the majestic river whose name, reflecting the meeting of two Auvergnat streams, the Dore and the Dogne, put me in mind of the confluence of the two Buddhist truths.

Within the confines of this work, it is not possible to give a full account of the history of the Buddhist doctrines and communities, so, as a first approach, I would recommend that readers consult the works of popularization that have already appeared on the subject. I will be emphasizing in particular two tendencies that seem to realize many of the potentialities of Buddhist thought and that at the same time reveal the dangers of any radical interpretation: Chan/Zen and Tantrism (or Vajrayāna). I will use the term "Chan" alongside or instead of "Zen" to remind readers of the Chinese origin of this movement.

Buddhism Forgotten

In a work entitled *L'oubli de l'Inde* (India forgotten), Roger-Pol Droit noted the paradoxical amnesia that seems to have characterized Western culture with regard to Indian thinking, and Buddhism in particular. More recently, in his *Le culte du néant* (The cult of nothingness), he has logged the various phases of that amnesia. What is the explanation for this strange phenomenon? First, the disaffection that the second half of the nineteenth century manifested toward India in reaction against the Romantics' enthusiasm for the "Oriental Renaissance": after all, in the days of high colonialism, neither India nor Buddhism could aspire to take the place of Greece and Christianity. Moreover, the colonial conquests were marked by a scorn that, in many cases, however, went hand in hand with a condescending appreciation of those colonies' past cultural greatness. In the field of Western imaginary representations, only Tibet, which escaped colonization, managed to carve out for itself the preeminent place that it still holds today. Finally, on the philosophical level, the Buddhist doctrine found itself unhappily classified under the heading of "nihilism," an error that was encouraged as much by a complacent ignorance as by the anti-Buddhist polemics of Christian missionaries. We are still suffering from the effects of this polemical distortion. "Buddhist philosophy," let alone Buddhist *culture*, are still not fully accepted in the West, and Buddhist "spirituality" often remains the province of fanciers of exoticism.

R.-P. Droit dates the epistemological rift that gave birth to Buddhism as a scientific object of inquiry to around 1820.[2] That rift was a real one, but it tends to mask the ongoing continuity of a more or less subtle Orientalist attitude and of tenacious prejudices that so-called scientific "objectivity" in many instances simply conceals. The "objectivity" in question was certainly not innocent of passing value judgments. To parody Karl von Clausewitz's "War is the continuation of politics by other means," you could say that the science of philology was Orientalism "by other means" just as Orientalism was already colonialism "by other means"—more dilute of course, but certainly Orientalism. It was a way of exonerating oneself at little cost and yet again reducing the unknown to the known (just as the missionaries, in their own way, did). To some degree, the same applies to the apostles of post-Orientalism. The debate over one particular book (Edward Saïd's *Orientalism*) and a chorus of mea culpas are not sufficient to put a definitive line through Orientalism, turn the page, and suddenly accede to true understanding.

The history of the discovery of Buddhism by Europeans to some degree constitutes the reverse of that of the Enlightenment. In the eighteenth century, the Europe of the Enlightenment took to lending an ear to Confucian China, in which it fancied it had found a model of enlightened government. Knowledge of Buddhism was gleaned essentially from the "edifying and curious letters" of the Jesuit fathers, who were themselves influenced by the Confucian critique, so Buddhism did not enjoy a good press. Buddhist monks, an Oriental version of clerical obscurantism, were perceived by the *philosophes* as a pack of tricksters and slackers.

Things were to change in the nineteenth century, thanks to what contemporaries, perhaps somewhat hastily, called the "Oriental Renaissance." This renaissance was marked by the rediscovery of India, now hailed as the cradle of all civilizations, the gushing source of all mysticism.[3] Amid this enthusiasm for Indian culture, which lasted for more or less the first half of the century, Buddhism was at first overlooked, but was soon to take its revenge. The first hints of change were detectable as early as 1817 in a pamphlet produced by Michel-Jean-François Ozeray entitled *Recherches sur Bouddou ou Bouddhou, instituteur religieux de l'Asie orientale* (Researches on Bouddou or Bouddhou, religious teacher of East Asia), a work that turned the figure not yet known as Buddha into a "distinguished philosopher," rather than just another vague Asian deity.

The first Indian Buddhist texts were not translated until the midnineteenth century. At that time, everything in this doctrine looked very new, for the abundant information provided in the preceding centuries by the missionaries in China and Japan had been virtually forgotten. There did not appear to be anything in common between the uncouth "superstitions" of the Chinese Buddhists and the noble humanism of the Buddha. Indeed, the Buddhist doctrine, as was apparent now that it was becoming better understood (or so it seemed), even provided a weighty argument that could be used in anticlerical battles. In reaction, however, this infatuation with Buddhism was about to give rise to a trenchant rejection on the part of the defenders of Western culture. A case in point is Jules Barthélémy Saint-Hilaire, a disciple of Eugène Burnouf, the famous "Buddhologist" and a specialist in Greek philosophy, which, in his eyes, was the only true philosophy. As Saint-Hilaire slashed away at the doctrine of the Buddha, he was really aiming at the emulators of the "Buddhist" nihilist,

Schopenhauer. At this point a polemic erupted around the "cult of nothingness," a polemic for which Hegel, as early as 1827, had given the signal, attacking Buddhism for making *nirvāṇa* "the principle of everything, the ultimate, final goal and ultimate end of everything."

Slightly closer to our own times, in 1898, Paul Claudel was writing from Japan as follows: "But those blinded eyes refused to recognize unconditional being, and it fell to the one known as Buddha to round off the pagan blasphemy." According to Claudel, "the Buddha found only Nothingness, and his doctrine taught a monstrous communion." "For myself," he added, "I find that the idea of Nothingness is linked with that of *jouissance*. And therein lies the ultimate, Satanic mystery, the silence of a created being retreating into an integral rejection, the incestuous quietude of a soul complacently ensconced upon its own essential difference."[4] But fundamentally, all these warnings were concerned to ward off an inner evil, not to repulse an external "Buddhist peril." Like the lion in the Buddhist fable, Europe feared no external enemy and could perish only from the worms that devoured it from within.

Toward the end of the nineteenth century, such negative Orientalism was to be succeeded by a positive Orientalism. Buddhism, for so long vilified, was now praised to the skies. Despite those for whom the doctrine of the Buddha represented a danger to Western thought, a growing number of admirers of Buddhism found in it an antidote to Christianity. In reaction to various forms of Neobuddhism in which the persistent influence of the occultism of the Theosophical Society was detectable, a modernist Buddhism, purged of its cosmological, magic, and irrational elements now became a "religion of reason." In 1893, the World Parliament of Religions, an international congress of religious studies, was held in Chicago, and, for the first time, was open to non-Western religions. This brought Hinduism and Buddhism (or at least certain aspects of them) to the notice of American public opinion. It was in the context of this congress that the Japanese scholar D. T. Suzuki, who was later to become one of the great interpreters of Buddhist thought, began his work of popularization. For over half a century, he acted among Western intellectuals as the herald of Zen (the doctrine that, for him, represented the finest flower of "Oriental" thought) and of Japanese culture. Others followed his example, and gradually Buddhism became acclimatized to Western attitudes.

A Persistent Orientalism

Since the end of the nineteenth century, two major types of discourse on Buddhism have developed: Western discourse, frequently characterized either by a primary Orientalism (that is to say, a reductionist view of Eastern "otherness") or else by a secondary Orientalism (an exotic idealization of that otherness), and national variants of Asian discourse, either Tibetan or Japanese, themselves often impregnated by second-degree Orientalism (reacting against Western discourse, but still influenced by it). A typical case in point is that of the Japanese historian Naitō Kōnan (1866–1934) who, in his work entitled *Shina ron* (On China), declared: "This book aims to study China, for the good of the Chinese and in place of the Chinese." In effect, Naitō simply took over the formula of Karl Marx, who, in *The Eighteenth Brumaire of Louis Bonaparte*, declared that Orientals "cannot represent themselves, so must be represented." For the Japanese leaders of the Meiji period (1868–1912), Buddhism became a foreign ideology, the influence of which had to be reduced: on the one hand by wiping out all traces of premodern syncretism between Shinto and Buddhism, on the other by dividing Buddhism up into sectarian, isolated, rival institutions, as had already been attempted by the preceding regime of the Tokugawa (1600–1868). "Eastern" (Indian) Buddhism in this way came to be reviewed and corrected by a Westernized "Buddhology" that presented the various Buddhist schools as so many perfectly "demythologized" philosophies. In this sense, "philosophical" Buddhism is itself a myth, whereas "mythological" Buddhism, for its part, is in many respects a philosophy of life. But that is a dimension that disappears when the Buddhist doctrine is too hastily reduced to its philosophical content, to the detriment of its literary and symbolic aspects. That type of rationalism obscures the extent to which textual, meditative, and ritual systems intermesh within the tradition.

Nowadays the study of Buddhism tends to split into the history of the tradition and "pure philosophy." In the Western philosophical domain, the nonhistorical approach of those such as Ludwig Wittgenstein has certainly proved very fruitful in that it put an end to the routine production of "histories of philosophy." However, in the case of Buddhism, a negation of history (and of anthropology) turns out to be particularly dangerous, for it opens the door to a number of forms of Orientalism by dint of representing certain eminently cultural or ideological themes as simply self-evident, natural, and unproblematic.

Thus, certain scholars, such as D. T. Suzuki and his Western follow-ers, have praised the superiority of Eastern thought, suggesting it to be a panacea for all the ills of the West. Suzuki's way of presenting Zen to West-erners smacks of a certain condescension. Yet many aspects of the Zen ex-perience, as he describes it to his American disciples, are simply Japanese adaptations of the Christian "mystical experience," which his fascinated in-terlocutors are unable to recognize beneath its "Oriental trappings." In any case, this Zen is itself only a "reviewed and corrected" version of traditional Zen, a response to the challenges of modernization and a later version of the "Neobuddhism" of the Meiji period.

I, for my part, certainly do not set out to exalt any kind of "Oriental" thought. To be sure, I do sometimes stumble into the pitfalls that I am busy denouncing, for to criticize the Orientalism of others by no means en-sures that one is immune to it. Likewise, it is hard to avoid value judg-ments when dealing with abstractions such as "Western thought." Rather than allot blame or praise, what is important is to see whether, without overly taking sides, it is possible to graft certain Asian concepts onto our own modern or postmodern discourse. The goal is twofold: to "defamiliar-ize" Western thought and to demystify Buddhist thought, to render it philosophically operational by stripping it of its false "Oriental aura." Per-haps we could then consider these two systems of thought not as different species doomed either proudly to ignore each other or to observe each other covertly from a distance, but rather as distinct forms of rationality that, given a chance, might interact with each other. Instead of seeking to reduce the one to the other, we might on the contrary make the most of the "play" that exists between them and the difference in their perspectives, thereby introducing greater depth or relief into our field of vision. Such an approach would allow us to advance into open terrain and explore new do-mains without altogether losing sight of the points of reference with which we are familiar.

Hegel is perhaps the most authoritative source of current misunder-standings about Asia. According to him, India's is a culture in which there is nowhere to be found "any mediation or way to pass from the inside to the outside and thence back inside oneself." China, for its part, certainly does have a history, but nevertheless maintains "an immediate and para-lyzing tête-à-tête between the internal and the external." In Asia, thought "slips uselessly from abstraction and as it does so never becomes anything more, never matures." Therein, for Hegel, lies its fundamental difference from European thought. "It will never occur to the mind of a European to place sensible things so close to abstraction." As Maurice Merleau-Ponty points out, those views of Hegels still carry authority. They fuel the seemingly endless amazement that China, despite its long head start over Europe, never managed to produce a scientific or industrial revolution. Yet Merleau-Ponty remains a Hegelian when he concludes that "the West invented an idea of the truth that obliges and authorizes it to understand other cultures and so to recuperate them as moments of one overall truth."[5] He nevertheless makes a considerable concession when he admits:

The philosophies of India and China sought not to dominate existence, but rather to constitute an echo or resonator of our relations with being. Western philosophy could learn from them how to recover that relation with being, the initial option from which it was born; it could learn to appreciate the possibilities from which we have shut ourselves off by becoming "Western" and also, perhaps, how to open them up again.[6]

A Difficult Crossing

By "Western thought" we generally mean "European thought," or what Americans call "Continental thought." That thought sometimes has difficulties in crossing the Atlantic. In 1984, a Franco-American colloquium was held at Johns Hopkins University. Its title was, precisely, "Crossing the Atlantic." One of the main participants was Richard Rorty, a leader of American pragmatism and the author of a book that has enjoyed considerable success, *Philosophy and the Mirror of Nature*. The fourth page of the introduction to the French translation of this book informs us that Rorty "attempts to do for the entire Western *epistēmē* what Michel Foucault, in *The Order of Things*, did for the *epistēmē* of the seventeenth century." No less! Rorty conceives of the "dialogue" between Western culture (in this case, above all, trans-Atlantic culture) and other cultures as follows:

We [pragmatists] . . . may say that things have been going better in the West over the past few centuries and we may suggest how they might further improve in the centuries to come. But if we are asked what all this has to do with the Chinese or the Cashinahuas, all we can say is that, for all one knows, exchanges with these peoples may modify our Western conceptions of the types of institutions that may embody the spirit of social democracy more satisfactorily. We are waiting, rather vaguely, for a time when the Cashinahuas, the Chinese and (as the case may be) the Martians will be part of the same democratic community. No doubt that community will have different institutions from those to which we are accustomed today, but we think that they will incorporate and amplify the kind of reforms for which we applaud our liberal ancestors. The Chinese, the Cashinahuas, and the Martians may have suggestions as to other reforms to introduce, but we should adopt these only if they succeed in adjusting to our typically Western sociodemocratic aspirations, working from a basis of judicious mutual concessions. We pragmatists believe that this moderate ethnocentrism is both inevitable and fully justified.[7]

According to Rorty, cultural differences are all relative and are basically no different from those to be found within a single culture. But in this text he envisages only the differences between old and new "theories," that is to say, those dated to before and after the Enlightenment, and does not address the gap that might exist within a single culture between worldviews that are irreconcilable. He opts to replace force by persuasion in relations with other cultures, to turn clashes into litigation, and to attach "linguistic islands" to the continent. The credo of this liberal vicar calls to mind that of one of the characters in Philippe Curval's book *Regarde fiston s'il n'y a pas un extra-terrestre derrière la bouteille de vin* (Have a look, sonny boy, to see if there is not an extraterrestrial lurking behind the wine bottle), who declares: "I passionately desire to meet with other beings, other civilizations, and to understand them, on condition that I myself remain the same." Jean-François Lyotard, another participant in the trans-Atlantic colloquium, was far from sharing Rorty's optimism: "Between the Cashinahuas and ourselves there exists a difference in the genre of discourse, and it is a fundamental one."[8] In particular, he took exception to Rorty's "soft" or "conversational" imperialism and accused consensus through persuasion, as recommended by Rorty, of being nothing but a disguised form of violence.[9]

Any comparative enterprise would seem to involve a double standard. In the case in which we are interested, it is clear that Buddhist thought is not judged according to the same criteria as Western philosophy. Buddhist thought is criticized for being tinged with religion, mythology, and mysticism—as if philosophy itself had not, throughout its history, been exposed to the same kind of influences. If it is cultural conditioning that is in question, what philosophy can ever have claimed to escape it? Can Rorty conceive of any dialogue with other cultures in terms other than those of American liberalism? Analytical philosophy, too, is affected by language and culture. Some would even say that the Cartesian *cogito* itself amounted to no more than a language game.

One cannot oppose or compare two systems of thought—Western thought on the one hand, Buddhist thought on the other—point by point. There are many reasons why that is so, the principal being that neither "thought" can be reduced to a "pure philosophy." Or rather, even if they have sought to purge themselves of all dross, in reality, they have been affected by many kinds of influences from a cultural context that they have, in return, helped to modify. Buddhist thought cannot be reduced to the philosophy of the Buddha. Nor can Western thought be reduced to philosophy.

The Western tendency to line up arguments for and against, which is sometimes said to stem from the confrontational warfare of the Greek phalanxes, is traceable in attempts to compare Western and Buddhist thought. A telling example is provided by the attitude that results in declaring that, once Buddhist thought has been reduced to its simplest expression, there really is nothing new about it. But why should we expect from Buddhist thought, thus caricatured, what we never demand of any Western philosophy, namely, that it should astonish and disorient us? Why not focus on the features that might enable it to be integrated into philosophical discourse and even to enrich the latter by radically questioning its premises?

The Authority Argument

It is said that the cowl never made the monk; nor, for sure, did it ever make a Buddhist master. The first Buddhist virtue is to reject all authority; the second is to obey one's superiors (or the other way round). One should beware of the "Panglossian" side of certain Buddhists. We recall Voltaire's Doctor Pangloss ("All Talk") who, amid the smoldering ruins of the Great Earthquake of Lisbon, explained to his disciple Candide that they were living, as Leibnitz's formula put it, "in the best of all possible worlds." To wish to change reality is to refuse, in the name of some ideal, to accept it. To accept it is, in some cases, to do as Pangloss does, but it may equally be to affirm life "despite everything."

It is essential to question even the reductionist interpretations that some Buddhist masters and their disciples provide for their doctrine. To parody the well-known quip, one might almost say that Buddhism is too important to be left to the Buddhists, since they are members of a religious orthodoxy, even if they reject that description. Understandably enough, Western experts on Buddhism usually place more emphasis on personal experience than on doctrine. Paradoxically, however, they tend to take refuge behind doctrinal generalities when questioned about their own experiences. Before accepting their normative description of awakening, it would be desirable to be sure that these Neobuddhist sages truly have themselves experienced what they describe. Without a priori denying the possibility of such experiences, we should surely note that those who lay claim to them for the most part remain in the domain of belief. Because I cannot myself claim to be a part of any orthodoxy or to speak in its name, I prefer to dwell upon what ought to go without saying, namely, that what I will be writing about is Buddhism as I see it, and that my interpretation, like all interpretations, is largely subjective.

Far from Shangri-la

Tibetan Buddhism, along with Japanese Zen, constitutes one of the main references of Western Neobuddhism. It was carried to the forefront of the political and cultural scene by the Tibetan tragedy, against a backdrop constituted by the Romantic image of Shangri-la, the mystical Himalayan paradise closed to all foreign influences. As a politico-religious institution, Tibetan Buddhism has been exonerated of its past, thanks to its identification with the person of an exceptional spiritual and political leader, the fourteenth Dalai Lama, Tenzin Gyatso. The present success that Tibetan Buddhism enjoys stems above all from the intense media coverage of this charismatic figure, who, in the eyes of worldwide opinion, has come to represent the cause of the entire oppressed Tibetan people. Despite the inevitable distortions to which it leads, the intense publicity that the Dalai Lama tolerates can be justified from a strategic point of view—and at any rate seems to produce more results than official diplomacy does. All the same, the personality cult that some of his Western disciples devote to him seems, several decades on, uncannily to echo the exalted prayer formulated by Antonin Artaud: "We are all your most faithful servants, O Great Lama; pray give us, bestow upon us, your enlightenment."

It is also fair to wonder to what degree the Dalai Lama, despite his sincere ecumenicism, is really representative of traditional Tibetan Buddhism, let alone of other forms of Buddhism. At a purely doctrinal level, he initially represented one specific school, that of Gelugpa, which came to predominate over the rest only after much sectarian rivalry. In this respect, the controversy currently dividing the Tibetan community in exile is significant.[10] The Dalai Lama recently banned the cult of a wrathful deity known as Dorje Shugden. This might be regarded as no more than an admirable decision made by a modernist mind struggling against "superstitions." But unfortunately the situation is not so simple. The deity in question, a protector of the Gelugpa school, is extremely popular in Tibetan Buddhism and was for many years revered by the Dalai Lama himself. The decision to prohibit his cult was made only following an oracle emanating from another deity, that of the Nechung monastery, a recognized protector of the Dalai Lama and his advisor in all important matters (for example, his decision, in 1959, to flee Tibet). So what in truth is involved here is a struggle between two deities and between two currents of Tibetan Buddhism, with the Dalai Lama caught in the middle. This internal quarrel has already produced particularly dire effects. The Chinese authorities, quick to see their interest in the matter, hastened to condemn the Dalai Lama for his intolerance toward an innocent deity—they who, for the past five decades, have been mercilessly persecuting local superstitions. The Dalai Lama's partisans, for their part, tried to smother the affair. However, taking a realistic view of the situation does not mean falling in with the stratagems of Chinese imperialism. In the long term, the cause of the Tibetan people has nothing to gain from an idealized conception of Tibetan Buddhism.

At this point, a little history, not all of it contemporary, may be helpful to our understanding of what is really at stake here. The Chinese obsession with its control over the marches of the Middle Empire can be partially explained, but not justified, by a long history of invasions. The Tibetans have not always been the pacific people whom we recognize today. In the past, they threatened China on several occasions, and in the eighth century even captured the Chinese capital. Subsequently, when the Mongols came to power in China in the thirteenth century, Tibeto-Mongol "Lamaism" became the official ideology in Beijing, the new capital. It was this spurt of Tibetan Buddhism in China, at the time of Marco Polo, that was used to justify China's first attempt to seize political control of Tibet.

The Western imagination has long been fascinated by the belief in the reincarnation of the lamas of Tibet. This is the belief that always dom-

inates discussions of the rationality or irrationality of Buddhism. Yet it
needs to be replaced in its specific cultural context. It is limited to Tibet
and the kingdoms neighboring it and has played virtually no role in either
Indian Buddhism or Indianized or Sinicized forms of Buddhism. In Tibet
itself, it was only in the fifteenth century, with the emergence of the institution of the Dalai Lama, that it assumed its full predominance. In particular, it enabled the fifth Dalai Lama to affirm his control over the
monasteries of other Buddhist schools and, with the support of the Mongols, to become the divine ruler of Tibet. The present Dalai Lama is regarded as his distant reincarnation and also as a manifestation of Avalokiteśvara, the mythical progenitor of the Tibetan race. This bodhisattva
(literally "being of awakening"), characterized by his compassion, vowed
to save all beings before he entered into *nirvān a* and subsequently became one of the Buddhist figures most revered in East Asia. The theory of
the reincarnation of the Dalai Lamas is simply a local development of the
doctrine of *karma*, which, in truth, is not specific to Buddhism. We would
do well to avoid confusing the doctrinal purity of Tibetan Buddhism, its
philosophical and religious superiority, and the political rights of the Tibetan people.

A Number of Other Purveyed Ideas

As we have seen, Buddhism is not solely Tibetan or even "Indo-Ti-
betan." It is also "Indo-Chinese" and "Sino-Japanese." From one point of
view, it is certainly tempting to concentrate primarily on Tibet and Japan,
each positioned at one of the two extremities of East Asia: In both countries, Buddhism made its appearance at the precise time when the state was
taking shape (one cannot really speak of Tibet or of Japan as entities before
the middle of the first millennium, that is to say, some ten centuries after
the time of the Buddha). So it was rapidly adopted as the official ideology
of both these new states. A similar phenomenon later occurred in various
other countries of East Asia. In contrast, at the beginning of the common
era, it took several centuries for Buddhism to become adapted to the Chinese culture, which was already highly developed and convinced of its own
superiority. It was this significantly Sinicized Buddhism that was transmitted to Korea and Japan, and also to Vietnam.

Is the Buddhist doctrine a form of pacifism? You could well believe it,
listening to the declarations of the Dalai Lama, who is constantly remind-

ing his more impetuous disciples of the virtues of nonviolence. Similarly, for Walpola Rahula, a specialist of Buddhist philosophy, Buddhism is "purely human," and that explains its tolerance, which, he claims, is the reason why "not one drop of blood has been shed in the two-thousand-five-hundred-year history of Buddhism." The Jesuit missionary Matteo Ricci made the very same claim for Christianity to his Chinese interlocutors, who, however, remained somewhat skeptical. Certainly, the emphasis that Buddhism places on compassion and detachment ought, in principle, to find expression in an attitude of nonaggression. But Buddhism's relations with war are complex. In the countries where it constituted the official ideology, it was expected to support all bellicose initiatives. Furthermore, Tantric Buddhism has developed a whole arsenal of magical techniques designed to overcome demons, and governments have always been tempted to assimilate their enemies to demonic hordes and to try to prevail over them by ritual warfare. Similarly, Buddhism, in its darker moments, has sometimes sought to eradicate local cults that stood in its way. In present-day India, finally, the Buddhist renewal results from the massive conversion of Untouchables transferring from Hinduism, and this tends to make it a religion of resentment. But overall, in this domain, it has been far more tolerant than other major religions or ideologies. It has seldom resorted to the notion of heresy and has never been led into the extremes of fanaticism that are so familiar in the West.

Should we see Buddhism as an atheistic humanism? That would be seriously to underestimate popular religiosity. In principle, to be sure, the Buddha is not a god, but in the reality of the cult he is often worshipped as a deity more powerful than all others. Unlike the latter, he can moreover create "Buddha fields" in which the faithful will be reborn, and this makes him a kind of demiurge—even if Buddhism rejects the notion of a creator. It is nevertheless fair enough to speak of humanism to the extent that, in early Buddhism, man was at the center of everything: The Buddha himself was perceived as a man who had realized all his human potentialities. Furthermore, as in the form of Buddhism called the Great Vehicle (*Mahāyāna*, in Sanskrit) by reason of its inclusive character, you could say that every human being is a potential Buddha—although that does not mean quite the same thing. Even beneath an animal or demonic mask—a mask that, alas, sticks to the skin—it is always a human being who transmigrates on the wheel of *karma*, passing in the course of innumerable lives through every degree of being. We should not be misled by the relatively humble status of the human condition as a fixed position on the ladder of beings: A human rebirth is the only kind that can eventually lead to deliverance. Other forms of rebirth (as demons, as animals, as gods, etc.) are basically simply dead ends. In this cosmic board game, even gods have to return to the square labeled "man" before they can accede to higher levels and leave the cycle of births and deaths forever.

The idea of an atheistic Buddhism is a tenacious countertruth (or at the very best a half-truth). The fact is that, according to the early Buddhist doctrine, atheism is an error, for it involves falling into an extreme. The idea results mainly from the rationalizations and extrapolations of historians incapable of grasping the reality of belief in all its complexity. It is a kind of "soft" dogma, a Buddhist *doxa* that mere observation of the day-to-day reality of Buddhist practices should suffice to dismiss.

Buddhism is not agnostic—let alone nihilistic. Indeed, in its Mahāyānist version, it is presented precisely as a form of access to reality, even a form of communication with the invisible. In some of its principal manifestations, it is an esoteric gnosis—quite the contrary of agnosticism. Nor, as is fortunately beginning to be understood, is it a kind of nihilism. Buddhism's "beyond good and evil" does not imply indifference to moral values, however much some Western experts, Schopenhauer for example, may in all good faith have believed it did.[11] Richard Welbon and R.-P. Droit have retraced the elaboration of this aberrant interpretation of *nirvāṇa*, which turns Buddhism into a nihilistic religion, a cult of nothingness. Nowadays, *nirvāṇa* no longer has such a bad press, and an institution such as the *Cahiers de l'Herne* has even devoted an entire issue to this theme—something that would have been unthinkable in past times. Nevertheless, the term continues, altogether mistakenly, to be bandied about on all sides—and not only with a psychoanalytic topping of the Freudian "nirvana principle," conceived as a desire for annihilation.

Is Buddhism at least an individualistic religion? If the Pāli tradition is to be believed, it initially stemmed from the spiritual quest of an individual whose teaching in time became first a religion, then a collective vision of the world. Nietzsche declared that a given thought should be judged according to its highest realizations. But in the case of Buddhism, to declare, as people often do, that that realization is nothing but an individual spiritual quest would be to underrate all Buddhism's collective and cultural aspects. A Catholic arguing that the Mass was no more than a late aberration would no doubt be violently resisted on all sides by his fellows. Even the least theological of his critics would object that the Gregorian Masses and the liturgy of Suger constitute a kind of "total social fact," a harmonious synthesis of art and faith, incorporating a mixture of economic, psychological, political, social, and philosophical elements. One certainly condemns oneself to understanding very little about Catholicism if one fails to see that Scholasticism, the ritual of Mass, and cathedral art are all aspects of the same phenomenon. The same applies to Buddhism. The much vaunted art of the Zen gardens, for example, reflects more than just an individual meditation on nature and naturalness. It implies a whole collectivity, a religion, a culture.

Despite its inherent rationality, however, Buddhism was no prefiguration of modern science. Its apparent modernity in no way alters the fact that Buddhism is a fundamentally traditional vision of the world. The Buddhist cosmology and mythology are not superficial ornaments that are by now superfluous, as is suggested by some modernist reformers, partisans of a "Protestant" Buddhism that would better suit the needs of modernization. It may be true that a demythologization is called for or may even be inevitable. In fact, the process has already been under way for over a century in a number of Asian countries. But we must recognize that this affects the very heart of Buddhist thought and will be, already is, extremely costly. When you condemn "outdated" rituals that, however, are supported by popular fervor—rituals such as the bathing of an effigy of the child Buddha, as is practiced every spring—you risk throwing out the baby with the bathwater.

Buddhism is not simply a psychology, a "science of the mind." The psychological and moral aspects of Buddhism, which are generally pushed to the fore and taken completely out of context, stem from a particular religious vision of the world, a metaphysics, and a cosmology. The lived reality of Buddhism is not confined to the monastic elite that constitutes its most advanced and modernist avant-garde.

Buddhism is not solely, even if it is also, a *pure experience*, detached from everything else. It is, to be sure, a utopia (in the strict sense of a truth that is "nowhere" to be found), but is *at the same time* an institution. Neobuddhism, for its part, is sometimes doubly utopian, in the current sense of the term—as a rejection of reality, in particular the reality of contemporary society, but also the reality of traditional Buddhism, which is reckoned to be insufficiently "spiritual." Neobuddhist enthusiasts avert their eyes from prayer wheels and other embarrassing signs of "popular superstition," raising them up toward spiritual realities of a more sublime nature.

Those who think that to free Buddhism from myth is the way to attain liberty and autonomy are forgetting the disciplinary aspect of Buddhism, as expressed in particular by the voluminous canonical corpus of the Vinaya. Buddhism is not a libertarian doctrine. It is true that a number of libertarian interpretations have seen the light of day, for example among the "mad" mystics of Tantrism and Chan. But we would be mistaken if all that we noticed about these eccentrics (in the twofold sense of individuals both bizarre and marginal) was their transgression, without at the same time noting the strict rules that constitute its framework. In a society such as our own, where an absence of norms has become the rule and is itself quasi-normative, transgression takes on a quite different meaning; at any rate it loses its Buddhist meaning.

Buddhism is at once an internal experience and a social structure. There is no universal "mysticism": Such an abstraction is to concrete religions what Esperanto is to real languages. There may be phenomenological and structural constants to experience, but they in no way prejudge the tenor of that experience. It would be mistaken to believe that such experience transcends the cultural framework. If the absolute, or whatever passes for it, happens to manifest itself, it always does so in an eminently concrete fashion. It is not just that its linguistic expression, a posteriori, fashions it according to the cultural norms. Right from the start, the latter informs all perception, be it normal or supranormal. Like Buddhism, of which it is but one aspect, Zen may originally have intended to bypass all "-isms." But for all that, it, too, very soon became a system that, as such, can and should from time to time be called into question.

Buddhism, the Internet, and the New Age

When Buddhism made its appearance on the Internet, Western Buddhist devotees found themselves faced with a new dilemma. The lightning development of this new form of communication, with all its potentialities and dangers, the impossibility of knowing whether it will be able to maintain and bring to fruition the utopian generosity of its founders or will, instead, lead to the individual falling under the control of mercantilism and state powers in a milder, yet castrating version of George Orwell's Big Brother—all the above make it hard to tell whether Buddhism will emerge enriched or impoverished from the experience. Is the Internet a modern version of the Great Vehicle or Indra's Net, each mesh of which is adorned by a pearl that reflects all the others—thereby symbolizing the perfect interpenetration of all phenomena? Or is the cyberspatial "Web" rather a trap set for us by Māra, the Buddhist Tempter? Is virtual reality nothing but a real illusion? Both interpretative grids remain possible.

Matters are not much clearer where the New Age is concerned. This phenomenon, likewise of Californian origin, does not simply constitute a new way of adapting religion to local cultures. On the contrary, it involves submitting traditional ways of thinking to one sole form of thought, that of modern, capitalist logic. So in truth, it negates local cultures. Western Neobuddhism, which flirts with this tendency without fully identifying with it, is inclined to become simply one of many forms of spirituality, a Buddhism à la carte, digitalized, flavorless and odorless (rather as money is). The almost obsessional preoccupation with a purely internal spirituality among the Bouvards and Pécuchets of the New Age, whose position is apparently the polar opposite of one of submission to the ideology of the body and its desires (as diffused by worldwide publicity) is perhaps just another form of the "will to well-being" that characterizes their contemporaries. But perhaps we should qualify that judgment. If Buddhism is to root itself in Western societies, it must clearly adapt—and purists are likely to regard any adaptation as a bastardization. It is not possible to doubt the sincerity of those who, like the Vietnamese monk Thich Nath Hanh and the Dalai Lama, are trying to meet the challenge of modernity in order to preserve the achievements of tradition. The success of a film as reductionist as Bernardo Bertolucci's *Little Buddha* is surprising, even alarming, but at the same time, it certainly testifies to the interest aroused by Buddhism—a lasting interest that will survive the fashions and clichés of Hollywood.

2

Buddhism and Rationalities

The semantic field of reason (rationality, knowledge, truth, logic, etc.) constitutes a domain so vast that it claims to cover the whole of reality. It brings to mind the magician who asked his king for just enough room to spread out his cloak and, when granted this, spread out a cloak that covered the entire kingdom. As Hegel put it: "Everything rational is real, everything real is rational." Yet this field, like all others, can be defined only by its limits. We now need to undertake a rapid survey of those limits.

Reason has already been judged—if all we needed was a verdict of guilty or not guilty. But just as the process of justice is tortuous, so, too, is the process of gradually revealing how choices have been made and the orientations followed by Western thought, all the intermediate positions that have been forgotten and all the other possible choices that were not made. At the risk of belaboring the point, let me replay a speeded-up account of that process, for it is doubly important to my project. It is on the one hand the story of the impenitent application of a certain type of rationality that is irreducible and proud of being so (or rather of Being), disinclined to recognize its limits, that continues to block any real access to other types of rationality. On the other hand, it tells of a constant blackmail applied by reason, a logical Manicheanism that drives those who are disappointed or dissatisfied to turn to the opposite extreme.

Certainly, to put the Enlightenment on trial in the way that John Saul does in *Voltaire's Bastards*, a violent attack against the tyranny of rationalization that traces such single-minded thought back to Voltaire and

Rousseau, makes little sense. Conversely, however, a too hasty exoneration of the *philosophes* also seems suspect. Furthermore, among the critiques of reason, we should distinguish between the fundamentalist critique, with its propensity for *idées fixes*, and the postmodern critique, which is the surest antidote to all fundamentalisms. In some respects, the Buddhist position is close to the latter critique. Doubtless, the philosophy of the Enlightenment was initially neither a body of doctrine nor a system. The "Voltairian" optimism of Flaubert's Monsieur Homais and Bouvard and Pécuchet was never shared by Voltaire himself, nor by Rousseau or Diderot. The counsels for the prosecution in the trial of the Enlightenment appear to have invented much of their evidence. The witch-hunt in which they engage is not unlike those that they denounce. Nevertheless, the Enlightenment, as an ideological movement, continues to be influential, and the very least that can be said is that the movement has not always been as richly nuanced as the thinking of its founding fathers.

The partisans of unconditional rationalism often think that they can brush aside critics by dismissing them as incurable obscurantists and meanwhile forget to ask themselves to what extent the critique might be justifiable. If rationalism can be denounced only in the name of a certain kind of reason, it must be said that the denunciation of irrationalism, for its part, is often irrational. Any critique of reason comes up against a preliminary objection: Insofar as it claims to be arguing against a particular state of things, it is itself operating within the field of reason, and can therefore express itself only in the language peculiar to that field. But let us not dwell upon that objection, for it is valid only for those who adopt a Manichean viewpoint. If you try to pin down thought between the hammer and the anvil, you sacrifice all intermediary positions and all possibilities of mediation and chances of compromise. For my part, I would like to examine some of the constraints that bear upon so-called rational thought and tend to make it lose the thread of its arguments or to undermine its claims: in short, anything that creates in reason what Ambrose Bierce calls a propensity for "prejudice" and inclines it "to weigh possibilities in the scales of desire."

The Reason of the Strongest

For a long time, reason claimed a monopoly over the history of philosophy. But that is no longer the case. Times change, and with them, so, too, does the status of reason. In a world that has become multipolar, despite those who believe the contrary, the language of reason (logic) is used only as a lingua franca by bilingual intellectuals—who thereby gain the advantage of being able to play upon or according to a number of different norms. Martin Heidegger once told a Japanese interlocutor that a dialogue with Asian thought could come only after the necessary dialogue with Greek thought. But it could be argued that the converse is true: It is through the mediation of Chinese thought (itself, as we now know, a thought of the detour) or of other Asian ways of thinking that, by dint of illuminating some of our own a priori positions, we may regain the access to Greek thought that (according to Heidegger) we have lost.[1]

Merleau-Ponty hoped that the "great rationalism" of the Enlightenment would be succeeded by a wider kind of reason that would be able to penetrate as far as the irrationality of magic and gift giving. It is worth noting, however, that for him, it was a matter of penetration (a metaphor that is still aggressive), rather than of opening up, although his intention was to write "in praise of philosophy" (which was indeed the title of his book). All the same, progress had been made. As a result of prematurely narrowing its inquiry, philosophy made it possible to establish something "other" that was not reason. Yet we should beware of an excessive rationalism that believes it can explain everything and imagines that otherness can always be reduced to what is the same, with nothing left over. That would be to forget too hastily the dark side found in all reality. "Great reason" needs to recognize its limits, to extend the field of what is known, to be sure, but then to halt before the unknown and, in particular, not bury the monuments of other civilizations beneath the sands of its self-identificatory discourse. The golden age of philosophy, in which reason was confused with an understanding of objective causality, is well and truly over. We now know how much that reason owed to history and to the particular state of capitalist society and Western culture. A philosopher knows that she is irreversibly caught up in that historical process, with no fixed point of rest from which, like Archimedes, she could playfully lift up the world. All things considered, it would probably be best to abstain definitively from any "great rationalism" and accept the existence of a whole scattering of rationalities.

There is one domain of Western rationality that has expressly devoted itself to understanding other cultures: namely, anthropology, with its discourse not so much on mankind in general, but rather on just a fraction of humanity, other people who have not yet acceded fully to the privilege enjoyed by modern Westerners, that is to say, full rationality, or philosophy. There is a fundamental grain of truth in the definition produced by Ambrose Bierce, who describes ethnology as "the science that treats the various tribes of Man, as bandits, robbers, swindlers, dunces, lunatics, idiots, and ethnologists." For confirmation of that opinion, one has only to reread Michel Leiris's *L'Afrique fantôme* (Phantom Africa), in which he describes the Dakar-Djibouti ethnological mission in which he took part from 1931 to 1933. There is something predatory about anthropological reason and about the look that Westerners cast upon others, all those of other cultures, one of whose shortcomings is to find themselves "preyed upon" by the sacred.

To be sure, ethnology as a discipline stemmed from the desire of the *philosophes* of the Enlightenment to reduce human differences by reintegrating "primitive" cultures into the great evolutionist schema—which was also used to justify missionary and colonial enterprises. Although anthropology often acted hand in glove with colonialism, it did affirm the dignity of "savage thought" and helped to reduce the racist prejudices of the West.[2] Nonetheless, the West continued to regard the domain of "pure," rational thought as its own particular preserve, meanwhile conceding to other cultures at least the right to opinions or views in the domain of aesthetics.

It was in order to distance itself more from mythical thought, epistemologically to cut itself off from the latter, that anthropological discourse sought inspiration from the scientific model. But the genealogy of scientific thought itself is somewhat problematic, insofar as origins are to be found in religious thought. The epistemologist Nayla Farouki has detected profound affinities between monotheist transcendence and the principles of philosophy and science, which she calls "transcendentals." Divine transcendence implies that God has withdrawn from nature. That withdrawal discloses a whole expanse of reality that becomes accessible to science. Nature is disaffected: It has become a huge wasteland that is no longer the primary source of what affects us. Nevertheless, science is not simply the daughter of theology. Although both movements developed from the same tendency, the opposition between monotheism and modern science remains profound.

Paul Valéry recommended "muzzling Reason," for according to him, the word "reason" (derived from *ratio*, measure) was synonymous with "to muzzle."³ The partisans of reason, among whom he in any case included himself, can always reply that to think against reason is still to think with it. But that point should not prevent us from drawing a distinction between rationality and rationalism or from being wary of the pretensions of the latter. There is no longer any reason for rationality to be narrowly Cartesian or Kantian. As has already been pointed out, other forms of rationality do exist, non-Western ways of philosophizing, some of which are quite close to our own Western way. Each has its own merits and defects. The dominant intuition of Western thought might at the same time constitute its blind spot. Light, while making it possible to see, is always likely to dazzle when it is too bright.

What we call "philosophizing" frequently does no more than retrace the history of philosophy. It is true that, except in a few rare cases, such as that of Wittgenstein, one can hardly consider oneself a philosopher if one has not paid tribute to one's ancestral lineage. Perhaps there is an element of magic in that invocation of the great ancestors. Even Wittgenstein, who so proudly paid no attention to that history of philosophy, was quickly recuperated by it (just as Socrates, the false ignoramus, had been long before). Whatever you say, philosophy is first and foremost a tradition. Every tabula rasa presupposes that of Descartes. You cannot proceed as though he never existed, or as though a number of others never did. To ignore them is still to claim descent from them.

Perhaps the same goes for reason as for so many other notions: You think you are speaking of the same thing and retracing its history, whereas in truth you are speaking of a number of distinct things that have nothing in common but their name. The Enlightenment's mistake was to have us believe in the existence of one single, indivisible Reason, where all that there was were various particular forms of rationality—which were not like fragments of a Greek amphora that needs to be reconstructed, but represented so many new creations, so many paths leading to the unknown. And, as Confucius says (more or less), it is man who, by using it, makes the path; he does not simply follow it.

The history of philosophy is purely Western. It is a lengthy account that leads us from Socrates and his obscure predecessors all the way to the Enlightenment and its brilliant heirs. But what if that history were merely a footnote to Plato, as has somewhat maliciously been suggested? However, footnotes generally have the merit of brevity, whereas what we have before us is an interminable commentary on Platonism, the paradoxical "doctrine of Socrates." Not that that prevents some scholars from tracking back to the Presocratics, in particular to the Parmenides-Heraclitus pair, the break that determined the history of a philosophy that opted for Parmenidean being rather than Heraclitean becoming. Had it plumped for the Heraclitean alternative, we might never have acquired our current interest in Buddhism, which is also a philosophy of becoming.

Socrates is sometimes said to have "killed" Parmenides, but even so, he was his heir. By anticipating slightly, it is possible to speak of Socrates' "double truth": "Out of Socratic thought, pursued in two different directions which in Socrates were complementary, came the Cyrenaic and the Cynic doctrines. . . . They developed into Epicureanism and Stoicism with their two opposing tendencies, laxity and tension."[4] In their representations of Socrates, most authors choose between a "rational" or "skeptical" view, and an "inspired vision." For some, he is the precursor of the Enlightenment, the apostle of reason, and the discoverer of subjectivity. We recall Erasmus's famous phrase "Saint Socrates, pray for us." For Hegel, for example, Socrates is responsible for the triumph of "the principle of subjectivity—of the absolute inherent independence of thought."[5] And that is precisely what Nietzsche holds against him, for Nietzsche regards the excesses of Socratic logic as a "veritable monstrosity." For others, in contrast, the mystical side of Socrates is paramount. In *Euthyphron*, Socrates is accused of being "a maker of gods"—and as we know, in all things he obeyed his own *daimon*. Like Joan of Arc and so many other mystics, the father of philosophy appears to have heard voices, or at any rate one voice, that of his own "good angel" (as Voltaire, with some irony, put it). It was a side of him that was far from pleasing to reasonable people such as Montaigne: "Nothing is so hard for me to stomach in the life of Socrates as his ecstasies and possession by his daemon."[6] In *The Two Sources of Morality and Religion*, Bergson, too, notes both aspects and likewise suggests that it is Socrates' mysticism that wins out.

Platonism is at once more and less than "the thought of Socrates." And that contradictory formulation brings us to the other great founder of philosophy, Aristotle, one of whose claims to fame was precisely the definition of the principle of contradiction and its corollary, the principle of the excluded middle. According to the first of those two principles, one cannot produce two contrary statements about one and the same thing. From this stems the second principle, according to which if one of those statements is true, the other must be false. We shall be returning to this question. For the moment, suffice it to recognize that, at the dawn of Greek thought, a choice was made. The "masters of truth" made way for philosophers, the ambivalence of mytho-logical thinking was replaced by the dichotomy between *muthos* and *logos*, false thought and true thought. That choice opened up grandiose and radically new perspectives and gave access to a new world. But an entire continent, a veritable mental Atlantis, foundered as the Europe of thought emerged. That critical (in both senses of the term) choice favored the rise of new forms of discourse such as philosophy and science. But that vision of the world, peculiar to the Greek city, also engendered a blindness that was peculiar to the Greeks and their heirs. The benefits of that epistemological turning point were certainly immense: In the long term, they made the Renaissance and the Enlightenment possible and prepared the way for scientific thought. But we are now beginning to count the cost and to balk at the fallout. In some sectors of the scientific domain, the sacrosanct rule of the excluded middle is increasingly openly called into question, or at least relativized. Yet for all that, it continues to hold a quite despotic sway over Western philosophy and ethics. What should now be brought into question is that very philosophical absolutism, if necessary by seeking inspiration from cultures that never made that critical choice between myth and logic, or at least opted for a more flexible kind of rationality.

The single and absolute truth of monotheism, from which the truth of Western reason, among other kinds of truth, is derived, can hardly be set in opposition to the plural truth (or truths) of polytheism—since an opposition still presupposes that the terms should be situated on the same level, which in this instance is not the case. Rather, we need to adopt an oblique approach to this truth, in the Chinese manner, or get at it through the "double truth" of Buddhist thought. In chess, the knight is my favorite because his approach is neither frontal (like that of the castle) nor purely oblique (like that of the bishop). A truly Buddhist approach would be like that of the knight, somewhere between Western logic and Chinese obliqueness. But clearly every piece has its role to play.

Another critical moment in the history of Western thought was that of the *cogito ergo sum*. With Descartes, not only a particular direction and a particular content of thought were determined, but also a particular tone. It was at this point that philosophy adopted the high and mighty tone that brooks no reply, which it has retained ever since. Like it or not, we are all Cartesian. It is not possible to "cut Descartes out," as one of James Joyce's characters in *Finnegan's Wake* suggests. Nevertheless, from a Buddhist point of view, you could just as well say "I think, so I am not," or "something thinks, so I am not: I am being thought." What I take to be *my* thought has multiple sources and *I* am at the best (or worst) but one among them. A Western individual is possibly that strange being who is so possessed by his/her thought (always supposing it is his/hers) that he/she is no longer accessible to other forms of possession. In Balinese rites, the priest sprinkles the villagers with holy water to prevent them from falling into a trance. The Western tourist, however, is not at risk, for he has a more powerful charm to protect him, his camera, which brings into play the reassuring objectivity of reality—a reality in which only what is visible is real, and spirits are allowed neither citizens' rights nor the right to incite others. Is the experience of the *cogito*, which is central to our Western culture, more important than the experience of possession, which is just as central to certain traditional cultures? And what if the one and the other were simply two faces of the same reality? What if thinking were a particular form of possession (and therefore of dispossession)? One cannot help but admire the efforts of certain philosophers such as Wittgenstein to think for themselves, to hear their own voice above the mental hubbub. But what if, strictly speaking, there were no ideas other than "received" ones? Then the only difference would lie in the manner of our receiving them, in the choice made between them.

Descartes's intuition—the certainty of consciousness—has been perverted by his reduction of that consciousness to a *cogito*, and ego-centered (and egocentric) thought fascinated by the external reality that it thinks it dominates. According to Buddhism, thought possesses one delicate probe that makes it possible to explore the darkest corners of consciousness (a term that, in Buddhism, includes the unconscious). Buddhist meditation is a way of plunging, while wide awake, into unconscious processes, to dream while remaining lucid—to enter into oneself without one's psychic processes being obscured by sleep. Perhaps that is what the real *cogito* is, a kind of floating attention, a "weak" thought that is eclipsed as soon as egocentric thinking, so-called "strong" thought, appears on the horizon of consciousness.

Then along came Kant, bringing us his Enlightenment and banishing metaphysics to the outer darkness. The story is too well known for us to need to dwell upon it. Let us approach him obliquely, him and his frontal *Critiques*, perusal of which has become an obligatory rite of passage for all philosophy students. That itself is something that passes all under-standing—the understanding that Kant was at pains to distinguish from reason and that Ambrose Bierce describes as follows: "A cerebral secretion that allows anyone possessing it to know a house from a horse by the roof on the house. Its nature and laws have been exhaustively expounded by Locke, who rode a house, and Kant, who lived in a horse." It is neverthe-less to Kant that credit must go for having restored to phenomena, held ever since Plato to be nothing but appearances, their value as apparitions— thereby bringing us closer to one strain of Buddhist and Sino-Japanese thought.

I really ought now to go on to discuss Hegel and his claims to ab-solute knowledge, but the courage and the will to do so fail me. It is worth noting, however, that he was among those who tried to abolish the principle of contradiction and that, through a superb stroke of irony, his house in Heidelberg has become, not a monument to his memory, but a multistory parking garage, a worthy enough symbol of instrumen-tal rationality.

Ever since Wittgenstein upset the applecart, philosophy has seemed just another language game. Despite its formidable interest, the game has by now been played so often that the moves have become repetitive and mechanical. In its most academic aspects, philosophy is not so much a quest for truth as an esoteric literary genre. Of course, there have always been considerable exceptions, some of them influenced by Christianity (Saint Augustine, Kierkegaard), others in reaction to it (Nietzsche).

Even challenges launched by such as Nietzsche or Wittgenstein were made in the name of philosophy. But that is no longer so in the case of what Paul Quignard calls "speculative rhetoric." According to him, this is an antiphilosophical erudite tradition that pervades the whole of Western history, a tradition whose theoretical emergence he dates to the early sec-ond century in Rome and to the letters of Frontinus to his disciple Marcus Aurelius. Quignard, a rhetorical poacher in the hunting grounds tradition-ally reserved for philosophy, himself identifies with this tradition. But why limit oneself, as he suggests, to "our" antiquity and neglect that of all other cultures, or indeed the resources that other present-day cultures offer us? According to Quignard, there is no need "to turn to the East, to Chinese Daoism or Buddhist Zen in order to think with greater profundity or to escape from the dead end of first Greek metaphysics, then Christian theology, and finally the Nihilism of the Moderns: There is a forgotten tradition, marginal because it is intrepid, persecuted because it is recalcitrant, that has been handed down through the ages, preceding metaphysics, but challenging the latter once it was constituted."[7] Such a shame that he cannot resist resorting to the argument of the excluded middle, prompted by an old reflex characteristic of the thought that he is denouncing. In practice, however, Quignard himself is far more open than most Western writers to the thoughts of East Asia.

What right has reason to look down its nose at everything, including unreason? Faced with what sometimes eludes our consciousness, sometimes erupts irrepressibly into it, so that we lose our grip on ourselves, philosophy remains at a loss. It suffers from a kind of mercantilism, obliged as it is to exchange ideas and concepts only at the official rate. Even Paul Valéry, in the wake of many others, demanded that mystical experience be reproducible, expressible in common terms, demonstrable—in a word, commodifiable. Perhaps that is what prompted Yves Bonnefoy to say that Valéry "was the only accursed poet of our times, no doubt sheltered from misfortune and the very thought of misfortune, but condemned to ideas and to words (the intelligible side of words), for lack of an ability to love things."[8]

Immanent Reason, Transcendent Reason

In *What is Philosophy?*, Gilles Deleuze and Félix Guattari present the whole of the history of philosophy from the point of view of immanence. "In the end, does not every philosopher lay out a new plane of immanence, introduce a new substance of being and draw up a new image of thought, so that there could not be two great philosophers on the same plane?"[9] According to them, that is what distinguishes philosophy from wisdoms or religions, which are still dominated by transcendence.

Deleuze and Guattari define religion as "thinking through figures." "Figures are projections on the plane, which implies something vertical or transcendent." They include the hexagrams of the *Yijing* as well as Tantric *maṇḍalas*. Figures stand in opposition to concepts, which imply no verticality, no transcendence, "only neighborhood and connections on the horizon." The immanence claimed by philosophy thus has very little to do with the immanence dear to Chinese thought to the extent that the latter becomes absolute only when transcendence is projected into it. According to Deleuze and Guattari, it is possible to speak of Chinese, Hindu, Jewish, or Islamic philosophy only to the extent that the thought of those cultures takes place on a certain plane of immanence. But that plane, which may be filled equally well by figures or concepts, is not purely philosophical. Philosophy remains "a Greek thing." Moreover, "only the West extends and propagates its centers of immanence."[10]

Whereas Gilles Deleuze and Félix Guattari oppose philosophy (conceived as pure immanence) to all forms of transcendence, Nayla Farouki, in *La foi et la raison*, tries to show that the same "transcendental" movement is at work in the concepts of philosophy and in the transcendental concept par excellence, the divine "transcendence" of monotheistic religions. She stresses in particular that scientific research is founded upon a desire to bypass empirical reality in order to reach an "other" absolute truth that would make it possible to justify the empirical world. But the imaginary representations of science, with its invisible atoms, are just as mythical (and require just as much credulity) as those of myth: The existence of the atom, like that of God, is accepted as a matter of principle. The transition from empirical concepts to antithetical ones and thence to transcendental ones (that is to say, formalization) offers obvious advantages in the scientific (hence empirical) domain. However, it proves less profitable in other domains, such as philosophy and the human sciences. Thus, Claude Lévi-Strauss, while stressing the rationality of savage thought and even suggesting that an essentially identical logic is at work in mythical thought and in scientific thought, cannot, in the last analysis, avoid reducing "savages" to budding logicians. By formalizing savage thought as he does, he establishes the grammar of myth as a language, but forfeits all the semantic, contextual, and dialogical richness of autochthonous speech.

"Disenchantment of the world" has become a much used expression since it was introduced by the German sociologist Max Weber. From time to time there is also talk of a reenchantment of a kind, to please the nostalgic. But if reenchantment is never as complete as one would like, disenchantment of the world is not so massive a phenomenon as has been suggested. Sociologically speaking, it affects only a particular level of society. Marcel Mauss made the point tellingly in response to a lecture on "primitive" cosmology given by Paul Mus:

We are thus in the presence of a concept of the world . . . that takes up a position other than that in which we or, to be more precise, those of us who are dissociated,

Cartesians, would place it. For the most humble fortune teller and even the young polytechnicians and seamstresses who listen to her also live in a different world from philosophers, even if it is a classical one. And when the fortune teller reads my future in the coffee grounds, she seeks it in a world that she herself has organized and, above all, that she has organized according to a predetermined tradition.[11]

The philosopher Vincent Descombes, commenting upon the work of the ethnologist Jeanne Favret-Saada on witchcraft in rural France, emphasizes that rationalist interpretations of magic make the mistake of everywhere detecting only relations between man and nature and failing to see the relations between human beings that underlie or are even inherent in men's relations with nature. Besides, "the laws of nature invoked by those who seek to demystify the world are themselves a countermythology designed to eliminate primitive mythology. The mythology of reason replaces the mythology of superstition."[12]

Belief in witchcraft may mark the social and psychological limits of scientific rationality in certain sectors of a society in principle dominated by the ideology of the Enlightenment, but in its own way, that belief, too, represents a certain rationalization of nature. The technical side of magic has often been stressed. The demonologists of the seventeenth century were well aware of it as they strove to tip magic to the side of the Devil. Belief in magic survived even the Devil, and its technical aspect explains how it is that, even today, it is possible to accommodate it alongside a particular kind of science. In truth, the Enlightenment's concept of the individual has never quite replaced the notion of a subject being inserted into all kinds of community networks: the systemic understanding of personality. When an individual has to explain a "spell of bad luck," he often needs some principle of explanation that is more satisfactory than blind chance; he urgently needs to discover the source of the evil so as to protect himself against it. Furthermore, individuals tend to personalize events. It is not purely fortuitous that even meteorologists baptize the typhoons and tornadoes that ravage some countries, giving them men's and women's names. In his description of the 1906 earthquake that devastated San Francisco and shattered the newly built Stanford University, where he had just arrived, William James evokes the seismic blast as though it were someone with a personal grudge against him. I underwent similar experiences in 1989 at Stanford and again in 1995 in Japan, albeit with considerably less enthusiasm than James. The earthquake erupted into my life like some kind of intimate enemy. All the seismological knowledge in the world could not change how I felt, for doubtless, like many others, I still have a Neolithic soul.

Freud reflected upon the sense of "the uncanny" (*das Unheimliche*) that often accompanies belief in occult forces and that, according to him, develops when repressed infantile complexes are revived by some impression or when outlived primitive convictions seem once more to be confirmed. He wrote as follows: "Today, we have passed beyond those modes of thought, but we do not feel very sure of our new convictions; the old ones live on in us, on the look out for confirmation." Freud soon excluded himself from those who are affected by such a feeling: "Conversely, he who has completely and finally dispelled animistic beliefs in himself will be insensible to this type of the uncanny."[13] But even if Freud, the theorist of psychoanalysis, was confident that he was immunized against such returns of repressed beliefs, we know that on several occasions Freud the man certainly did experience that type of feeling.

And how do philosophers fare, with their minds that are in principle so serene? Over and above the more or less dialectical opposition of ideas, Western philosophy probably consists essentially in creating a continuous tradition of thought integrated within a great history that confers upon it legitimacy or, as it were, its credentials of nobility (or democracy). To some extent this constitutes a reassuring, protective mechanism that confines thought (and being) to a well-defined domain of the physical and mental world. Even Sade, Nietzsche, and a few other rebels were eventually tamed by the tradition that subsequently developed. The "other" of reason can be apprehended only in the language of reason, the language of the "same."

The prodigious development of the instruments of empirical observation has certainly enabled science to discern the grain of things increasingly clearly, but that vision never penetrates below the surface. Even when a probe delves deep into the body, it still encounters nothing but surfaces. Objectivized understanding never gives us access to the secret of the thing in itself; reality remains opaque to us. Could another form of understanding be possible, which would itself belong to the order of secrecy and be submissive to it, just as dreams are submissive to "the orders of the night"? Would that still, strictly speaking, be understanding, in accordance with the "objective" definition of the term? "Understanding from the abyss," as Henri Michaux puts it, evokes the nescience of Daoism or Chan. But is it really possible to speak of unconscious understanding, is it possible to unveil unconscious thoughts without transfiguring and adulterating them, like those sea anemones that lose all their beauty once they are lifted out of the water? Is there something in between consciousness and unconsciousness, vision and nonvision, normal understanding and understanding "from the abyss" that would clear the way for a possible mediation?

Abstraction and Concepts

He who holds to True Righteousness does not lose the original form of his inborn nature. So for him . . . the long is never too much, the short is never too little. The duck's legs are short, but to stretch them out would worry him; the crane's legs are long, but to cut them down would make him sad. What is long by nature needs no cutting off; what is short by nature needs no stretching.
　　—Zhuangzi, *The Complete Works of Chuang Tzu*, translated by Burton Watson

What are the real advantages and disadvantages of conceptual thought outside the scientific domain? Should we not embark on a systematic critique of the concepts that, as Yves Bonnefoy observes, "give thought the vast power of words to enable it to escape from the house of things"?[14] Reasoning is constructed around an absence from oneself and from the world, rather like a doughnut around its central hole. As Valéry intuitively noted, it is possible to philosophize only because of "the impossibility of recording intuitions."

One of the best things about analytical philosophy is that it is a redoubtably efficient technique for fighting "against the fascination which forms of expression exert upon us."[15] But that becomes one of the worst things about it when analytical philosophy itself falls under the fascination of a particular kind of purely linguistic approach. In his definition of "family resemblance," Wittgenstein deals a severe blow to "the craving for generality" and the "contemptuous attitude toward the particular case" that characterizes scientific and philosophical procedures. He attributes many philosophical mistakes to the tendency to believe that there exists "something in common to all the entities which we commonly subsume under a general term . . . whereas games form a *family* the members of which have family likenesses."[16] He provides one of his typical examples: "If one asks what the different processes of expecting someone to tea have in common, the answer is that there is no single feature in common to all of them, though there are many common features overlapping. These cases of expectation form a family; they have family likenesses which are not clearly defined."[17]

In all probability, universal truths no more exist than universal man does. It has been said of Shakespeare that he resembled all men except in one respect, namely, that he resembled all men. A concept cannot grasp the presence of an object or its particular aura. Although that lack of feeling may be a positive quality in the scientific domain, it certainly is not in those of philosophy and the human sciences. The anthropologist Clifford Geertz has commented upon the founder of anthropological structuralism as follows: "His [Lévi-Strauss's] books seem to exist behind glass, self-sealing discourses into which jaguars, semen, and rotting meat are admitted to become oppositions, inversions, isomorphisms."[18] Similarly, the diagrams and other lineage charts so dear to anthropologists transform the artistic haziness of lived social relations into geometric figures with sharp edges.

The Thread of Logic

The principal claim to fame of Western reason is to have managed to formulate logic. We know that, for Hegel, logic was "the absolute form of truth." But to believe that is to forget that, in the magnetic field of culture, concepts, like iron filings, are oriented by the forces that pass through them; they do not possess the autonomy attributed to them. The notion of a single truth makes it impossible to grasp the permanent fluctuation of reality. The framework of logic rigidifies a discourse that would benefit from remaining as fluid as possible and sometimes even from resorting to paradox.

Reconsidering analytical philosophy, toward the end of his life, Bertrand Russell declared: "To argue interminably about the meaning that imbeciles ascribe to imbecilities . . . is certainly not very important." Of course we must allow for a measure of exaggeration here, but it is true that logical caviling does sometimes have the air of a rite of exorcism designed to set aside or call to order a recalcitrant, seething reality. The question of the inadequacy of a particular kind of logical thought in the face of reality calls to mind an episode in Eugène Ionesco's *Rhinoceros* in which, while a rhinoceros (or several) is/are at large in the town, a logician sets about calming the fears of its inhabitants with syllogisms. Even logicians sometimes resemble Voltaire's Pangloss.

However, let us not force the issue. It is perfectly possible to distinguish between a tempered use of logic that helps us to understand our language games better and professional analytical philosophy that has become a language game in and of itself. The analytical reflections of the later Wittgenstein and those of Vincent Descombes make it possible to set in order and exorcize the phantoms of philosophical Romanticism. However, we should reject the altogether desiccating and imperialistic side of a particular kind of logic that, rather than helping us to understand reality with all its nuances and degrees, impoverishes it and deforms it by imposing a straitjacket upon it. The truth of analytical philosophy perhaps lies in the sometimes maniacal detail of its demonstrations, rather than in their accuracy. To be sure, the discussions of grammarians, too, possess a therapeutic value: In the dark war years, Valéry devoted himself to the study of logic in order to ward off the all-pervading gloom.

From Aristotle to Leibnitz to Russell, logic is essentially a technique designed to produce linear thought, deliberately impoverished so as to become perfectly operational—rather in the same way that ascetics take a vow of absolute poverty in order to get to heaven. Logic is the art of directing one's thought without abandoning it to the mercy of associations of ideas. A similar way of proceeding is to be found in certain currents of Buddhism. "To think? . . . To think is to lose the thread." That quip of Valéry's can be interpreted in two ways: At one level, thought is multiple and overflows on every side away from the thread of logical reasoning; and conversely, at another level, thought, due to its sluggishness, causes us to lose the tenuous thread of a lighter, more airy consciousness. It was also Valéry who emphasized "the versatility of a thought capable of losing the thread" and opposed it to purely abstract thought, "which follows its thread and is nothing but what it follows."[19]

The rectilinear structure of logic could also be set in opposition to Chinese thought, which has been said to proceed obliquely and by detours, were it not that such opposition would still stem from the logic of the excluded middle. However—it will be objected—China did not produce a scientific revolution. This objection does not carry as much weight as is sometimes assumed. China's tardiness is due not so much to any intellectual deficiency as to the resistance of its social fabric. If scientific understanding—which got going far earlier in China than in Greece and can rightfully pride itself on its superior successes—did not topple Chinese feudalism as it was to topple European feudalism, that is, paradoxically, because China was better integrated socially and politically than Europe was. The Chinese "scientific" ideology had provided feudal domination with a "natural" long-term basis more solid than that of the European ideology of the "divine right" of kings. The invention of gunpowder—of Chinese origin, as was the printing press—may have sounded the knell for the feudal fortresses and armies of Europe, but in China, it was used above all for firecrackers to celebrate the New Year. The fact that linear scientific thought spread across Europe "like a trail of gunpowder" does not imply any intrinsic superiority over the concrete thought of the Chinese, which sought to cleave to the changing qualities of empirical reality rather than to discover the abstract principles behind it. Significantly enough, the Chinese term *li*, generally translated as "principle" and much used by Buddhists and Confucians alike, originally designated not an abstract principle, but the veins that run through jade.

The Principle of Contradiction and the Principle of Identity

Western logic rests upon the principle of contradiction and that of the excluded middle. The first is expressed as follows: "It is impossible for the same attribute to belong and not to belong, at the same time, to the same subject, with the same relationship." This principle of contradiction can neither prove nor refute itself. It needs to be accepted unconditionally for, Aristotle tells us, it is "unconditioned." The principle is valid only for discourse, not for the nature of things, not for extralinguistic reality. As Valéry has said: "There is no contradiction without diction, that is to say, outside discourse."[20] There can be contradiction only between one statement and another, not between one thing and another. Unfortunately, those two registers often tend to become confused. Vincent Descombes notes that in ordinary discourse, it is impossible to say yes *and* no, for the yes-no sequence does not mean the same as the no-yes sequence. The yes that comes *after* the no is not the same yes that it was before. The situation has been modified by the no—and vice versa.

Behind the principle of contradiction, or rather underlying it, is another: the principle of identity or of the unity of essence. This is a belief in the solid existence of things, founded upon common sense, *doxa*—what the Buddhists call "conventional truth." In short, all Western logic thus derives from a realist metaphysics. As Guy Bugault observes: "The principle of contradiction is an indivisibly logical, ontological, and anthropological norm."[21] It is also worth noting its juridical aspect. When you sign a contract, there must be no doubt as to your identity.

Although the principle of contradiction cannot logically be refuted, it nevertheless can be relativized. The Western tradition includes a number of thinkers, ranging from Nicolas de Cues to Hegel, who have sought to limit its field to an inferior form of reason. But it is probably in Buddhism that this intuition becomes truly central, since Buddhism challenges the underlying principle of identity and introduces the notion of two truths, the one relative, the other conventional. The fact is that once things lose their stability and everything is in perpetual flux, the principle of contradiction becomes inoperable. Moreover, even if it in theory remains relevant in the day-to-day world governed by conventional truth, it loses its *raison d'être* in the domain of the absolute, which is a matter of ultimate truth. Some Mahāyāna schools go even further: Since the two levels of reality (transcendence and immanence, *nirvāṇa* and saṁsāra) are no longer ontologically distinct, the real world, redefined as the domain of "transcendent immanence," now passes out of the jurisdiction of the principle of contradiction. With all things now perceived from the point of view of the absolute, it is possible simultaneously to deny and to affirm such or such a characteristic of any particular thing. However, this adoption of an absolute perspective expresses not so much a mystical experience as an act of faith regarding the reality of such a perspective. It authorizes a series of spiritual exercises, logical and epistemological permutations that, by encouraging the practitioner "not to abide anywhere," are supposed to enable him/her to accede to a higher plane. This entails a pragmatic decision for whoever seeks to pass beyond the level of conventional truth, in the same way as the principle of contradiction, far from constituting an absolute law, entails a pragmatic decision for whoever intends to remain at that level.

The Law of the Excluded Middle

The above English translation of the French *principe du tiers exclu* brings us closer to the Buddhist Middle Way, or rather in effect distances us from it. According to the philosopher John Dewey, that law of the excluded middle is "the source of more false reasoning in philosophical discourse and in moral and social investigations than any other kind of sophism."[22] The law is set out as follows: "It is not possible for there to be any intermediary between contradictory statements. One must necessarily either affirm or deny any predicate of a subject." In other words, if one of two contradictory statements is true, the other must be false. A door must either be open or shut; logically, it cannot be half-open (let alone half-shut). It is a matter of "either . . . or." One must either be or not be, so Hamlet, all unwittingly, turns out to be Aristotelian. However, this dilemma would be a false one to a Buddhist, accustomed as he would be to a tetralemma (A; B; both A and B; neither A nor B). The third term in this tetralemma states precisely that it is possible for a thing to be *at once* thus *and* not thus. If the thesis of our opponent implies a contradiction, the contradictory thesis (that is to say ours) is ipso facto verified. But it is precisely on this point that Buddhist dialectics parts company with Aristotelian dialectics. Thus, the Buddhist philosopher Sengzhao (fifth century) warns: "When you exclude an assertion, be sure not to include an assertion of the contrary." Buddhist dialectic refutation moves beyond the dilemma and constantly makes use of the tetralemma. Furthermore, it uses the latter only to pass beyond it. The tetralemma is conceived, precisely, to escape from the dilemma in which the principle of the excluded middle traps us. Aristotle, who clearly knew of the tetralemma, disapproved of it and mentions it only to rule it out and return to his own beloved debates.

But life is not an endless contradictory debate. In reality, the middle, assumed to be excluded, bursts in, engineering many returns for what has been repressed. Like it or not, it is a part of what is there. Reality bounces back, catching us on the hop. The law of the excluded middle impoverishes reality by guiding us away not only from error, but also from what appears, without due reflection, to be simply "beside the point" or insignificant. As has already been noted, reality is the domain of the more or less (a question of degree), not of the true and the false and the contradictory judgments characteristic of discourse. The arbitrary cleavages operated by language and thought in the tissue of reality are rather like those frontiers in the New World that were drawn with a ruler, with total disregard of the local geographical and human realities. That is why we must learn to handle a "contradictory logic" that, once detached from its commitment to the law of the excluded middle, can become more inclusive and open to the turbulence of reality.

The law of the excluded middle can be twisted rhetorically in a number of ways: by a chiasmus, by paradox, by repetition, or by speech that is "voluble" (from the Latin *volubilitas*, "a movement that twists, turns, rolls, and unrolls easily; that flows easily, with easy and rapid speech"). With that roundabout metaphor, we return to the detours of Chinese thought. Only this type of complex discourse can convey complex reality—etymologically, that is—the reality that is full of folds, as opposed to simple (*simplex*: "with only one fold"). We, too, are complex, that is to say, "folded in with," "closely linked with" that reality, and this makes us "responsible" or "complicit."

Reason and Grammar

"Buddhist thought" and "Western thought" are abstractions, misleading simplifications that stem from the desire to generalize condemned by Wittgenstein. They are somehow narrative figures, largely fictional, that tend to mask the multiplicity of the realities for which they stand: There are, after all, all kinds of Western, Eastern, and Buddhist thoughts. Yet these thoughts form—or seem to form—a system, as Nietzsche observes when he points out "the strange family resemblance" that Hindu, Greek, and German philosophies all share: "The separate philosophical ideas are not anything optional or autonomously evolving, but grow up in connection and relationship with each other. . . . However suddenly and arbitrarily they seem to appear in the history of thought, they nevertheless belong just as much to a system as the collective members of the fauna of a Continent."[23] We need not follow Nietzsche where his own prejudices encourage him to attribute resemblances and differences to physiological or racial characteristics. He shares with analytical philosophy the intuition that many philosophical problems stem from an inadequate comprehension of language. But whereas analytical philosophers believe that grammar provides the solution to this, for Nietzsche, grammar is the very source of the problem. It is because they place too much confidence in grammar and the system of language that philosophers allow reality itself to elude them. To seize upon it, you would have to free yourself from language or, as the Chan masters say, "cut across the path of words."

Émile Benveniste shows that Greek philosophy is determined (or at least informed) by the language it speaks. Aristotle's famous categories, for example, are simply grammatical structures of the Greek language: Where the philosopher saw categories of thought, there are really nothing but linguistic categories. The whole diversity of Western metaphysics stems from particularities of the Greek language, especially from those involving the notion of "to be," at once a verb of existence and a logical copula. But is that language really privileged from a philosophical point of view, or does it only seem so rich to us precisely because we still think through it? Does not its vaunted richness imply, as its counterpart, a certain poverty? What if the truths that etymology appears to reveal and the access to Truth and Being that, according to Heidegger, etymology affords us are, in fact, illusory? Do they not dig the trap or pit into which metaphysics and grammar cause us to fall?

Benveniste argues that the fact that thought is determined by language does not prevent us from thinking "differently." After all, the Chinese, despite their relying on categories such as the *dao* or *yin* and *yang*, are perfectly capable of understanding Western logic and setting in operation the sciences that stem from it. Significantly enough, however, Benveniste never envisaged the reverse: Yet it would be interesting to know whether Westerners, despite their own categories of thought, are capable of grasping Chinese thought.

Reason and Rhetoric

It is perfectly possible to lie to someone (or to lull him/her into belief) by telling the truth and nothing but the truth, and we are told that the devil himself is adept at citing the Bible. In Buddhist legend, Māra, the Cunning One, similarly takes on the appearance of the Buddha in order to deceive the faithful. Meanwhile, as the German philosophers Max Horkheimer and Theodor W. Adorno note in *The Dialectic of Enlightenment,* conversely, the "irrational" nature of faith may also become a rational device that those who are totally "enlightened" use to establish their influence over the faithful.

Nietzsche, among others, has drawn attention to the rhetorical nature of philosophical discourse. The term "rhetorical," in the widest sense, here designates a dialogical understanding of discourse and truth itself. Rhetoric implies a use of language that is not only referential, but also "performative." Instead of simply describing reality, language can modify it. In some cases, to say is to do, as when a judge declares the accused to be guilty.[24] Rhetorical language also acts upon the interlocutor, albeit indirectly. To the extent that it refuses to pay attention to the rhetoric that underpins it, all positivist discourse, whether philosophical or scientific, condemns itself to being blind to the transferences between itself and its "object." So it is that a dichotomy has appeared between science and rhetoric, or rather between a rhetoric that is "nothing but rhetoric" and a scientific discourse that succumbs to a myopic rhetoric of antirhetoric.

Nietzsche commented on the law of contradiction as follows: "We are incapable of both affirming and denying one and the same thing: that is an empirical subjective law, not the expression of some 'necessity,' but simply an incapacity."[25] But those are not sufficient grounds upon which to declare that the law of contradiction is aberrant, that logic is inadequate to cope with reality, and that all discourse is performative. For Nietzsche, the metaphysical critique seems to imply an end to the illusion that the language of persuasion (*doxa*) can replace that of truth (*epistēmē*). It is true that the language of truth no longer possesses its erstwhile glorious status; nevertheless, it is still not entirely eliminated. As a result, it becomes impossible ever to switch totally from one type of language to the other. Deconstruction leaves the reader suspended, as it were, between the two. Each of the two kinds of truth—the "epistemic" and the "doxic," can exist only through the other; each refers back to the other. The literary critic Paul de Man notes that the deconstruction of discourse does indeed reveal the error of reference, but still does so in a referential mode. It never quite manages to transform discourse into an action or an opinion.[26] The status of discourse remains impossible to decide: It is neither simply *epistēmē* nor simply *doxa*, never purely descriptive or normative, but seems condemned to oscillate between the two. This view seems to me to chime with the Buddhist notion of the two truths.

Dialogical Reason

Logical, conceptual, abstract reasoning is never as neutral as is believed, for it always contains an element of rhetoric. In one of his works, Jorge Luis Borges challenges those who transform metaphysics and the arts into a kind of interactive game: "Those who practice this game forget that a book is more than a verbal structure or a series of verbal structures; it is the dialogue it establishes with its reader and the intonation it imposes upon his voice, and the changing and durable images it leaves in his memory."[27] For example, the discourse of this or that philosopher, by making us "the interlocutor in a secret and continuous dialogue with nothingness or the deity," flatters our vanity and encourages an illusion of self. In this sense, all philosophical discourse is immoral.

In principle, the vocation of philosophy is to call us into question, to implicate us existentially. But we know that, since the eighteenth century, it has lost its pretensions to provide a rule for living and now limits itself to a role of knowing. For all their philosophical finesse, the great moralists of the seventeenth century remain confined to the narrow sphere of *doxa*. That is not the case of a Nietzsche or a Kierkegaard, but they remain exceptions.

Philosophy is no doubt not altogether wrong to be wary of "masters of truth." How can one seek the truth if one forgoes one's critical reason? But a shortcoming of a similar order is detectable in philosophical discourse itself. On the basis of what strange a priori decision can one act as if one believes that only the truth of discourse matters, as if the doctrine and the doctor were not intimately linked? Does not every philosophy imply belief in some individual and his charisma, and does not every philosophical school stem from the seduction exerted by some discourse (even the *Discourse on the Method*) or some way of behaving? Even so, surely we should not allow a critique ad hominem to replace a critique *ad doctrinam*, as Nietzsche does when he attacks the "prejudices of philosophers." He declares that "they [the *philosophes*] all pose as if they had discovered and reached their real opinions through the self-development of a cold, pure, divinely unconcerned dialectic (as opposed to the mystics of every rank, who are more honest and doltish—and talk of 'inspiration'); while at the bottom it is an assumption, a hunch, indeed a kind of 'inspiration'—most often a desire of the heart that has been filtered and made abstract—that they defend with reasons they have thought after the fact."[28] His diatribes against Kant and "Königsbergian thought," that "comical *niaiserie allemande*," are famous: "The equally stiff and decorous Tartuffery of the old Kant as he lures us on the dialectical bypaths that lead to his 'categorical imperative' really lead astray and seduce."[29] In *Beyond Good and Evil*, he criticizes Kant's presumption in taking as his starting point aesthetic definitions, despite lacking the requisite experience and necessary artistic sensitivity. He concludes his attack as follows: "There is a point in every philosophy when the philosopher's 'conviction' appears on the stage—or to use the language of an ancient Mystery, *Adventavit asinus / Pulcher et fortissimus* [The ass arrived, beautiful and most brave]."[30] All the same, Nietzsche knows full well that, on this score, no one is beyond criticism and that exactly the same could be said of himself. In a way, all philosophical discourse is a confession.

Despite the trenchant if somewhat unfair criticism, Kant has become a kind of sacred cow. In fact, as a crowning irony, the same fate has befallen Nietzsche himself, the very man who set out to attack all the sacred cows of the European tradition. You cannot criticize Kant without being Kantian, just as you cannot move beyond Nietzsche without being a Nietzschean. But do not ingratitude and a deliberate amnesia where influences are concerned constitute the very essence of philosophy? Is not rejection of all affiliation the philosophical gesture par excellence? Time and again it has recurred, albeit in weaker forms, ever since the Cartesian tabula rasa applied to Descartes himself and a few others in this very book.

Qu Boyu has been going along for sixty years and has changed sixty times. There is not a single instance in which what he called right at the beginning he did not in the end reject and call wrong. So now there's no telling whether what he calls right at the moment is not in fact what he called wrong during the past fifty-nine years. The ten thousand things have their life, yet no one sees its roots; they have their coming forth, yet no one sees the gate. Men all pay homage to what understanding understands, but no one understands enough to rely upon what understanding does not understand and thereby come to understand. Can we call this anything but great perplexity? Let it be, let it be! There is no place you can escape it. This is what is called saying both "that is so" and "is that so?"[31]

Maturity and Autonomy

Modernity has sought to complete the project of the *Aufklärung* (a term that it is always rather tricky to translate as "Enlightenment"), which, according to Kant, involved getting humanity to progress from its "minor" state to a state of maturity. In a short text entitled "What is Enlightenment?" (*Was ist die Aufklärung?*), Kant defined "minority" as "a certain state of our will that makes us accept the authority of someone else as our guide in domains where we ought to use our reason."[32] In his reinterpretation of this text, Michel Foucault likewise emphasizes the notion of "maturity," which, he suggests, is expressed by the expression "Aude sapere": "Have the courage, dare to know." He distinguishes the Enlightenment as a historical movement from Humanism as a general theme and insists that we should preserve the attitude of autonomy that characterizes the Enlightenment, rather than adhere to certain elements in its doctrines. And in any case, we ought to distinguish more clearly between the "elucidation" of the German *Aufklärung*, the English Enlightenment, and the French

Lumières: All are forms of a Western rationality that, while assuming themselves to be universal, are in fact eminently national (and at times nationalistic).

According to Foucault, we should remain faithful to Kant even as we oppose him. In particular, we should reject "everything that is presented in the form of a simplistic and authoritarian alternative." In the context that interests us here, that means, precisely, the entire Western tradition that is founded upon the "simplistic and authoritarian" opposition of reason to faith. It is perhaps just such a fidelity that Freud manifests when, point by point, he demolishes all Kantian pretensions to autonomy. All Freud's attempts at "elucidation" (*Aufklärung*) are certainly directly in line with those of the Enlightenment. But at the same time it is likewise Freud who calls into question the Western "'maturity' that we too hastily consider already acquired." Maturity has yet to be acquired and possibly never will be, for the unconscious is ever lurking.

Whereas Kant dreamed of humanity's rapid progression to maturity, Freud, almost two centuries later, takes it back it to its cradle by showing that all men and women remain fundamentally minors who continue to lull themselves with illusions. Not that this stopped him from sometimes claiming that he himself *had* attained to maturity. To acquire maturity, it is not enough to wish to do so. On the contrary. Philosophical maturity is rather like adolescence, which has been described as a prolonged attempt to avoid adolescence. Thus, immaturity may consist not only in submitting to authority, but also in a desire to do without the unconscious and to believe that one can easily elude irrationality. If the slumber of reason engenders monsters, it is perhaps fair to suggest that a slumbering imagination engenders immaturity.

Without necessarily subscribing to the theoretical or clinical content of psychoanalysis, this would seem to be the mode of thought that, to date, has offered the best alternative to the exclusivist logic of all discourse with scientific pretensions, such as that of the human and social sciences. To be sure, Freud, too, remains overly scientific and positivist (especially when speaking of religion), but it was he who first undermined the dogmas of Western universalism and triumphant individualism, as classically formulated by Kant.

How far can reason move toward madness in order to comprehend (in the sense of incorporate) it without foundering? Is reason a frog that tries to puff itself up as big as an ox, or even bigger, in order to swallow the latter? What if it were basically just a particular form of madness, just as music heard in the distance becomes just another kind of noise? Present-day psychoanalysis has not yet managed to get the true measure of the irrational, so instead tries to explain it away. Freud himself remains a positivist—despite all his brilliant (and sometimes hazy) intuitions. He never gives his patients credit where credit is due (in either sense of the term "credit"). Any negation on their part is interpreted as a disclaimer, any assertion is illusory. All the same, his definition of illusion does have the merit of highlighting the essential "duplicity" of all truth: A truth may become an illusion or even a lie when it is a response to certain psychic needs. Science and logic, whatever their objective value, may, in the same way as religion, become illusions for the subject, for their truth is always in danger of being perverted by the role that it is made to play. Although Freud opened up certain new avenues, he also closed others, sometimes falling into his own traps. After revealing the illusions underlying culture, he created illusions for himself in his desire to form a school and attempted to delude others in order to win scientific credentials for psychoanalysis.

Reason and Reasons

As we have seen, the advent of Greek reason marked the decline of myth. Whereas the latter was characterized by a productive ambiguity, philosophy managed to make a clear-cut separation between one level and another in order to rule out any confusion. At a stroke, myth forfeited any claim to speak the truth; it was reduced to vain words, the fantasies of an imagination too fertile to be true.

In similar fashion, the thought of the Enlightenment refused to recognize the validity of the arguments of its opponents. All those who criticized it were in error, for, as Descombes remarks, "Reason can be opposed only by bad reasons."[33] Despite those such as Foucault who have criticized that kind of blackmail, it crops up more or less everywhere, particularly as soon as the topic is "spirituality" or the New Age. Yet the latter movements, for all their problematic tendency to go astray, also manifest a legitimate spirit of resistance. But they would probably not have spread so widely had not emancipating reason been perverted into technical reason, an instrument of domination. It is therefore urgent that we recognize the coexistence of particular forms of rationality that are quite distinct from the ideal reason whose canonical form is claimed to be Logic.[34]

Since Max Horkheimer and Theodor W. Adorno, we have become familiar with the "dialectics of enlightenment," an enlightenment whose good intentions seem to have paved the way to our modern hell and that, in the belief that it was putting an end to myths that purveyed violence, has ended up doing violence to itself. According to these authors, reason, in its very principle, is totalitarian—hostile to the *totaliter aliter* (totally other). The multiplicity of reality has been replaced by a duality, a confrontation between a double unity, that of nature and that of the subject.[35]

Logic is by no means egalitarian, so philosophy has some grounds for adopting its characteristic patrician tone. In Athens, equality for citizens was introduced at the same moment as servitude for slaves. In the seventeenth century, John Locke, the theorist of liberalism, while advocating human liberty, nevertheless still reserved the expression "free men" for "English gentlemen." The underlying assumption became explicit when England was forced to consider the claims of its Indian subjects. Even today, despite the grand declarations of principles that favor human rights, it is conveniently forgotten that, both historically and in daily practice, liberal consumer society rests upon the economic and political servitude of the societies of the Third World. In this connection, it may be useful to recall the social or even ethnic origins of universalist liberty as revealed by etymology. According to Émile Benveniste, originally the word "free" did not mean "relieved of something." Instead, it indicated "belonging to an ethnic stock that was designated by a metaphor of plant growth. That belonging conferred a kind of privilege never experienced by foreigner or slave."[36] So it is hardly surprising if the universalist moral imperative of rationalist philosophy turns out to be an internalized form of an ancient social subordination.

Jean-Joseph Goux has tried to show that the emergence of a certain type of rationality (scientific rationality) was contemporaneous with a particular mode of exchange that involved a universal equivalent, whether this took the form of money or of concepts. In monetary commerce, as in algebra, it is a matter of suspending meaning. In a famous passage, Nietzsche defined truths as used, "white" metaphors similar to silver coins on which the effigy has been erased. He recommended a return to the original effigy, to the metaphorical meaning, through the abandonment of conceptual abstraction. We must reactivate live metaphor in our lives if we wish to avoid turning our thought into what Mallarmé called a "mental commodity."

According to Marx, "Logic is the *money* of the mind, the speculative *thought-value* of man and of nature, their essence indifferent to any real determinate character, and thus unreal; *thought* which is *alienated* and abstract and ignores real nature and man."[37] And, if we are to believe J.-J. Goux, there is an affinity between Western reason, the kind that is traced back to the Greek philosophers, and the institution of a "general equivalent."[38] Money has become the equalizing principle, the homogenizer of reason. What reason has brought about at the level of ideas, money has at the material level, producing a similar homogenization of reality. One reaction to the increasing abstraction of reality is to proclaim the distinctiveness of objects. But it is in the name of that very distinctiveness that the objects themselves become commodities—albeit stamped with a bogus emblem of nobility—in order to satisfy the desire for equalization. There is now a market for distinctive objects (in the auction houses of Drouot or Sotheby's), just as there is a market for branded commodities. It is not long before such a utensil is itself advertised as being distinctive, at which point the original is swamped beneath copies, each of which claims to be more distinctive than any of the others—like the Indian statuette that Tintin and Milou (*aka* Snowy) endeavor to track down in *The Broken Ear*.

Paradoxically, a generalized free exchange of ideas leads to the disappearance of local *doxa*, opinion that is shared by some, but is nevertheless singular because it cannot lay claim to the universality that pertains to truth. There was a time when *doxa* was the truth on the other side of the Pyrenees, but now the Pyrenees have been flattened on the world map of reason. In the supermarkets of reason, the truth is everywhere the same. Max Weber succeeded in demonstrating the link between the development of capitalism and the rise of rationality in Protestantism. With the advent of the democratic regime, all transcendence, divine and royal alike, disappeared. What Nietzsche was to call the death of God echoed the execution of Louis XVI in France.

Reason and the Irrational

In the book that made Michel Foucault famous, the author described the great divide between reason and madness and also the great "enclosure" of the latter.[39] For reasons both historical and epistemological, his thesis has often been challenged. The German philosopher Jürgen Habermas, for example, criticizes Foucault's presumption in using the language of reason to speak in the name of the "other" of reason. However, Vincent Descombes draws attention to the logical Manicheanism of Habermas, who confuses two different notions of otherness—the other (*alterum*) as one term in a pair, and the other (*aliud*) in the sense of something indeterminate that transcends any pair. Thus, the other of reason is not only madness (of which reason cannot speak), but also something that, further upstream from the distinction between madness and reason, transcends both "reason" and "madness" and that it ought to be possible to express through both. Descombes, for his part, prefers to avoid that indeterminate use of the term "other" and to stick to its particular uses. According to him, one should always specify the other "what." There is no such thing as a general irrationality. The various "others" of reason—myth, faith, and so on—do not constitute a generic "other" that can be termed "irrational." The most that can be said is that such or such a belief is irrational when it can be seen to be incompatible with the totality of the beliefs held by a given individual. And those beliefs are never, in practice, given as a closed system that is easily objectivized. That applies even more in the case of a mentality or culture.[40]

The same point of view is adopted by Ludwig Wittgenstein, who, in his *Remarks on Frazer's Golden Bough*, takes issue with the way in which James Frazer, one of the founders of English ethnography, treats magic and the religious concepts of people as "errors": "Was Augustine mistaken, then, when he called on God on every page of the *Confessions*? Well—one might say—if he was not mistaken, then the Buddhist holy-man, or some other, whose religion expresses quite different notions, surely was. But *none* of them was making a mistake except where he was putting forward a theory." For, Wittgenstein added, "a religious symbol does not rest on any *opinion*. And error belongs only with opinion."[41]

In any case, you cannot get rid of the irrational by denying it. Irrational beliefs are not simply repressed; they shift in the strangest way and are hard to seize upon. You think you have rid yourself of them, yet you continue to entertain them by ascribing them to others. For instance, we continue to believe in Santa Claus for the sake of and through our children. One typical case is that of Casanova who, while posing as a magician one stormy day, was panic-stricken when lightning struck close by. Convinced that he truly had invoked malignant forces, he thought he owed his safety to the fact that he had not stepped outside the magic circle that he had drawn on the ground. Another paradigmatic example of a man hoist by his own petard, given by Claude Lévi-Strauss, is that of Quesalid, an Indian of the American Northwest, a man with a mind of his own, who was irritated by the superstitions of his fellow tribesmen. Having passed himself off as a shaman with the aim of revealing the fraudulence of other shamans, he ended up caught in his own trap, believing in the magic that he had set out to ridicule.

Theoreticians who thought they were dealing magic a severe blow by describing it as an inept pseudoscience (or, at best, a useful illusion) did not realize that they were seriously off target. In the human world, magic really can kill, and the power one man holds over another may certainly be real. All credit to Jeanne Favret-Saada, whose luminous study of a subject as shadowy as witchcraft has revealed these power relations and shown that one enchanted archipelago continues to exist in our disenchanted world.

Meanwhile, even when the internal coherence of human reasoning appears to be beyond question in one particular field of thought, we should not be misled into thinking that reasoning as a whole is truly well founded. There is no way of proving that it is well founded, but neither is there any way of proving that it is erroneous. The idea that belief in reason is, in its very principle, irrational appeared as early as in the work of the Daoist thinker Zhuangzi. Along the same lines, Paul Mus has written as follows: "Behind plenty of disciplines that have wished to do without metaphysics, there was a metaphysics, that of clear ideas."[42] The discourse of Habermas and, more generally, of analytical philosophy as a whole seems to me to stem from that metaphysics of clear ideas and perfect communication.

The circle of reason, like a magic circle, or what Buddhists call a *maṇḍala*, is subject to certain laws. Kant was one of those who traced out that circle on the ground, a circle out of which one could not step on pain of being ruled out of the game. So it was, after all, just a game! But outside the game, life goes on, although, short of a miracle, the players will never realize that.

As critical thought, philosophy ought to aim for the furthest limits of thought and being. To fall back on the sphere of evidence, certainties, and tautologies is to renege on that aim, for it leaves the way open for all kinds of latter-day gnoses, yet deprives one of the possibility of challenging them or distinguishing between them. The idea of restricting philosophy to grammar, repeating the same structures over and over again in a quasi-obsessive manner, calls to mind the obsession with detail analyzed by Freud in connection with his remarks on ritual. Paradoxically enough, a better understanding of ritual thought would perhaps help to provide an escape from this ivory tower. But of course that does not mean that we can dispense entirely with philosophical grammar.

Western thought (that is to say, rational thought, logical philosophy) asserts itself through confrontation, in accordance with the principle of the excluded middle. By so doing, it casts into outer darkness a number of human realities such as imagination, dreaming, literature, and myth, and—last, but not least—the "thought from/of the outside," for instance, ritual thought. These various domains, allegedly irrational, are the ones that Buddhist rationality will enable us to explore—without however, entirely leaving our own philosophical "preserve."

3

Buddhism and Chinese Thought

If we consider the Buddhist tradition from the point of view of its geographical and doctrinal expansion and not solely from that of its ideal proximity to its Indian sources, we notice that it has suffered serious prejudice at the hands of historians. As has been noted above, Buddhism, which originated in northern India in about the fifth century before the common era, spread throughout the whole of Asia in the course of the following ten centuries. Yet, except for Chan/Zen, the East Asian Buddhist tradition has to date been strangely neglected by sinologists and "Buddhologists" alike.

Nobody dreams of questioning the credentials of Christianity in Western culture just because it originated in the Near East. Yet that is exactly how scholars frequently behave when they examine the relations between Buddhism and Chinese culture. Of course Chinese Buddhism is not all there is to Chinese thought, but without the latter, Buddhism would have been nothing, just as Chinese thought would have been incomplete without Buddhism. Chinese Buddhism is impregnated with Confucianism and Daoism, and the historical development of the latter cannot be explained without taking the Buddhist influence into account. Just as Western thought has been nurtured by Greco-Roman and Christian influences, Buddhist thought has assimilated two cultures that could hardly be more different, those of India and China—not to mention a number of peripheral cultures that are themselves highly original in many respects, such as those of Tibet and Japan. To understand this global and globalizing thought, along with the local strands of resistance to which it gave rise and that at once complicate and revivify it, we therefore need to consider East Asia as a whole.

The thought of East Asia is usually divided into three great doctrines: Buddhism, Daoism, and Confucianism. But to be more comprehensive, those need to be complemented by three forms of thought that, at the point where the established ideologies intersect, have totally altered the intellectual and religious landscape of Asia: the Tantrism of Vajrayāna, Chan Buddhism, and the cosmological thought of *yin* and *yang* (in Japanese *onmyōdō*). These derived from the three above-mentioned major doctrines, but cannot be reduced to them, for they managed to combine with them in an altogether original fashion. Chan Buddhism, for example, maintained productive, albeit somewhat competitive relations with Confucianism and Daoism. Tantric Buddhism, even though as a school (Zhen'yan, the school of "true words" or *mantra*), it flourished only briefly under the Tang dynasty, from the seventh century to the ninth, nevertheless exerted a considerable influence upon the Chinese and Japanese cultures and was, in return, influenced by them. Finally, the cosmological thought of *yin* and *yang* influenced Sino-Japanese Buddhism just as deeply as it influenced Confucianism and Daoism. It is therefore no longer possible simply to reduce Chinese thought to Confucianism or even to the duo that it forms, on the *yin-yang* model, with Daoism. We must reject both the monochrome vision of Buddhism seen as an autonomous Indian philosophy and the notion that Confucianism is all there is to Chinese thought. To that end, we could perhaps imagine Chinese thought as a fabric whose "warp" is constituted by three kinds of threads: Confucianism, Daoism, and Buddhism (the meaning of *jing*, sacred texts, Confucian classics and Buddhist *sūtras* is, precisely, "warp"). Meanwhile the weft is also constituted by threads that form three motifs (or bands): Tantrism, Chan, and the cosmological thought of *yin* and *yang*. However, this model is valid only from the seventh century onward, since prior to that, the weft was purely cosmological.

When Buddhism was introduced in China around the beginning of the common era, it was at first considered to be a variant of Daoism, an autochthonous religion that tradition traced back to the legendary Laozi. But from the fourth century on, the differences became clear, and rivalry between the two religions soon increased. The controversy peaked with the fantastical theory of the conversion of barbarians: Laozi was said to have gone off to the West to convert barbarians, taking the name of the Buddha. To punish them for their initial lack of faith, he allegedly condemned them to celibacy (a subterfuge to deprive them of descendants). Indian Buddhism was thus represented as no more than a barbarian version of Daoism, a dubious alloy that Chinese goldsmiths rejected. The Buddhists counterattacked, maintaining that Laozi and Confucius were in reality disciples of the Buddha whom the latter had sent to China to prepare the way for the Buddhist doctrine. This controversy, the futile aspect of which should not mask the importance of what was at stake, dragged on for centuries. Only in the twelfth century was it brought to an end, with the triumph of Buddhism.

In the course of its implantation in China, Buddhism had to confront various other difficulties, in particular the question of the independence of monks. Unlike in India, where the clergy (whether Hindu or Buddhist) was recognized as the ultimate power in the spiritual domain, in China, the emperor, known as the Son of Heaven, was positioned at the summit of both the spiritual and the temporal hierarchies, so monks owed him total obedience. As can be imagined, they did not submit unquestioningly to this. Many monastic pamphlets appeared, declaring, with the backing of canonical texts, that "monks should not prostrate themselves before the emperor." However, the battle was lost from the start. By the fifth century, Buddhism, by now domesticated, passed under the close control of the state apparatus. What the emperors sought from this new religion was not so much deliverance from the bonds that kept them in this world, but rather an increase of their own power here below.

Despite its popularity, in the eyes of the Confucians Buddhism always retained the stigma of a foreign religion and because of this periodically became the object of governmental persecution. Under Emperor Wuzong, in particular, in 845, over two thousand monks and nuns were defrocked and many temples and statues destroyed. Closer to our own times and in an altogether different political context, the Cultural Revolution likewise inflicted terrible ravages. But although severely hampered in its day-to-day practices, Buddhism was anchored in the mores of the Chinese sufficiently deeply and has survived all those ideological and political storms.

The Adventures of Immanence

Thanks to the works of François Jullien, certain aspects of Chinese thought are becoming better known.[1] His books have the double merit of focusing upon a number of particularly interesting features of the Confucian tradition, which he describes as a thought of immanence, allusion, and detours, while also providing this tradition with its philosophical credentials, without—however—slipping into facile comparativism. All the same, we should beware of believing that this is *all* there is to Chinese thought, thereby repeating Confucianism's own gesture of exclusion with regard to Buddhism, Daoism, and popular religion.

It is widely held that there is, strictly speaking, no philosophy or religion at all in China: In China, one allegedly finds none of the conceptual oppositions (such as theory and practice, cause and effect, ends and means, the world of ideas and the perceptible world) that first Greece, then Europe generally managed to elaborate. And above all, China is said to know nothing of divine transcendence and to offer us only an example of a "total, all-encompassing immanence."

The reciprocal influences between Buddhism and other kinds of Chinese thought (Confucianism, Daoism) should prevent us from too hastily assimilating "Chinese thought" to a quasi-immutable philosophical system (even if—particularly if—change constitutes its principal object) and from then being subjected to the ideological effects of such thought. The subtlety of the thought of Confucius and his heirs should not blind us to the stultifying side of Confucian orthodoxy, which dominated Chinese society for almost twenty centuries. As the descendants of Voltaire, we would be wrong to allow the affinities that attracted the *philosophes* to Confucianism to continue to mask the pluralism of Chinese thought.

Socratic definition, the basis of Western thought, stands in sharp contrast to what François Jullien calls Confucian "modulation." Whereas the notion of a single truth presupposes some immutable essence, a variety of views makes it easier to accommodate a constantly changing reality. "Shifting speech" makes it possible to embrace reality from every angle and to cleave to the spontaneous movement of things. At the same time, however, Jullien draws attention to the perverse effects of circumlocution and periphrasis once political prudence becomes second nature to the speaker and prevents him from speaking frankly. Although it may be true that all poetry tends to become political, that is not to say that politics becomes poetical. One cannot but sense how much ideological violence may be hidden behind such "harmonious" discourse and the apology for naturalness. It was against such a stifling atmosphere that a "straight-talking" Chan master such as Linji Yixuan (ninth century) tried to react until he was himself "recuperated" by a politically and spiritually correct exegesis.

As a subject of knowledge and curiosity, Chinese thought has long occupied a privileged position in Europe. Despite its manifest differences from Western thought, it is after all not as foreign to us as is often suggested. Or perhaps we could say that it has long been "recognized" as other and has, by the same token, been tamed as a figure of otherness. The Jesuit missionaries were already seeking to reduce that otherness when they translated the Chinese authors into Latin, thereby turning Confucius (better known, until Ricci, by his real name, Kongfuzi) into *the* "philosopher" of the Chinese (*Sinarum philosophus*).

The Jesuits' exclusive interest in Confucianism, later followed by that of Western sinologists, singled out one particular type of Chinese discourse, which monopolized access to knowledge and truth. This has favored the eclipse of other forms of thought that are just as relevant and has obscured Chinese intellectual and cultural reality, rather than revealing it.

The eminent "Daologist" Isabelle Robinet draws attention to this problem when she deplores "the misunderstanding into which Western historians of Chinese thought are led . . . when, to varying degrees, they ascribe an unduly privileged position to Confucianism and make it the center and touchstone of Chinese thought to the point where other currents are to some extent drained of their content. . . . In consequence, Daoism is denied the place that it rightfully deserves in the history of Chinese thought, being reduced simply to Laozi and Zhuangzi, and never taken into account. Yet its philosophical dimension, which has yet to be studied for what it is, has remained vibrant throughout that history to which, precisely, it presents a different, complementary facet."[2] It is perhaps worth adding, however, that that very complementarity itself belongs to our preconceived ideas about Chinese thought, masking, as it does, its other components and its essential plurality. As a literate tradition, Chinese Buddhism may be seen as operating in counterpoint to the Confucian tradition in some respects and to the Daoist tradition in others.

The allusive subtlety of Confucius's *Analects* stems largely from a somewhat laconic oral tradition upon which written commentaries were subsequently grafted, developing endless complexities. Did Confucius himself consciously introduce that subtle wisdom into his works, in expectation of an ideal disciple who would pass it on, or was it read into them retrospectively by the Confucian tradition? Appealing to the supposed intentions of an author is always a tricky business. To put that another way, has not the canonization of the Sage led to a quest for (and consequently the discovery of) more subtlety in the text than it really contained? In truth, all exegetic traditions do just that: They create meaning in the belief that they are merely revealing it. Is the indirect access provided by exegesis really access at all, and if it is, does it lead to what it thinks it has discovered or to something quite different—rather as Christopher Columbus discovered America instead of India? Not that that necessarily removes all value from the discovery, and not that such a deviation is necessarily a bad thing.

Outside Confucianism, a similar tendency is detectable in the "subtle" ravings of commentaries on the sayings of the Chan masters, such as the *Biyan lu* (Record of the Emerald Cliff). This is an anthology of "cases" (*gong'an*, or *kōan* in Japanese), the famous riddles that a Chan initiate must resolve (or rather dissolve) in order to achieve awakening. The Sinicization of Buddhism probably reached its climax in the "literary" Chan of the Song dynasty (tenth to thirteenth centuries), in particular in its recourse to classical (Chinese or Buddhist) poetry or to Chan poems, which were sometimes collected together in anthologies in which disciples could delve freely in order to convey their insight to their master. Attention is frequently drawn to the artificial and, as it were, perverted nature of so bookish a response. However, in the best instances, it was not really the case that a disciple would mechanically fall back on a ready-made response. Rather, through the powerful suggestiveness of the poem, he would be brought to a state of awakening and would then convey this to others. A similar practice appears to be traceable back to Confucius, who encouraged his disciples to delve freely into a prestigious anthology of poetry known as *The Book of Odes*. All the same, this practice undeniably soon tended to become stereotyped. So we should perhaps do well not to regard these sometimes laborious literate refinements as representative of Chinese thought as a whole.

On the other hand, neither can we ascribe the emergence of imagination to the West without overlooking a number of Chinese (and non-Chinese) religious currents for which the world of images (*xiang*), situated in between the relative and the absolute, remained a reality that could be reached through visual meditation and symbols. François Jullien rightly stresses the part that Buddhism played in rendering the imaginary increasingly accessible to the Chinese, especially as described in novels.[3] In various Buddhist schools, the visualization of Buddhas, deities, and "demonic" beings who represented superior energies played an important role. So the contrast drawn between China and the West seems too clear-cut and to some extent metaphysical. According to Jullien, in China, the transcendence of Heaven in relation to man stems from nothing external; it is simply the totality of immanence at the level of the whole world. Although as a result of its taste for immanence Chinese thought has not produced any other metaphysical level (such as the level of Buddhist essences or that of the Platonic Ideas), we nevertheless find in it a religious Beyond that does constitute a form of transcendence. At about the time when Confucius was discoursing on *ren* (humanity), emperors who died took with them hundreds of slaves who were supposed to serve them in the Beyond. (A number of tombs have yielded up their decapitated bodies.) That Beyond certainly represented a different ontological level. Similarly, Chinese drama originally (and even today, as performed outside temples) essentially constituted a representation of the divine; it was a communication with the other world, a manifestation of "the other stage." In Buddhism, the world is composed of three spheres (or levels): that of desire, that of form (or matter), and that of the formless (or immaterial—which, however, is still not quite transcendent). The *nirvāṇa* that was sought by certain Chinese Buddhists was located beyond those three levels.

Jullien has certainly shown that the "Chinese" (for which read "Confucian") tradition opted for "referential" interpretation rather than the "symbolic" kind found in the West. Where a Western commentator looks beyond the obvious meaning to discover a more abstract, metaphysical truth, a Chinese commentator instead seeks for an allusion to a precise political situation. However, counterexamples are not hard to find. In Chan, in Linji Yixuan's works, for example, one finds apparently "political" poems interpreted allegorically to convey a purely spiritual meaning. This leads one to wonder whether the Chinese choice of immanence might not to some extent be linked with the corpus of works (Confucian, Daoist, Buddhist, or other) that sinologists select to study. Buddhism seems to have introduced into China the very transcendence that we are told does not exist there. Terminology may also have something to do with this situation.

As Isabelle Robinet remarks: "If transcendence is understood in the generally accepted sense of recognition of something not completely knowable,
something whose nature one does not understand, something situated beyond all known or knowable frontiers . . . then the Chinese must be very
arrogant if they disclaim all knowledge of transcendence. Rather, surely, it
is simply that some of them are interested in not-knowing (or not-under-
standing), while others are not." This kind of "Chinese thought" is, all in
all, essentially a philosophy of the literati, so we may surely be justified if
we interpret it ideologically. Much leisure time is assuredly requisite if one
is to discuss the world's "process." The Chinese discourse on "naturalness"
is a means of anchoring certain social relations of power in the great laws
of the universe, instead of resorting to mythology and the sacred, as the
Japanese do.

On the other hand, a rapid glance at China's "other," in this instance,
Japan, shows us that China's otherness still preserved too much that was
just the same, too much that had simply been tamed. In contrast, what
could be more foreign to Western sensibilities than the Japanese mythology of the *Kojiki* (Record of Ancient Things, dated 712), particularly once
it became the national ideology (*kokugaku*), around the seventeenth century? Yet in the name of a purely Japanese *esprit de finesse*, what that ideology rejected, precisely, was Chinese thought (including Buddhism), which
it called *karagokoro* ("Chinese spirit"), because it was too rationalistic and
too alien. Greater subtlety than one's own can always be found, and to
some Japanese, Chinese subtlety certainly seemed pretty flat. With respect
to Chinese rationalism, those Japanese were not altogether mistaken. One
should, for example, note the logic that presides over the elaboration of the
hexagrams of the *Yijing* (The Book of Changes) and the rationalizing tendency that stemmed from their interpretation—to such a degree that Leibnitz fancied he detected in it affinities with his own thought. As soon as it
distances itself from pure divination (and so from a certain divine transcendence) and sets out to "naturalize" the cosmos, the thought of the *Yijing* imposes an abstract rational schema—complex and subtle to be sure,
but nevertheless eminently logical. Thus, the *Yijing* has quite naturally
found its place among game software.

Zhuangzi and Chan

In the course of developing the potentialities of Mahāyāna, Chinese Buddhism to a large extent opened up to a number of non-Buddhist influences, in particular the thought of the Daoist writer Zhuangzi. We should no doubt resist exaggerating the distance separating Zhuangzi and Confucius. One of the differences between these two figures, if not between their respective ways of thinking, is that whereas Confucius was always seeking the company of powerful people (in order to advise them) and good disciples, the regular company of Zhuangzi calls to mind of a den of thieves: brigands, cripples, one-armed men, butchers, idiots, vagabonds. We find the same kind of rather seedy individuals involved with Chan. Zhuangzi often pokes fun at Confucius and his doctrine, criticizing the latter for limiting itself to the visible world without seeking to understand its origin. However, some of his dialogues that set on stage Confucius and his favorite disciple, Yanhui, present a more nuanced picture of the Sage. In one of these dialogues, after Yanhui has set out his plan for reforming the regime of a local tyrant, explaining the method he intends to adopt (virtue and imitation of the Ancients), Confucius tells him that his plan is doomed to failure because it leaves no room for "the fasting of the mind." Pressed by Yanhui to define this, he says: "Make your will one! Don't listen with your ears, listen with your mind. No, don't listen with your mind, but listen with your spirit. Listening stops with the ears, the mind stops with recognition, but spirit is empty and waits on all things. The Way gathers in emptiness alone. Emptiness is the fasting of the mind."[4]

Despite Confucius's warning, this fasting of the mind, which is a truly Daoist feature, also crops up in another of Zhuangzi's anecdotes, one that relates to Prince Wenhui and his cook. When cutting up an ox, the latter wielded his knife with a rhythm that called to mind the great music of ancient times. Watching him at his work one day, the prince went into raptures and questioned him about his art. The cook set down his knife and replied:

What I care about is the Way, which goes beyond skill. When I first began cutting up oxen, all I could see was the ox itself. After three years I no longer saw the whole ox. And now—now I go at it by spirit and don't look with my eyes. Perception and understanding have come to a stop and spirit moves where it wants. I go along with the natural makeup, strike in the big hollows, guide the knife through the big openings, and follow things as they are. So I never touch the smallest ligament or tendon, much less a main joint.

A good cook changes his knife once a year—because he cuts. A mediocre cook changes his knife once a month—because he hacks. I've had this knife of mine for nineteen years and I've cut up thousands of oxen with it, and yet the blade is as good as though it had just come from the grindstone.[5]

For Zhuangzi, a sage is one who has acceded to the highest truth, to that through which things come to exist. The notion of "that through which" (*suoyi*) also plays an important role in Confucianism, but only the Daoists, following Zhuangzi, underline the importance of nescience or nonknowledge in attaining to that highest truth. Ordinary knowledge, as recommended by the Confucians, can never understand what it is that makes it possible. This negative path was to constitute a deep vein running through Chinese thought and in particular to influence the non-thought of Chan.

One of Zhuangzi's most famous apologias is that concerning Hun-dun (indistinction, primordial chaos): The lord of the center, Hundun, had two friends, the sovereign of the Northern Sea and the sovereign of the Southern Sea. One day these two, having met in the land of Hundun, who had treated them with great kindness, decided to recompense him for his warm welcome, and they said to each other: "'All men . . . have seven openings so they can hear, eat, and breathe. But Hundun alone doesn't have any. Let's try boring him some!' Every day they bored another hole, and on the seventh day Hundun died."[6] The cosmos was born out of chaos; a symbolic body came from an organless body. In Chan/Zen, there is one type of *stūpa* (funerary monument) described as ovoid or seamless, which symbolizes the body of the deceased that has been made perfect by death (which is assimilated to awakening), that is to say, the chaos to which he has now returned. The Chan Master Zhongfeng Mingben (1263–1323) compares the Chan teaching to Hundun:

Somebody came and delivered a blow to the head of Chan, another a blow to the feet of Chan, a third a blow to the heart of Chan. Finally, someone else came along and put three dots above those marks (already made). Upon closer examination, Chan, thus ornamented, no longer resembles its original appearance. Subsequently, others came and added new marks to those already there. Sometimes they put them in the wrong place, and they began to criticize one another and to give names to those marks, calling them "Chan of the Tathāgata (or Buddha)," "Chan of the patriarchs," "literary Chan," "heretical Chan," "Chan of the Auditors," "worldly Chan" . . . "Chan of the shouts and blows."[7]

Here Mingben is critical of attempts to classify the teachings of Chan into a doctrinal system and a hierarchy, instead of showing that Chan, in its truly chaotic essence, is beyond all hierarchies. But his comparison of Chan to primordial chaos goes somewhat wide off the mark, for the Chan in question here already has eyes, feet, and so on, whereas in Zhuangzi's parable the organic differentiation of the originally organless body is the very cause of Hundun's death. Mingben deserves his own criticisms to the extent that his discourse leaves marks upon the smooth body of Chan. This corporeal metaphor was further strangely developed by a later Zen master, Manzan Dōhaku (1636–1715). Manzan compared the nine Buddhist schools of his period to the nine orifices of the body and Zen to its heart. But he failed to explain precisely which schools, according to him, corresponded to the lower orifices.

The other form of Buddhism that, while remaining very Indian, exerted a major influence upon Chinese culture was, without doubt, Tantrism (or the "Diamond Vehicle," Vajrayāna). It was largely through this intermediary that Indian culture spread throughout Asia, all the way to Japan, which then proceeded to adopt part of its phonetic system. Under the Tang, the Zhen'yan school, or school of *mantras*, was even adopted as the Chinese Buddhist orthodoxy, but clashed with Confucian anticlericalism. Unlike Chan, it never recovered from the persecution of 845. However, Tantrism did not disappear from the Chinese scene either as rapidly or as completely as is usually believed, and in the thirteenth century, under the Yuan dynasty, another, Tibeto-Mongolian version was introduced. This was the "Lamaist" Buddhism observed by the young Marco Polo. Furthermore, some Tantric rites and beliefs were assimilated by popular religion and Daoism. That is not surprising, because the Tantric practices presented many affinities with Daoist sexual practices, in particular the use of alchemy and "the art of preserving the vital essence." Both doctrines came under attack from a prudish and rationalistic Confucianism anxious to stamp out superstitions. But on this point, the Confucian ideologists clashed with the fascination with spiritual and magical powers that was evinced by the sovereigns of China. Although Zhen'yan, as a school, virtually disappeared from the religious scene, Tantrism continued to make its presence felt in Daoism and its rituals, in the Chinese theater, and even in popular religion.

Ideally, it would desirable to write at greater length about the Chinese contribution to Buddhist philosophy (and the reverse: the Buddhist contribution to Chinese philosophy) and, in particular, the numerous philosophical works produced by the various Chinese Buddhist schools. One could then move on to the Japanese contributions, and we ought also to make room for the literary or mythological contributions of the Chan and Tantric "madmen," dialogical thought, and the theme of transgression. But a whole other book would be needed to tackle all these subjects.

From the Middle Empire to the Empire of the Self

Basically, it is neither Europe nor China that I have come to seek here, but a vision of China. I have it in my grasp and am sinking my teeth into it.
    —Victor Segalen, *Oeuvres*

In its "amnesia" where Buddhism is concerned, present-day sinology is heir to a long Chinese tradition that, in the wake of Confucianism (and Daoism), considered the Buddhist doctrine to be a vulgar heresy or—worse—a barbarian religion. That tradition found particularly eloquent spokesmen in the West, among them Victor Segalen.

In one chapter, devoted to the art of the Wei, of his *The Great Statuary of China*, Segalen holds forth with some complacency on what he calls "the Buddhist heresy" and its damaging influence on the Wei kingdom. Similar analyses appear in another work, *Résultats archéologiques en Chine occidentale* (Archeological results in western China), in which the Wei kingdom is criticized for having marginalized itself in Chinese history by welcoming in "China's major heresy, sinfulness, and slavery, Buddhism." When Segalen visited the great Buddhist temple of Yungang, all he descried there was "the repetition of a single monotonous type." Nor did Longmen, another great rocky Buddhist site, escape his sarcasm: "In short, in this cave, all that is purely Buddhist is *ugly*. The decor, on the other hand, is extremely interesting. Whatever is secular and Chinese is *beautiful*." According to him, even the site was nothing but a monumental mess: "The mountain, the pure mountain, with its felling areas, its laws, its architecturally contrived 'order,' was no longer any more than an empty sponge, a place putrefied by the works of man."[8]

Segalen passed similar judgment on the nonmonumental Buddhist statuary highly valued by Westerners, who wrongly believe it to be Chi-

nese. "These products of the Hindu apostolate were credited with an autochthonous value. Since they represented men in stone for the first time,
attention was chiefly paid to the most exclusive human attribute: the face.
People were grateful to them for introducing the human face to 'Chinese
art.' But because these faces of Buddhas, which are expressionless both by
nature and by dogma, cannot be called beautiful in a material sense, they
were credited with a spiritual beauty, 'spirituality.' People went into ecstasies over them. The rest was up to the dealers." After his aesthetic critique of Buddhist art, Segalen moved on to attack Buddhism generally,
contrasting its current decadence with the pure teaching of its founder. In
his "Notes for an Essay on Chinese Sculpture," his jottings ran as follows:

Consider Buddhism in China as a sickness in Chinese thought; a sickness of Chinese Forms.—Double borrowings, triple borrowings all cascading over one another.—The pure origin is the southern canon.—Then the legends of the North
unleashed all those gods with misshapen attributes. The whole mishmash has already been well stirred. Soon it will be incomprehensible or, worse still, we will
understand it all: It will be a religion. A religion of the "for the weak" style, a sop
for the disinherited![9]

Already, in his *Journal des îles* (Journal of the Islands), written while passing through Ceylon (Sri Lanka) in 1904, Segalen, outraged by the devotion
of the Singhalese to the relic of the Buddha's tooth, had remarked: "From
the master I descend—and it truly is a great fall—to the cult, to the manifestations of the populace, to relics." And he concluded as follows: "In the
future, then, I will violently separate out the formless conglomeration of
myths, cycles, counted years, and all the many episodic Buddhas—everything that clutters and crushes the work of the Master. What a shame it is
that there is only one word, Buddhism, to designate so many different
things, and that that word itself is comical, squat, pot-bellied, paunchy,
and smug. In the future then, I will remind myself: This is the teaching of
Siddhartha, the man-who-attains-his-goal."[10] During that visit to Ceylon,
Segalen had written a drama in five acts entitled *Siddhartha*, which he offered to the French composer Claude Debussy, but the project fell through.
The creation of such a dichotomy between "original" Buddhism and popular "superstitions" constituted a violent distortion of the living reality of
historical Buddhism in the name of a purified and angelic ideal. There is
not, nor has there ever been, any Buddhism set apart from those who practice it, and anyway, in reality, all that appears to us to stem from "supersti-

tion" (the cult of relics, for instance) was to a large extent the creation of scholar-monks.

In his diary, Augusto Gilbert de Voisins, the friend who accompanied Segalen on his 1909 archaeological expedition, sheds a rather different light upon the disgust that Segalen manifests for Buddhist tawdriness. Having stumbled upon a magnificent wooden Buddha in an abandoned temple, the two friends deliberated as to what to do:

"This statue must be ours! We cannot leave it behind as if it were just a bronze pot! We won't leave without it! This we swear, in words that commit our honor and that are binding." "That is all very well, but how shall we set about it? Carry it off? Steal it? We could not possibly even lift this block of wood!" "Right, then shall we cut off its head?" We immediately found an axe in our baggage and set about the sacrilegious task. With all my strength, I struck the first blow on the golden neck, but left hardly a mark on the age-old block of wood. In vain we struggled. Segalen took his turn with the axe, but to no avail. He puffed and panted. I was exasperated, our hands were burning, and no progress was made. We persevered for half an hour and were probably on the point of giving up when, to put us completely at our ease, two passing peasants, drawn by the noise, came in.

We were very embarrassed, for there are limits even to cynicism, and I imagine that our ashamed faces showed it. To defile a temple by defacing the statue of its god is an action that is hard to excuse. But the newcomers, far from manifesting anger and indignation, on the contrary behaved in a way that stupefied us. They offered us their assistance! First they got us to understand that it was hopeless to try to decapitate this heavy Buddha while it stood erect. They laid it down on its stomach, with the head resting on a log, slipped some blocks beneath its ribs, steadied it with bundles of straw and finally, laughing at our ineptitude, relieved us of the axe. A few well aimed strokes, some cracking, then a dreadful rending, and the deed was done. The beheading was completed![11]

The two accomplices fled, with the head stashed in their bag. As they went along, Segalen made up a story based on this incident, and Augusto Gilbert de Voisins tells us that its horrific ending seemed to assuage his sense of guilt. The decapitation scene does indeed appear in Segalen's *Imaginaires*, in a story entitled "The Head," the hero of which is an autobiographical character called Robert. The scene, which is inserted into a love story featuring Robert and a young woman called Annie, ends in an altogether fantastical fashion. Robert tells Annie that on the way back from this expedition, as night was falling, his horse stumbled, and, as a result, the head was dropped, rolled down a slope, and disappeared into a ravine.

When Robert peered down into it, he beheld the Face, smiling as it floated gently up toward him. Gradually it faded, and finally, twisting round, merged with his own face, thereby imparting supreme knowledge to him. Robert now proposed sharing this knowledge with the woman who, spellbound, was listening to his tale.

The incident involving the decapitated statue is also recounted in a letter (dated August 29, 1909) from Segalen to his wife (the Annie of the short story), a letter written at the end of a "delightful day." Subsequent letters make no further mention of the short story prompted by that incident. At one point Segalen even thought of writing a "Buddhist novel set in our own times" about the discovery of Buddhism by two lovers and the manner in which they then sublimated their love by renouncing it. Its provisional, somewhat arrogant title was *The Initiation of Our Lord, Buddha*, which was later altered to *Imitation of the Buddha*. In this account, a new twist that was added to the story spoke volumes about Segalen's sense of being pulled this way and that between spirituality and sexuality. "The end is poignant: If they do not renounce their great love, they will lose merit, fall into lower existences, perhaps even descend to the Buddhist hells, which, for the first time, they can now imagine. . . . But come what may, they will descend to it, still loving each other."[12]

In passing, it is perhaps worth noting the significant differences between A. G. de Voisin's diary version of this incident and Segalen's romantic and epistolary versions. In the latter, culpability is sublimated in a facile manner, and the sacrilege is transformed into a superior kind of transgression that leads to the fusion of the guilty party and the victim in a kind of ultimate enlightenment. But the main impression left is that of Segalen's idealization of the Indian Buddha and his pure "spontaneity," which is accompanied in real life by deep scorn and a remorseless profanation of the religion of Chinese Buddhism in its cultic aspects. Inasmuch as this Chinese Buddhism is regarded as being neither truly Chinese nor truly Buddhist (since it is no longer Indian) and consequently no longer sacred, it is not possible to profane it. It is nothing, or deserves to be nothing, so there is no harm in consigning it, whether passively or actively, to oblivion, to the nonexistence from which it should never have emerged. As this clearly shows, it is possible for an overly conservative and idealistic conception of Buddhism to wreak considerable ravages.

4

A Hybrid Teaching

"Philosophical" Buddhism

Usually philosophy is defined as rational, autonomous discourse, free from all religious authority, but with Buddhist thought that is not the case. Yet Nāgārjuna (second to third century), Candrakīrti (eighth century), and other Buddhist logicians do bear comparison with their Western fellows. To be sure, Buddhism remains a spiritual quest, and attempts are often made to discredit Buddhist thinkers because they venture into a terrain that "true" philosophers would refuse to enter. But in that case, we would also have to recognize that no more were Socrates and Plato really philosophers, or Augustine, Spinoza, Pascal, Nietzsche, Kierkegaard, and Bergson. We must either reject this system, with its double measures and double standards, or else, as I now propose to do, we must include in it the two Buddhist truths. The notion of a twofold truth should allow us to bypass the old dilemma of faith and reason and to rediscover the "external thought" of Buddhism, that is to say, ritual thought.

The thought of the Buddha, like that of Descartes, according to Merleau-Ponty, "is one of those institutions that, the longer they last, continue to grow and to transform within themselves all the events by which they are confronted until such time as, imperceptibly, the movement is reversed, and the excess of situations and relations that they fail to assimilate over those that they can absorb changes them and gives rise to a new form that, however, could never have developed without them."[1]

The earliest European historians of Buddhism tried to recover the historical Buddha from beneath the embellishments added by tradition. But that "minimal" Buddha is nothing but a fiction—and a Western one at that—one that lacks even the legitimacy of autochthonous fictions, yet displays a typical Orientalist arrogance toward those. We must leave behind the kind of erudite tradition that claims to lead all the way back to the sources and on that account believes that it knows more than Buddhists themselves about the Buddha's real personality and all that Buddhism truly is. By reconstructing the life of the founder and his original doctrine, nineteenth-century Orientalists were killing two birds with one stone: They demonstrated the degree to which, by reason of all their uncouth superstitions, the Buddhist peoples whom they had colonized had fallen from their original philosophy and thus also the extent to which they were now therefore in need of the European Enlightenment. In the case of India, for example, they set Buddhist rationalism in contrast to Hindu ritualism. At the same time, in the rational ethic of Buddhism they discovered a religion after their own hearts: the Buddha became the model of the free thinker who does not hesitate to oppose age-old traditions, rejecting all forms of social determinism, and Buddhism became a religion for the individual, the rationalism of which formed an illuminating contrast to Christianity (ritualistic Catholicism, in particular).

In truth, in this respect, Western historians are not always solely responsible, for the autochthonous religious elites likewise display a tendency to negate anything in the Buddhist tradition that seems in the slightest mythological, ritualistic, or metaphysical while, on the contrary, stressing all the particularly rational, philosophical, psychological, and ethical aspects of Buddhism. These modernist authors, mostly from the educated middle classes, seek in all good faith to redefine Buddhism as a religion of reason and to reject the Buddhist cosmology and cult as outdated superstitions. The apology for "philosophical" Buddhism is perfectly justifiable when it is a matter of winning recognition for Buddhism as a movement of thought in its own right. However, it becomes problematic when it insists on limiting itself to a narrowly rationalist, demythologizing and antiritualistic approach, thereby misrepresenting what Buddhism is and always has been. It forgets one crucial thing—that mythology, metaphysics, and ritual constitute a living whole and that, without them, the Buddhist "Three Jewels"—the Buddha, the *Dharma* (the Law or doctrine), and the *Saṅgha* (community)—lose their meaning in the eyes of the faithful. Reconstructed (or rather distorted) in that fashion, Buddhism has become no more than a museum piece.

The question of whether, in its essence (if there is such a thing), Buddhism is a "philosophical" doctrine clearly rests upon the type of materials taken into account. Paul Mus has shown that once research faced up to the study of monuments and texts, it was able to produce all kinds of data bearing upon a number of by no means secondary aspects of Buddhism (myths, symbols, rituals) that confirm its resemblance to other religions. Conversely, a reading of the textual documentation, no longer as deposits of "Oriental wisdom," but rather as "monuments" that reflect a particular form of culture, leads one to restore Buddhism to its cultural and sociopolitical context.

An objective approach to Buddhism must not be deterred by its more embarrassing aspects. In the living reality of Buddhism, the philosophical and the religious, the rational and the magical, the profane and the sacred, go hand in hand, however much this may affront our logical minds. What Buddhism, as a middle way between two extremes, manages to rise above is precisely the traditional opposition between philosophy and religion. It is neither solely a philosophy nor solely a religion, but is *both at once*, or perhaps *neither*. It is perfectly possible to be religiously philosophical or philosophically religious. However, the implications of this quadrilateral logic are not always made sufficiently clear. In order to avoid some of the blind alleys into which an exclusive emphasis upon Indian Buddhist "philosophy" would lead us, we must construct the object of study differently, placing the accent in particular upon Chinese and Japanese influences. Mus's view of Buddhism was that "India produced it, India will explain it." But that will no longer do. Even if Buddhism remains incomprehensible without India, India, on its own, no longer suffices to explain it.

Philosophy, this so-called "love of wisdom," is sometimes a fear of truth, a retreat in the face of reality, an example of what the Chinese call "a love of dragons in paintings." The expression is a reference to a Chinese painter who loved nothing more than painting dragons and had acquired such skill that his dragons appeared to be alive. Hearing of this, a dragon king decided to reward him by appearing before him. But the sight was so upsetting to the painter that instead of making the most of it to revise his paintings in the light of this live model, he fled without more ado. His interest in dragons was illusory. Yet even when conventional and illusory, such an interest may sometimes lead to reality, for it is the only chance of meeting a dragon.

Like dreams, philosophy and wisdom sometimes operate as guardians of sleep. Despite his rejection of all metaphysics, the philosopher remains fascinated by the society game known as philosophy. One who is "awakened," in contrast, is someone who has touched bottom and has settled himself on the granite bedrock of reality. He is no longer duped by the philosopher's fascination with philosophy or by the sage's fascination with wisdom. He no longer plays that game—or if he does, it is with full knowledge of the facts. But does that not come down to saying that he no longer really knows how to play the game, since his taste for it is gone forever and he has lost the ability to become immersed in it, lost the *illusio*? Whether Buddhist or not, a sad saint is a sorry excuse for a saint—let alone for a Buddha. That is why, once early Buddhism's emaciated, unworldly Buddha, contemptuous of the world, had been replaced by the smiling Buddhas of Mahāyāna, it took but a step to reach the tubby, laughing Buddha of the Sino-Japanese tradition (Budai in Chinese, Hotei in Japanese). Whereas his Indian colleagues mostly remain seated in meditation, Budai is often to be found strolling through the marketplace, amid all its worldly tumult. This is a theme that is also dear to the Daoists: Their immortals, too, frequent the marketplace, where there is nothing to distinguish them from the common man except—for those who have eyes to see—their square pupils.

Buddhist Religion and the Sacred

The time has come to change tack: to affirm both the importance of Buddhism as a religious and cultural system and also, over and above that, the need for an inclusive approach. Most of those who have approached the Buddhist doctrine as philosophers have, unsurprisingly, found in it nothing but philosophy. Others, in reaction, abandoning all philosophical rationality, have been bent on drawing attention to the irrational, mystical character of certain forms of Buddhism and have been mystified by it. This tendency explains the attraction exerted by Zen and Tibetan Buddhism in the alternative culture of the 1960s and among its New Age Buddhist enthusiasts. In both cases, the Buddhism thus recreated in Western circles has frequently had very little to do with reality. For a religion, Buddhism is rather philosophical, but for a philosophy, it is extremely religious. Even the greatest Buddhist philosophers and logicians, such as Nāgārjuna and Candrakīrti, set their method of reductio ad absurdum (the reduction of a thesis by showing the absurdity of its necessary consequences and their perverse effects) in a religious context—a fact that, in the eyes of Western philosophers and logicians, clearly indicates the flawed nature of their reasoning, if not of their taste. Efforts are actively made to forget this aspect of Buddhist thought in the same way that scholars, for many years, sought to conceal Socrates' *daimon* and Kepler's fascination with the "music of the spheres" and other interests of an occult nature.

The textbook alternative—philosophy or religion?—makes very little sense where Buddhism, by nature a plural phenomenon, is concerned. Philosophy and religion can be kept separate only within an ethnocentric perspective from which, precisely, the nondualistic thought of Buddhism enables us to detach ourselves. Furthermore, it is important to see that this is not an altogether neutral question, since it frequently implies a denial of the religious aspect. The reason why I nevertheless raise it is that we still need to consider some of its implications, for these continue to obstruct a better understanding of Buddhism.

In 1904, the monks of Sri Lanka (then Ceylon) presented the following petition to the king of England, Edward VII: "According to the laws of the Buddha, the laity is not a part of religion. The members of the *sangha* are the sole living representatives of Buddhism on earth." Throughout the history of Buddhism, that declaration and others of the same ilk have been vigorously rejected. It should also be noted that, in Buddhism, the borderline between monks and laity is far less impermeable than in Christianity. A Buddhist monk can easily renounce his vows. In Thailand, for example, entering monastic orders is regarded as an obligatory rite of passage for all young men, but for most of them, it is a temporary state. There is nothing shameful about defrocking oneself. In Japan, monks may marry, and some lead extremely active sexual lives, and a wide range of intermediate statuses exist between that of an orthodox monk and that of a layman. Buddhism is certainly a clerical religion with marked esoteric tendencies, but it is important to note the growing importance of lay people in Mahāyāna and particularly in Chan. The lay ideal, represented by Vimalakīrti, the ideal "head of the household," sometimes meets with resistance on the part of the clergy.

Is the current interest in Buddhism part of what is somewhat too hastily called "the return of the religious" (which is by no means a return of the already established religions)? The somewhat theatrical aspect of these pretences of leaving and so-called returns (of the "death of man" and the "return to individualism" type) suggests that they belong more to the domain of myth than to that of history. But even if the traditional conceptual equipment of some manifestations of the religious phenomenon may seem somewhat outdated, religion does seem to belie the tales of its imminent death. On the whole, it is in quite good shape to the extent that it stems from epistemological structures that are still operative in our modern world, in fact, that even define it.

Mystical Experience and the Sacred

Before deciding to what extent Buddhism is religious or even constitutes a religion, it is important to reach a measure of agreement as to the categories represented by *religion, the religious*, and *the sacred*. The diversity of phenomena covered by the term "sacred" is conveyed well enough by the tongue-in-cheek "definition" provided by Ambrose Bierce in his *Devil's Dictionary*: "Dedicated to some religious purpose; having a divine character; inspiring solemn thoughts or emotions; as, the Dalai Lama of Thibet; the Moogum of M'bwango; the temple of Apes in Ceylon; the Cow in India; the Crocodile, the Cat and the Onion of ancient Egypt; the Mufti of Moosh; the hair of the dog that bit Noah, etc."

Are we talking here about religion, or religions? The religious phenomenon, while eminently unique, is also irremediably plural. The domain of religion, long sacred and secret, has become a sort of wasteland where both historians and philosophers of religion seek to put up their flag, with psychoanalysts, anthropologists, and sociologists hard on their heels. There are, fortunately, fewer theories of religion than theorists of the same. The comparative study of religions has at last sanctioned the idea that religions are first and foremost cultural factors, symbolic constructions, and systems of representation that deserve to be studied as such. The on the whole recent interest in ritual and myth has been encouraged by a widespread agnosticism, a kind of polytheism of values that implies a retreat on the part of faith and makes a measure of detachment possible. If we can now assert the value of the religious phenomenon, that is precisely because religion has by now virtually lost its hold on our society. The militant, Promethean atheism characteristic of the scientific thought and philosophy of the nineteenth century is, by the same token, now felt to be somewhat tasteless. The prevailing intellectual fascination with "religion*s*" is simply the other side to our tendency to distance ourselves from *the* religion of the West, Christianity. The renewed interest in things spiritual implies a secularization. Our disinterested study of the religious phenomenon is prompted by a basic lack of interest and is a distant effect of the Enlightenment, the combative vigor of which has been lost, leaving only a praiseworthy (but somewhat abstract) desire to understand humanity.

Indo-European Roots

Let us begin, fittingly enough, with etymology. It has to be recognized that, despite those who favor the hypothesis of a *homo religiosus*, there exists in Indo-European languages no common term for "religion." Religion, as an institution, was at first not distinguished from other institutions (such as law). The religious was everywhere, not yet perceived as a separate, sacred sphere. It was just such a phenomenon that inclined Christian missionaries to declare that there was no religion in China. For us, meanwhile, as Jacques Derrida has noted, to think "religion" is to think the "Roman."[2]

Benveniste has called into question the (quasi-religious) etymology that linked *religio* with *ligare* (to bind). He favors a different, more ancient etymology already proposed by Cicero. This explains *religio* by *legere*, "to collect, assemble."[3] Far from designating "religion" as a whole, *religio* originally simply designated the scrupulous attitude of the diviner toward the oracle. It thus meant "a hesitation that restrains, a selective scruple that warns." Hence *religere*, "to re-collect," that is to say, "to return for a new choice," "to reconsider a prior enterprise." And that, Benveniste concludes, is a good definition of a religious "scruple." With this meaning, we may say that Socrates, with the scruples dictated by his *daimon*, was a perfectly religious man in the Roman sense. But how should we explain the success of the other meaning, derived from *religare*, which underlines the binding aspect of religion, a bond either with the divine or with other human beings? According to Benveniste, "this is because the content of religion itself has changed. For a Christian, what characterizes the new faith in opposition to the pagan religions is the bond of piety, this dependence of the faithful on God, this *obligation* in the true sense of the word. The concept of *religio* was remodeled on the idea that man made for himself about his relation to God, an idea that was totally different from that of the old Roman *religio* and prepared the way for the modern sense of the term."[4]

In the Indo-European languages studied by Benveniste, the notion of the sacred had a semantic field quite different from that of religion, and here again, one is struck by the diversity of the terms used to designate the various aspects of the sacred. Sometimes the sense of an inflation, plenitude and, by extension, prosperity is conveyed. The sacred being or object is a being inflated by an overflowing and superabundant force, an exuberant and fecund, life-bestowing power. However, with Latin, things changed. An opposition between sacred and profane now became manifest, an opposition that, following the works of Emile Durkheim and Mircea Eliade, has seemed so self-evident that we tend to regard it as a universal polarity. Latin is also the source of the ambiguity of the "sacred" (*sacer*), "consecrated to the gods or carrying an ineffaceable defilement, august or accursed, something worthy of veneration or that arouses horror." This ambivalence opposes "sacred" (*sacer*) to "holy" (*sanctus*), understood to result from a human sanction imposed by law.[5] The Latin notion of "sacred," which implied a setting apart, a withdrawal into isolation, a separation within a precinct, and an opposition to the profane (what is "outside the temple," *pro-fanum*), does not altogether overlap with the Greek notion that is expressed above all by the term *hieros*. The latter designates "a property, sometimes permanent, sometimes temporary, that might result from some divine influx, some divine circumstance or intervention." A man condemned to death was as *sacer* as a sacrificial victim, but he was not *hieros*. The semantic diversity prevents us from acceding to any "common prehistory of the sacred." All the same, behind that diversity, in all Indo-European languages we do find the same opposition between "what is filled with a divine power" and "what is forbidden contact with human beings."[6]

It is the latter sense that dominates in the notion of sacrifice. Durkheim's analysis of the sacred in *The Elementary Forms of Religious Life*, which appeared in French in 1912, owes much to the study of sacrifice by Henri Hubert and Marcel Mauss, itself inspired by a monograph by Sylvain Lévi on Vedic sacrifice (based on the *Veda*, the holy scriptures of Hinduism). That affiliation explains why Vedic ritual gets the lion's share of Hubert's and Mauss's attention in their attempt to pinpoint a general mechanism of sacrifice. It is not possible to go into this extremely complex question at this point. Suffice it to say that their analysis applies chiefly to its main subject, Vedic sacrifice; it is less relevant when they attempt to extend the Indo-European data to Hebrew sacrifice (and implicitly to Christianity), and it eventually loses its way in generalizations of an anthropological nature.

It is nevertheless possible to make one prudent generalization in the case of Buddhist ritual. According to a widespread belief, Indian Buddhism may be defined by its trenchant rejection of Vedic ritual. But in truth, it is not particularly original in this respect, given that a similar rejection characterizes Vedantism, a philosophical Hindu movement that followed in the wake of the Vedic religion. A Hindu ascetic is one who has "extinguished his fires" and so no longer practices the ritual involving domestic fire. Instead, as the Indianist Charles Malamoud has shown, he has "cooked" himself, consumed his passions and offered himself up for sacrifice.[7] What is involved here is thus an internalization of sacrifice, rather than a negation, it is a rejection of external sacrifices in favor of internal sacrifice in the fire of consciousness. The same procedure characterizes a Buddhist renouncer, in particular, a devotee of Tantrism. Where some observers fancy they detect a rationalist critique of Vedic ritualism, we should instead see a sublimation of it. Even if, in some cases, this sublimation leads on to negation pure and simple and a down-to-earth materialism, those are on the whole marginal tendencies.

Religion and Power

As we have seen above, Kant considered submission to a book or to a master to be typical forms of immaturity. Although the former type is more obviously characteristic of "religions of the Book," it is also to be found in other contexts: Essentially, every religion is canonical. Unconditional obedience to a person or a rule immediately calls to mind certain recent tragedies that have given rise to much comment on the part of the media. One feature of cults and sects is a dispossession of the self in favor of a spiritual master or *guru* (literally, "a man of weight"). In Buddhism, each individual is in principle responsible for his/her own salvation. However, in practice, the virtue of humility fostered among disciples is apt to lend itself to personality cults that seem a far cry from Kantian maturity. Through what kind of strange reversal could such radical heteronomy lead to autonomy? "Young sprigs need a tutor," we are told, or "As in the army, you have to learn obedience so as to be capable, one day, of giving orders." To which the retort of the partisans of radical autonomy is that it is never too early to think for oneself and that, where unscrupulous masters are involved, placing one's freedom on deposit might lead to radical bankruptcy. You cannot invest in shares of truth or liberty on the stock exchange. There are, unfortunately, no objective criteria for distinguishing a true *guru* from a charlatan. Even in Chan, power relationships have always existed. In psychoanalysis, in principle the cure can work only if the patient to a certain extent becomes dependent upon the psychoanalyst. In the spiritual domain, however, even among the masters, *gurus* have their detractors as well as their partisans. Krishnamurti, for instance, spent his whole life trying to persuade his followers not to idealize him, and Linji likewise recommended that his disciples should not be taken in by false masters (although he was, of course, referring to others, not to himself). Like Krishnamurti, Linji spoke from the height of his magisterial chair, possibly out of compassion, but not without condescension: So maybe there was a measure of power involved here, too.

The Christian missionaries in China found no religion there, nothing but, on the one hand, what seemed to them a heterogeneous collection of superstitions and magical practices (which at that time were not yet classified as popular religion, as they are today) and, on the other, doctrines of a moral and metaphysical nature—"philosophical" Confucianism and Daoism. They despised the religious element in Daoism, retaining from it only what seemed to them to constitute a distant echo or prefiguration of the true religion, the belief in a single and transcendent principle, the *dao*.

It is for rather similar reasons that some people continue to declare that Buddhism is not a religion: It consists on the one hand of superstitions and magic, which are marks of decadence. On the other, at the heart of its doctrine, it constitutes a philosophy and an ethic. We find here the same attempt to separate the grain from the chaff as in James Frazer, Émile Durkheim, and all those who have sought in vain to distinguish religion from magic. Even while opposing Kant by attempting to prove the social origin of our categories of thought, Durkheim remains profoundly Kantian in his conception of religion as an essentially moral phenomenon. But in doing so, he projects on to other times and other places a concept of morality that is that of the bourgeoisie of the Enlightenment. In *The Elementary Forms of Religious Life*, where he describes the rites of the Australian Aborigines, he is really trying to understand the simplest mechanisms of social cohesion in order to draw from them lessons designed to reform modern society. The historian Dominic LaCapra comments that Durkheim "became the Plato of the Australian Blackfellows, only to emerge as the Docteur Angélique of the consensual society."[8]

The "Exit from Religion"

The idea that religion basically implies a secularization is to be found in a number of authors. But it is probably in a work by Marcel Gauchet, *The Disenchantment of the World,* that it is carried furthest. In his title as in his thinking, Gauchet is inspired by Max Weber, who regarded Protestantism as an essential phase in this process of the "disenchantment" (*Entzauberung*) of the world, a process that began with ancient Judaism and that, in agreement with Greek scientific thought, rejected as so many superstitions all magical means of attaining to salvation.[9]

The disenchantment began when the transcendent God withdrew from the world, as happened with monotheism (which Nietzsche called "monotono-theism"). Marcel Gauchet's main thesis engineers a Copernican revolution. He declares that the advent of "universal religions," far from representing progress on the religious level (as was argued by, for instance, Henri Bergson in *The Two Sources of Morality and Religion*), on the contrary constitutes so many stages in the loosening and the calling into question of "the religious." The zenith of religiosity, he claims, was attained in primitive societies, not in premodern Western society. Christianity, the universal religion par excellence, is precisely the one in which this "exit from religion" was able to take place.

Gauchet suggests that this movement was prompted by a more or less historical event, a great sociopolitical shake-up, as it were, that brought the mythical world to an end, opening up an irreversible rift, first within myth itself, then between myth and reason. The responses to that initial event were of two kinds: those that strove, ultimately in vain, to fill in the divide, and those that, on the contrary, dug it ever deeper, as Christianity did. As Gauchet sees it, in this schema, Buddhism offers a compromise between "the otherness vis-à-vis the world and the salvaging of the One." It tries to fill in the gap in two ways, two ways that are, in principle, opposed: either by introducing all kinds of mediation (gradualism) or else by maintaining that there is no gap and never has been (subitism—a term coined by Paul Demiéville from the Latin *subitus,* "sudden"). A rationalist and demythologizing Buddhism is thus opposed by an esoteric Buddhism in which the distinction between the religious virtuosi and the faithful masses is considered to reflect the constitutive "duplicity" of reality.

The relations of Buddhism with myth and reason are as complex and conflictual as those involving monotheisms. Christianity, for example, is a religion of distance between men and the divine only if one looks no further than the abstract formulations of its theology, without taking into account the manifestations of popular piety. As is well known, on the Protestant side, Luther, even while loudly calling for the demythologization (and demystification) of Christianity, refused to allow any room for reason in the domain of faith. Yet Max Weber drew attention to the rationalist tendencies of Protestantism. And while this German sociologist sought the origins of capitalism in the Protestant ethic, as Bernard Groethuysen saw it, the "bourgeois spirit" emerged from the very heart of Catholicism. The "exit from religion" began in France in the seventeenth century at the time of the controversy over mysticism, and one of the main phases in this evolution was the controversy that set the Jansenists against the Jesuits on the question of the nature of God. The all-powerful God of the Jansenists was forced to give way before a new God, that of the Jesuits, a God more inclined to accept human reason and pride.[10]

The important role played by Jesuit missionaries in the propagation of faith in Asia is well known. Some of their detractors took offense at the way in which Matteo Ricci and his successors contrived to win the esteem (if not the faith) of Chinese elite groups, not so much by preaching holy truths as by demonstrating their scientific skills. The famous "rites controversy" was designed to discredit the Company of Jesus by revealing the extent to which the missionaries had compromised with Chinese customs: the Jesuits dressed and behaved in every respect as Confucian scholars and exhibited the same scorn for Buddhism as did the latter. But for the defenders of pure faith, it was a matter of a rearguard action. The Jesuits were really pointing the way to the future. Even as they proclaimed their Christianity, they were draining it of part of its contents. The *philosophes* were in no doubt at all on this score and, despite their fierce anticlericalism, were fervent readers of the "edifying and curious" letters sent from China by the Jesuit missionaries, whose scorn for superstitions and idolatry they themselves shared.

The secularization of Western societies has led to a diversification of what religion has to offer. There is no longer any need to "explain" religion, as there was in the days of Durkheim and Bergson, for religion has so to speak dissolved as a result of historical and anthropological knowledge: From one culture to another, there is no longer any way of telling for certain what is religious and what is not, let alone of collecting together so-called common elements and turning them into *the* religion, highly valued by an immutable *homo religiosus*. The vague mysticism constructed by those means is not much use as an explanatory tool. The retreat of Christianity, the theology of which has cut itself off both from the scientific world of causality and from the ethics of social realities, has left the field open to all kinds of ideologies. Even if Buddhism is regarded as a soft ideology, it is possibly one of the best able to fill in the gap between the material and the spiritual that was created by Christianity and then widened by Cartesianism.

The "Return of the Religious"

While Marcel Gauchet considers the modern world to be carried along by a movement that leads to the inevitable exit from the religious, Jacques Derrida, for his part, reckons that the logic of the religious chimes with that of modern technology. In his "Faith and Knowledge," his thought develops within a framework formed by two works, one by Kant (*Religion within the Limits of Reason Alone*), the other by Bergson (*The Two Sources of Morality and Religion*). One of the merits of his thinking is that it establishes a link between the question of Western rationality and the "double truth" of religion. Derrida returns to the problem, originally posed by Kant, of a rational understanding of religion and the religious. He ponders the so-called "return of the religious" and the violent reactions that this arouses on the part of "enlightened" minds, those "who believed naïvely that an alternative opposed Religion, on the one side, and on the other, Reason, Enlightenment, Science, Criticism (Marxist Criticism, Nietzschean Genealogy, Freudian Psychoanalysis and their heritage), as though the one could not but put an end to the other."[11]

But it is not a matter of a simple alternative, a choice that each individual might make once and for all "in his soul and conscience." Derrida examines in particular the relation between religion and abstract thought, or what, significantly enough, he calls "the evil of abstraction." Those relations are by no means simple, since in relation to all forms of abstraction, "'religion' is at the same time involved in reacting antagonistically and reaffirmatively outbidding itself."[12]

Well before Bergson, Kant noted that there are two kinds of religion and that it is regrettable that they are so often confused: on the one hand, the religion of simple cults, dogmatic, eminently self-interested, basically in quest of "favors from God" and worldly profits; on the other hand, moral religion, founded upon a "reflective faith" and essentially preoccupied with the right way to conduct one's life. According to Kant, only the latter is in perfect accord with practical reason and the categorical moral imperative. It is hardly surprising that Nietzsche dismissed both Kantian morality and Christian morality! Yet with his "moral" definition of religion and his choice of Christianity as the "moral religion" par excellence, Kant is in good company. As Derrida points out, Voltaire shared that view: "In short, a little in the manner of Kant, believe it or not, Voltaire seems to think that Christianity is the sole 'moral' religion, since it is the first to feel itself obliged and capable of setting an example. Whence the ingenuity, and at times the inanity of those who sloganize Voltaire and rally behind his flag in the combat for critical modernity—and, far more seriously, for its future."[13] How surprised Kant and Bergson would have been to discover that deep down they were Voltairians ...

It is worth noting in passing that this reduction of religion to morality, which dismisses all the rest of it as superstition, also characterizes various forms of the recuperation of Buddhism. Like a Christianity reduced to the Sermon on the Mount, Buddhism is all too often reduced to an ethic or a disillusioned rationalism. That is true in particular of the Neobuddhism spread these days by those who favor a doctrine better adapted to the modern world and purged of all its cosmological elements. According to them, the Buddha was an eminently pragmatic sage who recommended tolerance and a kind of pre-Stoicism. However, although morality may be one of the components of the Buddhist doctrine, it is neither the only nor the principal one. The concept of a moral religion implies that all forms of esotericism and, a fortiori, of orgiastic religion constitute no more than a resurgence of magic and the baser human instincts, an intrusion of demonic (or even demoniacal) forces into the sacred, sanctified precinct. But historically, Buddhism is massively esoteric, even fundamentally "superstitious" (in the etymological sense of *superstes*, "one who survives, who has seen and lives to bear witness"). The rationalistic devaluation of *superstitio* came from the Romans, who, as Voltairians *avant la lettre*, denied all credit to the ancient cults. On this point, where paganism was concerned, Roman Christianity simply took over the arguments and prejudices of its predecessors.

Derrida, too, stresses the double origins of religion. But unlike his predecessors, he does not separate the sources: "For here origin is duplicity itself, the one and the other."[14] He emphasizes the elliptical nature of religion, its double center, the double, contradictory possibility that implies on the one hand an absolute respect for life, on the other, sacrifice.

Monotheism, Atheism, Polytheism

God is dead, Nietzsche announced, adding that religion would follow, albeit possibly much later. In support of this, he adduced the fact that Buddhism, the shadow cast by the Buddha, has survived its founder by over two millennia. But we cannot rule out the possibility that the death of God and the so-called return of religion may simply be two aspects of one and the same phenomenon.

Both faith and unbelief are eminently social phenomena, epistemological, a priori factors that lie beyond the control of the individual (or that even fashion him or her). Like it or not, we live in an age of suspicion, although that does not justify turning suspicion into the truth. The doubt that Nietzsche applied to an unthinking adherence to truth may equally be applied to suspicion, but even doubt thus duplicated does not produce certainty.

Saint Bernard declared, "There is no middle term; either you burn forever with the impious, or you rejoice forever with the saints": an application of the excluded middle that is certainly as valid as any other. In the Manichean world of "either . . . or," the limbo that once provided refuge for those who were neither impious nor saintly has disappeared. But according to the Buddhist idea of a nondual absolute, it is not even necessary to repent in order to obtain salvation. The identity between contraries is well expressed in a story by Jorge Luis Borges entitled "The Theologians" in which an Inquisitor and his declared enemy, a heretic, turn out to be one and the same person in the eyes of God.[15] In the same way, atheism and monotheism, despite their "radical," irreducible opposition, are perhaps two versions of the same phenomenon, a phenomenon that is characterized by a shift to the level of radical abstraction—whether that of transcendence or reason. In both cases, we find the same rejection of mediation and a similar constitutional idealism. In *La foi et la raison*, Nayla Farouki reveals the deep affinities that exist between Western rationality and monotheism. However, the conclusions that she draws differ somewhat from mine. If, as Nietzsche insisted, "despotism always clears a path to some kind of monotheism," to me, the reverse seems equally true. Meanwhile, in between the all-or-nothing of monotheism and atheism, the middle way of polytheism comes into view.

Like the three great monotheisms, Buddhism arose originally as a religion of transcendence. It is true that *nirvāṇa* has nothing in common with the sphere of births and deaths. Seen from this point of view, Buddhist logic seems opposed to pagan logics that, even if they do recognize a lack of continuity between the world below and the Beyond, do not hold that this cuts the former off absolutely from the latter. However, unlike the other major religions, Mahāyāna Buddhism came around to suggesting a (neither monist nor dualist) identity between the relative and the absolute, *saṁsāra* and *nirvāṇa*. By the same token, it became a religion of "transcendent immanence."

Apart from these essentially theoretical models, the religious practice of popular Buddhism articulates the visible and the invisible, the profane and the sacred, as two regions of a structurally diverse reality: two sectors topologically distinct, but linked by countless connections. So in the last analysis, Buddhism, too, stems from a "pagan" or polytheistic logic. It has managed to climb back down from its great universalist and abstract principles to accede to a sacredness that is concrete, local, and immanent. It has thus achieved a compromise between two very different concepts of sacredness, rediscovering the deep anthropological structures that underlie the various Asian cultures.

Religion, Mysticism, and Psychoanalysis

If Bergson's distinction between the two types of religion presents problems, so, too, does the distinction between "true" mysticism (that is to say religious and—what is more—monotheistic mysticism) and "wild" or "natural" mysticism (fusion with nature, but without God). With his critical experience of drugs, the "miserable miracle" that, for all its misery, allowed him to accede to a veritable "understanding through the abyss," Henri Michaux, for his part, turned to that "natural" mysticism. But that understanding amounted to no more than a glimpse, and this had to be complemented by asceticism, the best form of which was apparently that of certain Eastern religions such as Hinduism: "What has come, as a gift, effortlessly, and even as a result of abandoning all effort, has to be recovered by effort and by renouncing all easy and natural methods, namely, by the transcendental way." Michaux constructs an interesting contrast between Western monotheisms and Hinduism. But what particularly draws him to the latter is precisely its Promethean character, a quality that at first sight seems very Western (even if it has mostly tended to find expression outside the strictly religious domain):

In many respects, it [the Hindu religion] is set apart and is destined for a renewal (once most of its now useless gods have been eliminated).

Why?

Above all because it is *Promethean*. Its starting point is man winning hidden strengths, and not solely through Yoga. Most of its sacred books feature the ascetic, equal with the gods, seeking within himself for hidden forces of being.[16]

Michaux stresses the will to autonomy that, he says, characterizes Hinduism (but that others have attributed above all to Buddhism), and he suggests that this is what explains the affinities that seem to exist between traditional Indian thought and modern Western thought. But where Buddhism, at least, is concerned, this interpretation stems in part from a misunderstanding, and I mention it only because it is representative. Except in movements such as Chan, fundamentally, Buddhist liberation has very little to do with individual autonomy in the modern and Western sense. Buddhism is not a "Promethean" doctrine, nor could it become one without negating itself. Even if it does imply a measure of voluntarism (unlike, for instance, the praise heaped upon "spontaneity" that is to be found in certain currents of Chinese thought), it does not proceed by dint of breaking up reality, and the only doors that it kicks in are already ajar (or illusory). The Buddhist ideal—as defined by Mahāyāna at any rate—is to be in accord with the "thusness" of things, the emptiness of reality. But this does not make it a fusional kind of mysticism.

All mysticisms privilege emptiness, but there are different kinds of emptiness. The Buddhist emptiness is not that of Christian mystics such as Master Eckhart. Nor can all monotheisms be reduced to one and the same reality: The God of the Christians is not Allah, whatever the claims of syncretist intellectuals and other theo-sophists. Nor is he the *dao* of the Daoists, nor the Brahman of the Hindus. Let us return to the distinction that Nayla Farouki draws between antithetical concepts (such as, for example, "immortality" as opposed to "mortality") and transcendental concepts (constructed in a purely logical fashion and without regard for the empirical world): Is the concept of emptiness antithetical, or is it purely transcendental (or is it both at once)? One kind of emptiness is simply a negation of plenitude and of objective reality; the other kind is an absolute emptiness, prior to all determination, and Daoism similarly recognizes both a nonbeing that is incommensurable with being and a nonbeing that is the source of being.

The Freudian Illusion

Freud was one of the most fervent critics of both "wild" mysticism and established religion. He tackled the religious question in a number of works written toward the end of his life, following a tumultuous period of inquiry that led him from a study of the nervous systems of the eel (1877) and of the crayfish (1882) and from his discovery of the therapeutic effects of morphine to an excavation of the bases of human civilization—along the way taking in his discovery of the unconscious.

In *The Future of an Illusion* (1927), Freud sets out to show the fundamentally illusory nature of all religion. He asks himself wherein lies the powers of dogmas such as the *credo quia absurdum* and the "as if" philosophy—all those practices that we observe without believing in them, but acting "as if" we did. He suggests (or rather asserts) that these illusions serve to fulfill erstwhile wishes, so it matters little whether or not they are founded in reality. This enables him to avoid tackling the question of their truth head-on: Whether they are true or false makes no difference to their psychological function.

He concludes that the religious illusion is a "universal obsessional neurosis of humanity," a neurosis that, like the obsessional neurosis of a child, stems from the Oedipus complex, the child's reaction to his father. Having reached this conclusion, he slips back into the evolutionist theories that dominated the day: Religion, a phenomenon in the growth of humanity, is destined to disappear when the species reaches maturity. By succumbing to this universal neurosis, a religious individual contrives to avoid individual neuroses, but at what a price: through "the violent obsession of a psychic infantilism and his inclusion in a mass madness."

As for the hypothesis, *horresco referens*, that science, too, might be an illusion, Freud, having envisaged the possibility for form's sake, responded with a firm *Vade retro*. What he told his imaginary interlocutors was, in substance, that science can teach us things about reality that will enable us to increase our power and improve our existence. If this belief is illusory, then, he admitted, I am in the same boat as you are, but—he hastened to add—that is not the case, for science, with its many significant successes, has already provided sufficient proof to the contrary. The circularity of his argument is certainly significant: It tackles neither the question of meaning or truth nor that of the psychological function of a scientific belief, but is content simply to invoke the objective results of science. And as if to convince himself, he repeats, "No, our science is no illusion. But an illusion it would be to suppose that what science cannot give us we can get elsewhere."[17] In this respect, Nietzsche shows greater perspicacity, for he believed that "every age has its own divine type of naïveté, for whose invention other ages may envy it." And paradoxically enough for a man famous for his diatribes against Christianity, he then went on to say: "And how much naïveté, venerable, childlike, and boundlessly clumsy naïveté lies in the scholar's faith in his superiority, in the good conscience of his tolerance, in the unsuspecting simple certainty with which his instinct treats the religious man as an inferior and lower type that he has outgrown, leaving it behind, *beneath* him—him, that presumptuous little dwarf and rabble man, the assiduous and speedy head-and-handiworker of 'ideas,' of 'modern ideas!'"[18]

Oceanic Feeling

Upon receiving a copy of *The Future of an Illusion*, Romain Rolland wrote to Freud admitting the illusory nature of religion, but regretting that the author had forgotten to take into account certain noninstitutionalized forms of religiosity such as the "oceanic feeling" with which he himself was familiar and that he believed he shared with millions of human beings. On the basis of this feeling, he added, one can claim to be religious even while rejecting all belief and all illusion. Freud was much struck by this expression, which, he claimed in a letter in 1929, allowed him no rest. In fact, it was this unease that prompted him to write *Civilization and Its Discontents*. He sent a copy of the second edition of this work to Romain Rolland, dedicating it as follows: "To his great oceanic friend, from the terrestrial animal, S. Freud." In it he admitted at the outset that he could discover in himself no trace of this "oceanic" feeling.[19]

At first sight, such a feeling seems to call into question the reality of the self and its autonomy and fits in well enough with Buddhist doctrine, which regards that self as a fundamental illusion. Freud, too, accepts that the autonomy of the self is a trap to the extent that the conscious self opens internally onto the unconscious, but he maintains that, externally, the self must affirm itself vis-à-vis the world by tracing out very clear boundaries. This progressive demarcation characterizes the psychic process by which a child passes beyond his/her "primary narcissism," his/her initial feeling that he/she incorporates the whole world, and eventually, after many repressions, comes to accept the "reality principle." All the same, Freud recognizes that this initial psychic state, this primal self, may have been preserved, buried beneath subsequent psychic strata. He suggests that the oceanic feeling might be a desire to return to that primary narcissism and that its connection with religion is, in short, simply a secondary phenomenon.

Freud also invokes the testimony of another of his friends, who assures him that the practice of yoga will allow him to regress "to primordial states of mind which have long ago been overlaid." But he immediately distances himself, saying: "It would not be difficult here to establish relations with many obscure modifications of the life of the soul, such as trance and ecstasy. But for my part, I feel moved to identify with Schiller's words, and exclaim: 'Let him rejoice, he who breathes up there/In the rosy light!'" Freud says that he feels "impelled"—but by what, precisely? He admits that he is forced to turn away from those depths without pondering upon the nature of such a constraint, which is founded upon an equally profound fear of transgressing some ancestral taboo. The next lines of the poem are significant: "For underneath is horror,/And man must not tempt the gods/Nor ever, ever desire to see/What they see fit to cover by night and terror."[20] Yet it is precisely that kind of plunge into the depths that Freud strove throughout his life to accomplish by dint of his analytical methods. So how should we explain his instinctive retreat? Why on earth is he so ready to deny all reality to that oceanic feeling, using a scientific rhetoric (interspersed with poetical references) that, as he surely knows, has the ability to conceal so very much? Such a denial clearly constitutes a tactic of avoidance that is a matter, precisely, for psychoanalysis (or, as a Buddhist might say, reflects an incapacity that possibly stems from *karma*).

As the Indianist Michel Hulin notes, a strange complicity full of second thoughts exists between Freud and Romain Rolland.[21] Freud's protestations of friendship are at odds with the critical tone of his letters. When he exclaims to Romain Rolland, "How strange to me are the worlds in which you evolve! Mysticism is as closed to me as music is," Rolland is not altogether duped, and replies: "I find it hard to believe that mysticism and music are strangers to you. . . . Rather, I think that you are wary of them for the sake of the integrity of the critical reason that you use as a tool."[22] Romain Rolland had rightly sensed that his notion of an "oceanic" religiosity was deeply upsetting to Freud. Lobbing the ball back into Freud's court, he in his turn wonders why Freud is so resistant: "You doctors of the Unconscious, instead of becoming citizens of this limitless empire, the better to possess it, simply never set foot there except as strangers imbued with a preconceived idea of the superiority of your own side. . . . The wariness that certain masters of psychoanalysis manifest toward the natural free play of the mind that rejoices in its self-possession . . . unknown to them betrays a kind of back-to-front asceticism and 'renouncement.'"[23]

The interpretation to which Freud resorts initially allows him a measure of reassurance: According to him, if he has no oceanic feeling, that is simply because his psychic constitution has preserved fewer infantile vestiges. The phenomenon of mysticism, for him, becomes a simple flight to what Baudelaire called the "green paradise of childish loves." Unlike the Daoists, who perceived in the newborn child an image of the state before the fall into culture, Freud ascribes no truthful value to such infantile states. He rejects the idea of a possible return to that original self following an initiatory process of unlearning—as conceived by the Buddhists and Daoists, who aim to reconstruct an immortal and androgynous embryo within themselves by annulling sexual difference. For the circumcised Freud, the desire to regress to the maternal womb is no more than a culpable illusion. Nowadays it may be medically possible to reverse physical circumcision, the ritual event that introduced the child into patriarchal society and that prefigures the maternal weaning. However, psychic circumcision and the cleavage of the self is irremediable. The split subject never recovers. Freud could have addressed the same critique to a notion that is quite widespread in atheist circles according to which man simply projects outside himself the forces of his own self and thus imagines God in his own image. For Ludwig Feuerbach, for example, what is important is to be aware of that projection in order to reassemble all the pieces of the puzzle of consciousness and to achieve the reintegration of the subject. However, in certain of his definitions of the "nirvana principle," Freud seems to envisage the possibility of psychoanalysis leading to a kind of fulfillment, a transition beyond the real, the imaginary, and the illusory by dint of which the subject would find himself, as André Akoun puts it, "liberated from all substance, all weight, and figures of all kinds."[24]

There is, without question, a conflict of interpretations regarding religion between those who believe that "everything is social" and those who advocate the "inner experience" of transcendence. To return to but one example: Marcel Gauchet's analysis in terms of a self-imposed "heteronomy" and his grand narrative of the "exit from religion" as a progress toward autonomy make perfectly good sense within a particular (nonreligious) framework of thought. Such an analysis fits into a system from which it cannot be separated. But it will doubtless seem absurd to a religious mind that perceives heteronomy as an integral part of the order of things and autonomy as the ultimate arrogance. Such a person could address to the philosopher the same reproach that Claudel addressed to the Buddha, taxing him for his "incestuous" autonomy. In this context, the desire for autonomy is regarded as a Promethean or Oedipean arrogance, the consequences of which will have to be blindly borne. Within a religious framework, the only autonomy possible is what passes by way of a desired and accepted heteronomy, obedience to or harmony with a superior law.

5

The Major Schools

Buddhists have always sought to control the diversity of their doctrinal history by means of classificatory schemata, sometimes going so far as to represent Buddhism as a doctrine that has developed *more geometrico*, in a perfectly logical fashion. The Japanese historian Takakusu Junjirō presents the various schools of what he calls "negative rationalism" as falling quite naturally (and even chronologically) under the four rubrics of the "tetralemma"—that is to say, the four propositions of Buddhist logic, namely: A—not-A—both A and not-A—neither A nor not-A. According to him, Indian Buddhism can be separated into schools that 1) affirm being; 2) affirm nonbeing; 3) affirm both being and nonbeing; 4) affirm neither being nor nonbeing. Clearly, this kind of schema represents a purely intellectual view, for, in truth, the whole point of the Buddhist tetralemma is to show that, in the last analysis, reality transcends those four rubrics.

The traditional distinction between Hīnayāna (Lesser Vehicle) and Mahāyāna (Greater Vehicle) is said to reflect a whole series of dichotomies, such as ancient doctrine and new doctrine, conservatives and progressivists, monks and laymen, and opposed tendencies such as atheist and theist, philosophical and devotional, realist and idealist. It also assumes the reality of two clearly distinct entities for whose existence there has never been any proof, despite the many attempts that have been made to trace their origin and evolution. In the eyes of a historian, such a distinction is marred by many defects. However, its merit is that it does at least express an important structural opposition. The structure (about which there will be more to say) is that of a twofold truth, the one conventional, the other ultimate. But the appearance of a doctrinal classification here is misleading: The purpose of the distinction is really of quite a different nature—to upset and disturb, to mobilize and set in motion the Wheel of the Law, to transform a sectarian dichotomy into a dialectics of transcendence. For the sake of clarity and at the risk of falling into the same trap as traditional historians, I will now present the Buddhist doctrine under three headings, in an altogether conventional fashion. The headings are realism, idealism, and the doctrine of emptiness.

Landmarks in Emptiness

Awakening and *Nirvāṇa* are hitching posts for donkeys.
—Linji Yixuan, *The Zen Teachings of Master Lin-chi*

It is helpful to bear in mind what early Buddhism owes to its Indo-European origins. The Buddhist doctrine is called *dharma*, a Sanskrit word that corresponds to "law"—a term that, in India, is used in law, in technology, in religion, and in philosophy. The term is derived from the Indo-European root *dhar-*, "to hold," and, depending on the context, means "custom," "rule," or "usage." It expresses the concept of "order," according to Émile Benveniste the order that, like the Chinese *dao*, "rules the ordering of the universe, the movement of the stars, the periodicity of the seasons and the years, as well as the relations between men and the gods and also between men themselves."[1]

At a doctrinal level, the traditional division of Buddhist history into three periods, marked respectively by the emergence of Hīnayāna (Lesser Vehicle), Mahāyāna (Greater Vehicle), and Vajrāyāna (Vehicle of Vajra, in other words, Tantrism), has the disadvantage of emphasizing the differences and masking the similarities between the three movements. It also conceals a number of value judgments that are conveyed by various teleological models. The name "Hīnayāna" was originally a nickname that Mahāyāna Buddhists used to designate those who favored the opposing tendency, although the latter presumably did not, for their part, consider themselves to be supporters of any "lesser vehicle." All the same, provided it is disengaged from all pejorative connotations, "Hīnayāna" does, better than all other terms suggested to replace it, serve to define this tendency as regards its relations with other, rival ones.

According to the model that is most widespread today, Hīnayāna is essentially a moral system (a quasi-Kantian one) that preaches the autonomy of the individual and rejection of all ritualism. Mahāyāna and, even more, Vajrayāna are represented simply as pietist, ritualistic, and in many cases lax deviations from this "original" Buddhism. But in reality, the situation is more complex, for right from the start, certain tendencies that were later to characterize Mahāyāna are detectable. A second model, characteristic of studies of Sino-Japanese Buddhism, certainly regards Hīnayāna as a moral doctrine, but also as a somewhat sterile and complacent rationalism. In contrast, Mahāyāna, and in particular the Buddhism of the Pure Land schools, which proclaim the possibility of rebirth in the paradise of the Buddha Amitābha (or Amida in Japanese), are said to constitute a more authentic and democratic religious form. A variant of this model is used to explain the evolution of Japanese Buddhism—from the more or less Hīnayānist schools of the Nara period (710–794) toward the ritualistic Tantrism of the Heian period (794–1185) and eventually into the popular "new Buddhism" of the Kamakura period (1185–1333). A third model is used by all those who see Vajrāyāna as the apex of Buddhist thought, the ultimate result of an evolution that progresses from the austere individualism of Hīnayāna to the compassion of Mahāyāna, the instrument of a salvation still too distant, finally to reach the superior soteriology of Vajrāyāna, according to which it is possible to become a Buddha "in this very body." Obviously, not one of these evolutionary models suffices to retrace the complex history of Buddhism, which is an eminently pluralistic and diffuse tradition that defies any linear representation of its evolution.

The "Realism" of Early Buddhism

Esoteric Buddhism, strongly associated with symbolic and initiatory art, stood from the outset in opposition to "realist" Buddhism, with its negative view of the world of the senses (and of women, the latter's enticing emanation). Such a view might well have inspired the following lines by Charles Cros: "Let us proclaim the principles of art/And let us all agree upon this: /the curves of women are just fat. Flesh is only meat". Lest such pronouncements should remain purely theoretical, Indian Buddhists would train themselves "to contemplate impurity" by observing the various phases of decomposition of the corpses left on charnel grounds. As is well known, death is still ever-present in India, even today, for it is everywhere for the eye to see and for fire to feed upon in cremation sites such as the ghats of Benares.

It is hard to know what to say, briefly, about early philosophical Buddhism, as elaborated in particular in the scholasticism of Abhidharma. To avoid mentioning the four "noble truths" seems impossible. All too often it is these that are discussed to the exclusion of all else, a fact that certainly does Buddhist thought a disservice. At first sight there is nothing particularly original about these four truths: suffering, the origin of suffering, the cessation of suffering, and the path that leads to the cessation of suffering.

The first of these truths indisputably has the air of a prime truth. In the Buddha's India, it was known all too well that to exist is to suffer. What set the Buddha apart from other Indian thinkers was chiefly his analysis of the causes of suffering, or rather of ill-being, considered as a sickness, his remedy to bring it to an end, and the healthy state that resulted from this (*nirvāṇa*). Suffering was linked to the illusion of the existence of a self (*ātman*): This was the first divergence, but a radical one, from Hindu thinking, which regarded the *ātman* as a piece of the ultimate reality. The Buddhist self, for its part, was seen as no more than a collection of physical and psychical aggregates: form, sensations, perceptions, mental constructs, and consciousness. We will be returning to this question of subjectivity.

All suffering stems from desire, or what Buddhists, more concretely, call "thirst" (the thirst for pleasure, but also the thirst for existence and for nonexistence). The second truth also seems to go without saying, but Buddhists added a wealth of detail to the description of the process through which desire causes suffering. In truth, desire itself results from a more profound cause, namely, ignorance. This to some extent plays the role of a first cause, although in principle, Buddhism rejects any notion of a first cause. Nothing exists of itself: Everything is conditioned, at once the cause and the effect of something else. This is the basis of the famous formula of "codependent origination" (*pratītyasamutpāda*), a twelve-linked causal chain that explains the way in which all the elements of individual existence emerge, one by one. This formula, which many have sought to attribute to the Buddha, along with many other scholastic elaborations, is the basis for the notion of *karma* (or retribution for actions).

René Char wrote, "You die when you are forty from a bullet in the head that you shot at yourself at the age of twenty." A Buddhist would say, "at whatever age, you die from a bullet that you shot at yourself in an earlier life." At twenty, you think that your life lies before you, but already you are dining alone with Death—the undesired guest who, the texts say, visits us sixteen times in the space of a single moment, in a single breath. But an individual's death is not the end, for it is followed by one if not many rebirths: By virtue of the old principle of "whoever once drank will drink again," an illusory self whose past existence was caused by "thirst" is condemned to be reborn in order to suffer and possibly to exhaust the effects of its past actions.

If it is true that suffering is caused by desire, it is above all important to sever the latter at its root. The "radical" metaphor masks the gradual nature of this process, whereas the fourth noble truth stresses its complexity of the process. It describes an eightfold path (perfect comprehension, perfect thought, and so on), a path that was later usually subsumed under the three rubrics of morality, concentration, and wisdom. At the end of this path lies *nirvāṇa*, the reality of which constitutes the third truth and about which, in principle, nothing can be said except that it is deliverance from all suffering—without, however, being nothingness. All that the Buddha vouchsafes to his disciples is that there is such a thing as "a nonborn, a nonbecoming, a nonmade, a noncaused."

It is important to note the oral and analytical aspect of early Buddhist thought. In this respect, Buddhism remains very Indian. In *Un barbare en Asie (A barbarian in Asia)*, Henri Michaux waxes ironical about the Indian tendency to split hairs, starting with the example of the twelve links in the Buddhist chain of causality. In this respect, Buddhist scholasticism in no way lags behind Christian scholasticism. Western readers nevertheless tend to be surprised by the rationalizing nature of Abhidharma and of the disciplinary canon (the Vinaya), which is almost surrealistic in its listing of unusual details. Likewise, the enumeration of the four truths, the representation of the fourth as an "eightfold path," and countless other similar lists, all testify to the vigor of the oral culture of the Buddha and his disciples. Indeed, most oral cultures feature didactic counting rhymes of the "one, two, three, we are off to the sea" variety. It may be that, with the transition from orality to writing, the very truth of Buddhism changed—not just the way that it was expressed, as those who believe in a timeless "essence" of Buddhism would have it. We ourselves are still living in one of those written cultures, but the changes being brought about within and around us by the information revolution (and its apparent return to a kind of orality in the audio-visual domain) might result in yet another mutation in Buddhist truth.

We are already dealing with a double truth, even though early Buddhism did not theorize about it, as such. From one point of view, the four noble truths may seem simplistic, but from another, they prove to be the sticking point that cannot be got around, so that all the later developments of Mahāyāna may appear as empty words, hollow dreams: not even a conventional truth that can be transcended, but an irreversible deviation away from the central point, the eye of the storm, the original intuition—which has turned into a blind spot as a result of being imprinted too soon upon a sensitive retina.

Yogācāra "Idealism"

Within Mahāyāna, the school known as Yogācāra, or "the practice of Yoga," preaches the inexistence of things, or rather of the elements that constitute objective reality, but takes for granted the reality of consciousness. Its major thesis is that the external world does not exist, is simply a representation created by us. Hence the other names given to this school: *cittamatra*, "nothing but thought," and *vijñānavāda*, "the way of consciousness." Everything is like a dream, an optical illusion, but that illusion is itself produced by our own consciousness, like "flowers" created in space by blurred vision. However, even if the world is a dream, the sleeper, for his part, is certainly real. Illusory representations emanate from a vast psychic reservoir, the "storehouse consciousness" (*ālayavijñāna*) into which they are eventually absorbed. From that storehouse consciousness arises a discriminating consciousness, polarized into subject and object, and also five sensorial consciousnesses corresponding to the five sense organs.

The mind is thus seen as a skillful, but unfocused artist, a kind of Pygmalion in love with his creation or a Narcissus fascinated by his own reflection. The *Mahāyānavimśikā* declares: "Like a painter terrified by the terrible monster that he is painting, the commoner is appalled by the cycle of births and deaths (*samsāra*)."[2] Is the sculpted rock in the garden a Buddha, or is it just a rock? One Chan master replies: "Don't you know that the rock itself is in your mind?" "If that is so," another Chan master retorts, mockingly, "your head must feel heavy!" One day, the sixth patriarch Huineng (who died in 713) passed two monks arguing, close to a flagpole, about whether it was the flag or the wind that was moving. When the monks asked him his opinion, Huineng said, "Your mind is moving." His reply can be interpreted either in an idealist sense, as indicating the ultimate reality of the storehouse consciousness, or else simply as a way of telling the monks that they are wasting their time with such ludicrous questions.

Yogācāra texts use various metaphors to explain the functions of the different forms of consciousness. Empirical consciousness "wanders in the objective domain like iron attracted by a magnet"; "mental consciousness, with the five sensorial consciousnesses, forges a visible world and constitutes a theater stage."[3] Consciousness is also frequently compared to space:

> If all this is nothing but consciousness, upon what does the world
>   rest?
> Why do we see men coming and going on earth?
> Just as a bird moves as it fancies through the sky,
> With no point of support, never stopping, just as one moves on
>   the earth,
> So all the living, with the aid of their differentiating thoughts,
> Move in their own consciousnesses, proceeding in the same way
>   as a bird in the air.[4]

According to this schema, deliverance consists in bringing about a "revulsion of the support," in somehow getting consciousness to swivel round. As the following lines of Asanga (fourth century) put it:

> Among childish beings, what has no reality appears everywhere,
>   hiding Reality,
> Whereas among the bodhisattvas, it is Reality that appears every-
>   where, pushing non-Reality aside.
> Let it be known that the disappearance of what is false and the
>   appearance of what is true
> Is the revulsion of the support and is liberation, for then one acts
>   as one wishes.
> That is how the "revulsion of the support" comes about.
> As soon as one understands that all is nothing but consciousness,
>   differentiating thought is no longer operative,
> And as soon as thought ceases to function, there is a toppling [of
>   the support], there is no longer any support.[5]

To what extent can such idealism concern us today? That couple over there, deep in conversation, outside a café, with a sleeping dog at their feet, against a background of red and green geraniums: Are they a projection of my thought, an effect of my *karma*? But why should I be projecting this? What have they to do with me? In what past lives may I have met them, so that my mind summons them up here, this evening, in the fading light of the setting sun, in a small provincial town lost in the immensity of reality—in a scene that is so strangely familiar, and for good reason, since I am supposed to be organizing it. This thought, implanted in me by Buddhist idealism, is a strange one. At what level of my consciousness is this scene being played out? And those lights playing on their faces, are they the same that lit up other faces in other centuries, other places, where I was already—without being there altogether, as in scenes in my dreams? . . . All that is very hard to believe—and besides, if I really believed it, I would probably not write it down, since to write it down implies an opposed belief in an objective reality confronting me and my mind. All the same, it is hard to reject it. Is it not the same as what happens in dreams? The same attitudes, the same multitude of details and colors that seem so "true" (even the "maddest" of them)? In my "waking" dream, it seems that some characters dream only in black and white. I need to change that ...

Descartes is watching: I think, therefore I am. "But," a Buddhist would protest, "you can be, yet be asleep"; "to sleep, perchance to dream ..." According to Yogācāra, all dreams are illusion, only the dreamer is real. But a dream, however illusory or unreal, may have very real effects—as is testified by Buddhist (and Christian, for that matter) penance manuals, so preoccupied, as they are, with wet dreams ..." The *cogito* does not imply lucidity, not even that of a "lucid" dream, let alone that of a state of wakefulness. If it is true that evil exists because of wrongful thoughts and that I myself am contributing to such thoughts of violence, jealousy, desire, and hatred, the time has come to put a stop to it all. If the world is the dream of an idiot, the nightmare of a sleeper, and if I am that sleeper— then it is high time I woke up. All the rest—even good thoughts, words, and actions—apparently simply fuels the dream, fuels a clear conscience (which, like any limited conscience or consciousness, is a bad thing), perpetuates the sleep of the "great reason" that has engendered these monsters. Busy-ness [*affairment*] is a simply a form of stupor [*effarement*].

The Middle Way (Mādhyamika)

Mādhyamika, the school founded upon the notion of the Middle Way and said to go back to Nāgārjuna (second to third century), consists essentially of a critique of a number of philosophical positions that were adopted on reality. Its doctrine is described as a negative way that seeks to indicate (without ever succeeding in expressing) the absolute point of view by reducing all "relative" doctrines to absurdity. For Nāgārjuna, every phenomenon is empty in that it results from predetermined conditions. But not even a negative way can content itself with negation. It is possible to realize emptiness only when one has rejected all affirmation and also all negation, given that they both stem from conventional truth; that is the way to accede to ultimate truth. Mādhyamika is the school that theorized the notion of the "two truths," which constitutes the central (yet elliptical) metaphor of the present book.

The Mādhyamika point of view is to be found in a number of canonical writings. To give but one example, here is one that illustrates the Buddhist tetralemma: "Can awakening be achieved starting from being? No. From nonbeing? No. From *both* being *and* nonbeing? No. From *neither* being *nor* nonbeing? No. Then how can one grasp its meaning? Nothing is graspable. To grasp the ungraspable is what is called 'achieving awakening.'"[6]

The dialectical tendencies already at work in Nāgārjuna increased in his successors, logicians such as Dignāga and Candrakīrti. Nevertheless, we must be careful not to reduce Mādhyamika to mere philosophical dialectics, as is all too frequently the case. The doctrine of Nāgārjuna and his successors is always designed to serve a soteriology, a practice that aims for salvation. According to Paul Mus, "The logical construction, once completed, provided the necessary overall base for the jump in levels. Let us not look for the bases of this discontinuous logic in the general values of philosophy: they are to be found in magical practice."[7] One must take into account a conscious exaggeration on Mus's part. In good Mādhyamika practice, it is best probably to send packing both the purely logical interpretation and the magical interpretation.

In his controversies with the representatives of Buddhist scholasticism (Abhidharma), Nāgārjuna, like Aristotle in his disputes with the Sophists, finally resorts to the pragmatic argument: You can say what you like, using many words and grandiose theories, but in practice, common sense reclaims its rights. You cannot do whatever you like. Yet this is exactly the kind of argument—founded upon common sense, conventional truth—that can be used to counter the dogma of the absence of self, or emptiness: The aggression of others and of the external world is perhaps nothing but wind, the wind of our own *karma*, but such a wind is strong enough to blow the horns off an ox.

As we have seen above, Aristotle rejected the tetralemma in favor of the dilemma: Without the dilemma, there is no salvation. Nāgārjuna, in contrast, passes beyond not only the dilemma, but even the tetralemma, which he also reckons to be too dichotomous.[8] As a general rule, he excludes the law of the excluded middle—even though, on occasion, in the heat of a contradictory debate, he uses it as a dialectical weapon (which, to be fair, is in no way contradictory to the idea of twofold truth). We should also note that Nāgārjuna himself does not speak of double truth, even if his successors (in particular Candrakīrti) do. He sticks to the notion of "two truths" so as to avoid any hint of synthesis. The reason why I prefer to use the expression "twofold truth," even when speaking of the Mādhayamika teaching stemming from Nāgārjuna, is chiefly because it allows me to link this problem metaphorically with that of the double as developed both in the West and in Buddhism. But I should like to make it quite clear that, despite the obvious temptation to systematize Buddhist thought, there can be no question of my attempting a synthesis between the two truths (or rather the two aspects of a twofold truth that remains irremediably open). It is just a linguistic ploy and involves no ontological option.

In Nāgārjuna, emptiness is simply an "evacuation" of the theses of thinkers who are too full of themselves. However, plenitude, or "essential" emptiness (which comes to the same thing), like what is bred in the bone, comes out in the flesh, even in that of Buddhists who claim to be followers of this Indian master. In Chan Buddhism, for instance, emptiness becomes a domain devoid of all entities. The sixth patriarch, Huineng, trying to explain the content of awakening, comes to the conclusion: "Fundamentally, there is nothing at all." Here, emptiness has become ontological, as in Daoism—but this is not emptiness in the nihilistic sense. As in the *dao* or in Zhuangzi's primordial chaos, it is a domain in which one can "roam" in peace and quiet. However, this ontological emptiness lends itself easily to metaphysical, cosmological, and mythological interpretations, which Nāgārjuna, for his part, rejects.

The more a Buddhist practitioner is detached, the more, in a way, he is "interested" (or involved) (if, as Emmanuel Levinas does, one derives this term from *inter-esse* "to be among or between," to realize that our existence is "caught" in a tight network of relations). Nāgārjuna ascribes this sense of interrelatedness to emptiness, which he describes as "codependent origination." In the last analysis, Nāgārjuna's negative dialectic remains too pure and, by the same token, has no affective impact. It covers the relative domain without affecting it at all: With or without it, life goes on, and his dialectic even helps to preserve the *status quo* (apart perhaps from awakening a few exceptional individuals). To have any liberating effect, this logic needs to refuse to carry formalization to its limit. In truth, that is just what Nāgārjuna does do by prefacing his philosophical stanzas by a religious dedication. It is also necessary that the two truths should constantly overlap one upon the other, producing intermediate levels—and that is something that he seems to deny.

Despite appearances to the contrary, Nāgārjunian logic is not the same as ours, in particular in the following respect: Instead of fixing the terms of the interrelatedness, it draws attention to their constant fluctuation. Whereas in a tautology or an algebraic equation, the terms must turn out to be equal, in Buddhist logic, no terms ever do. The fundamental difference (always supposing that there is still a "foundation") is that Buddhism by and large values orthopraxy (correct practice) more highly than orthodoxy (correct opinion) and, in particular, ritual more highly than doctrine. The doctrine of emptiness is first and foremost a religious doctrine, a soteriology.

Chan: In between Immanence and Transcendence

Chan stands at the confluence of a number of currents of thought, some Indian, others Chinese. The Jesuit missionaries regarded it simply as a Chinese version of Indian Vedantism. In reality, while on the Buddhist side Chan doctrine clearly inherits much from the Yogācāra and Mādhyamikta schools, it is also heir to various tendencies in Chinese thought. Chan dialogues often call to mind the *Analects* of Confucius. In other respects, the fantasy, humor, and eccentric use of language of the Chan masters are irresistibly reminiscent of Zhuangzi. This paradoxical body of thought is too strongly individualized to be described as syncretic, yet it manages to combine the transcendental vision of Indian Buddhism (in which two levels, the relative and the absolute, are clearly distinguishable even if, in the last analysis, they are collapsed into each other) and the "immanent" vision of Chinese philosophical thought. In contrast to Indian and Tibetan Buddhism, Chinese Buddhism is dismissive of the logical approach. Even if a Chan master such as Linji retains a dialectic framework, he glosses it in a typically Chinese manner with snatches of Chinese poetry, and in this way destabilizes it: Poetry takes over from logic, and scholasticism ends up as riddles.

The Master gave an evening lecture, instructing the group as follows: "At times, one takes away the person but does not take away the environment. At times, one takes away the environment but does not take away the person. At times, one takes away both the person and the environment. At times, one takes away neither the person nor the environment."

At that time, a monk asked, "What does it mean to take away the person, but not take away the environment?"

The Master said, "Warm sun shines forth, spreading the earth with brocade. The little child's hair hangs down, white as silk thread."

The monk asked, "What does it mean to take away the environment, but not take away the person?"

The Master said, "The king's commands have spread throughout the realm. Generals beyond the border no longer taste the smoke and dust of battle."

The monk asked, "What does it mean to take away both the person and the environment?"

The Master said, "All word cut off from Ping and Fen—they stand alone, a region apart."

The monk said, "What does it mean to take away neither the person nor the environment?"

The Master said, "The king ascends his jeweled hall; country oldsters sing their songs."[9]

But even if Chan in some respects marks the ultimate development of Buddhist philosophy, through its anti-intellectualism it also represents an attempt to pass beyond it. This school manifests a fundamental distrust of language and a desire for a direct perception of reality. The quick-fire repartees of Chan, like the laughter of the Buddha, are impervious to all intellectual attempts to understand reality. Laughter, like silence, transcends speech, and many texts refer to the laughter of the Buddha, that immense laughter that rocks the world to its very foundations. But, we are told, "it is for a grave reason that his whole body laughs." Without being a bitter laugh, the laughter of the Indian Buddha retains a tragic element that is absent from the laughter of the Chinese or Tibetan Buddha. The Tibetan master Drügpa Kunleg, famous for his eccentricities, used to say: "My conduct has been in conformity with these words, without aim and without attachment, a burst of laughter: Long live joy, long live joy!"[10] Meanwhile Chan's myth of origin, for its part, celebrates the smile of the Buddha's disciple, Mahākāśyapa. When the Buddha was trying to pass on his Dharma, he picked a flower and showed it to his assembled disciples. None of them understood the meaning of his action except Mahākāśyapa, whose face broke into a wide smile. Buddha then declared: "I hold the Treasure of the Eye of the True Dharma, the deep and subtle spirit of *nirvāṇa*, and I now pass it on to Mahākāśyapa." This episode became the source and model for transmissions from Chan masters to their disciples. A smile is worth more than long speeches.

"Classical" Chan claimed to be a single tradition that "set down no written letter" because it was based on a "special kind of transmission outside the scriptures" that passed from "mind to mind," and a practice "aimed directly at the mind" that allowed each individual to "see his/her own nature and become a Buddha." This explains the importance of the relationship between master and disciple and that of the patriarchal lineage. In the last analysis, it is the legitimacy of the transmission that determines the authenticity of practice, and not the other way around (as in traditional Buddhism). As it happens, this preoccupation with genealogies was typical of the Chinese context in which Chan developed.

Paradoxically, this doctrine, which claims not to be a doctrine at all and to be beyond words, has itself produced a vast literature—the volume of which accounts for over half of the Sino-Japanese Buddhist canon. It consists principally of "recorded sayings" of Chan masters, essentially collections of *kōan* (in Chinese: *gong'an*, literally "juridical cases" that serve as precedents), riddles of a kind, which the disciple has to resolve in a nonintellectual fashion, since thought is regarded as the source of all our evils: riddles such as "What is the sound of one hand clapping?" or "What was your original face before birth?" These *kōan* constitute the essential core of "dialogues" such as the one between Linji Yixuan and one of his disciples: "The Master ascended to the hall. A monk asked, 'What is meant by this matter of the sword blade?' The Master said, 'Fearful! Fearful!' The monk was about to speak, whereupon the Master struck him." Linji is famous for his use of tough measures, laying about his disciples with a stick and in some of them thereby producing a sudden awakening, as well as bumps and bruises. The use of *kōan* has come to characterize the Zen of the Rinzai School (Rinzai is the Japanese rendering of Linji, the name of its founder), while the practice of *zazen*, or seated meditation (with or without *kōan*) is considered characteristic of the Sōtō School. As practiced in this school, *zazen* is not so much a form of introspection, but rather a ritual imitation of the awakening of the Buddha. So it is not a *means* to attain a goal (awakening), but a concrete manifestation of that awakening, an awakening that has always already been realized.

What was it about figures such as Bodhidharma, Huineng, and Linji (the three great masters of Chan) that prevented each of them from becoming a Socrates and playing a founding role for not just one particular doctrine (Chan/Zen), but for an entire culture? Bodhidharma's ignorance and his scorn for customs certainly bears comparison with Socratic ignorance. "Who stands before me?", the emperor asks him, to which he replies, "I do not know." A Chan poem expresses the same idea as follows: "As naturally as a bee making for a flower, Bodhidharma says 'I do not know.'" The Indian patriarch was more radical in his behavior than Socrates, but did manage to avoid the vengeance of those in power (although according to one tenacious tradition, he was eventually assassinated by jealous colleagues). Huineng was plainly illiterate (and possibly not altogether Chinese)—but that did not prevent him from filching the title of sixth patriarch from under the nose of the erudite Shenxiu. As for Linji, unlike Socrates, he never had the luck (or the bad luck) to see his teaching taken up by an overzealous disciple such as Plato.

Zen succeeded in establishing itself in Japan, in the thirteenth century, only once it had become impregnated with Confucianism. The Chan that had reached the Japanese archipelago in the ninth century was too rustic for the delicate taste of the aristocrats of Heian. Only after becoming more refined in China under the Song, and having attracted the interest of a less cultivated Japanese social category—the warriors (*bushi* or *samurai*), was it able to take root. But it was the "cultural goodwill" of the new ruling class influenced by Zen that produced the aestheticism of Nō, the arts of flower arrangement, tea ceremony, and the art of gardening. Those so-called "Zen" arts constitute a kind of betrayal of the clerics, for the fact is that Zen abandoned its sense of raw, immediate reality in favor of a secondary, domesticated reality. Paradoxical though it may seem, it is generally intellectuals who prize intuition the most highly (possibly because they themselves possess so little of it). So the naturalness of the Zen monasteries so much revered by tourists is in truth that of a still life, a *nature-morte*, or at least one that is moribund.

"Transcendental" Concepts

Moving on from the somewhat simplistic schema of the double structure of Buddhist thought, let us now examine a number of major concepts that might be described as "transcendental." The first "transcendental" Buddhist concept that springs to mind is of course that of *nirvāṇa*, initially defined as pure extinction, about which nothing can be said except that it possesses none of the features of this world. Hence the tenacious image of Buddhism as a form of nihilism. Compared with *nirvāṇa*, death itself is regarded merely as "a rather shallow stream," wrongly maligned. *Nirvāṇa* is not annihilation, but the perception of a world where, to borrow the words of Rilke, "the dark and the light, the flower and the book—all is at rest," or, as Michel Leiris's gloss puts it, "*Nirvāṇa*—all vanities vanished, there are no nights, no dreams, no future, no shores ..."

However, the nondualist logic of Mahāyāna was unable to settle for the dualism implied by the opposition between *nirvāṇa* and *saṃsāra*, or the cycle of births and deaths. To reduce that separation, the idea of the nondual identity of the two terms was introduced: Now *nirvāṇa was saṃsāra*, not some superior state of being or nonbeing; awakening was no different from defilement; the holy was no different from the profane. According to the *Vimalakīrti Sūtra*: "Attraction for *nirvāṇa* and repugnance for *saṃsāra* make two. But absence of attraction for *nirvāṇa* and repulsion for *saṃsāra* constitute a nonduality. Why? To speak of liberation, one must be bound, but if one is completely free of bonds, why seek liberation?"[1] Similarly, according to Nāgārjuna's *Madhyamakakārikā* (Verses on the Middle Way):

> During his life, as after his extinction, the Buddha is inconceiv-
> able; one cannot say he exists, nor that he does not exist,
> nor both at once, nor neither the one nor the other. That is
> why:
> There is not the slightest distinction between *nirvāṇa* and
> *saṃsāra.*
> There is not the slightest distinction between *saṃsāra* and
> *nirvāṇa.*
> The limit of *nirvāṇa* is the very limit of *saṃsāra.* Between the
> two, one can find not even the most subtle dissimilarity.[2]

But Mahāyāna goes further, introducing a veritable mental revolution: The indefinable *nirvāṇa* is now defined by four terms: permanence,
enjoyment, subjectivity, and purity. Point by point, these contradict the
characteristics that early Buddhism attributed to reality (impermanence,
suffering, absence of self, impurity). So we seem to be in the presence of a
concept that is not only transcendental, but also antithetical, that is to say,
obtained not from observation of the world of the senses, but by negating
an empirical concept.

In Mahāyāna, the notion of *nirvāṇa* is identified with that of awakening, in other words, with that of an ineffable experience that, instead of
bringing to an end the world of the senses, sanctifies it and takes its place
at the heart of this world. The Zen master Dōgen (1200–1253) said: "When
a man achieves awakening, it is like the moon reflected in the water: The
moon is not wet, the water is not disturbed. The light of the moon, although infinite, is accommodated in a tiny quantity of water. The whole
moon and sky can lodge in the dew on a blade of grass or in a drop of water. Just as the moon hollows out no hole in the water, awakening does not
disturb man at all. He no more resists awakening than the drop of dew resists the sun or the moon."[3] Far from constituting a rejection of the world,
awakening becomes a sovereign enjoyment of the world, purified of all its
negative aspects, which are false perceptions caused by illusion. As the layman Vimalakīrti tells a disciple of the Buddha who is unduly obsessed
with purity: "Son of a good family, without venturing into the great sea, it
is impossible to reach the precious stones that lie beyond one's appreciation. Similarly, without entering the sea of passions, it is impossible to produce omniscient thought."[4]

Karma and Causality

Once there was a man who was afraid of his shadow and who hated his footprints, and so he tried to get away from them by running. But the more he lifted his feet and put them down again, the more footprints he made. And no matter how fast he ran, his shadow never left him, and so, thinking that he was still going too slowly, he ran faster and faster without a stop until his strength gave out and he fell down dead. He didn't understand that by lolling in the shade he could have gotten rid of his shadow and by resting in quietude he could have put an end to his footprints. How could he have been so stupid!

—Zhuangzi, *The Complete Works of Chuang Tzu*, trans. Burton Watson

All in all, *nirvāṇa* remains a concept that is too vague for most practicing Buddhists, a distant goal mentioned only for form's sake, an absolute setting used above all to relativize existence and set it in perspective. Action (*karma*), or, to be more precise, retribution for actions, provides a far more helpful concept, since it makes it possible to explain the structures of both this world and the other, social inequalities, and the destinies of individuals. Without calling the social hierarchy into question, it sanctions the hope for improvement in the destinies of individuals in both this life and those that are to follow. But it also provides the foundation for morality and strengthens all ideologies of domination: One is born into poverty or slavery because this is what one deserves. There is no longer any justification for revolt; far better to endeavor to reform oneself in the hope of a better rebirth. The accumulation of merit, good *karma*, of course allows one to hope for the final deliverance that is the avowed aim of Buddhist practice. But in reality, what one expects from it is an improvement in one's present or future existence—honors and wealth if one is a layman, the acquisition of spiritual or magical powers if one is a monk and ambitious.

Up to a point, *karma* has also served to "disenchant the world" by introducing an inexorable rationality. *Dura lex, sed lex*—the law is hard, but that's the law. All things considered, this law cast in bronze is preferable to the daunting whims of the gods and demons of archaic mythologies. The unknown is more terrifying than anything, and an infernal but familiar Beyond, humanized despite its inhuman tortures, may on the whole be preferable to the deep anxiety produced by the vague idea of a world of shades such as the Jewish Sheol, the Greek Hades, or the ancient Japanese *yomi no kuni*. The Christian Hell, for its part, has inherited many features from the hells of Buddhism.

To palliate the anxiety aroused by death, Buddhist doctrine offered not one, but two cosmological schemata: that of the six paths and that of the wheel of existence. Without entering into the details of this cosmology, which, however, by no means constitutes an ancillary aspect of Buddhism, as is all too often believed, what we need to remember about the notion of *karma* is its pragmatic value. Not only does it provide a metaphysical foundation for morality, but it reintroduces a longer-term perspective into human existence: an illusory perspective, it may be objected, but nevertheless one whose effects are on the whole beneficial, for they confer meaning upon human existence (without, however, having God intervene) and at the same time discourage any tendency to declare "Après moi le déluge," since even after me it is still and always will be me who is involved. The only being who can make such a declaration with full confidence is the Buddha as he enters *nirvāṇa*. But as we will see, as Buddhism became implanted in the world, even this ultimate way out became increasingly rare. In Mahāyāna, the Bodhisattvas and aspiring Buddhas no longer take the great leap into the void of *nirvāṇa*, but remain right here in this world, and Buddhas themselves, against all expectations, return to it. If ever the deluge occurs again, it will simply be a premonitory sign announcing the imminent apparition of the future Buddha, Maitreya, and the hope of all and sundry will be to be reborn at that moment in order to benefit from his teaching and warm themselves in the rays emanating from his saving presence.

It is therefore important to underline the pragmatic aspect or even the performative value of the idea of *karma*. However, the long-term perspective of *karma*, which suited Indian thought quite well, seemed less well adapted to the Chinese context. So in Chinese "subitism," about which I will soon have more to say, there developed a tendency to deny not just all actions said to lead to retribution, but the very relevance of the law of *karma*. The Chan master Linji probably represents the most radical example of this reinterpretation:

You go all over the place, saying, "There's religious practice, there's enlightenment." Make no mistake! If there were such a thing as religious practice, it would all be just karma keeping you in the realm of birth and death. You say, "I observe all the six rules and the ten thousand practices." In my view, all that sort of thing is just creating karma. Seeking Buddha, seeking the *Dharma*—that's just creating karma that leads to hell. Seeking the bodhisattvas—that, too, is creating karma. Studying sutras, studying doctrine—that too is creating karma. The Buddhas and patriarchs are people who don't have anything to do.[5]

Followers of the Way, the *Dharma* of the Buddhas, calls for no special undertakings. Just act ordinary, without trying to do anything in particular. Move your bowels, piss, get dressed, eat your rice, and if you get tired, then lie down. . . . If, wherever you are, you take the role of the host, then whatever spot you stand in will be a true one. Then whatever circumstances surround you, they can never pull you awry. Even if you're faced with bad *karma* left over from the past, or the five crimes that bring on the hell of incessant suffering, these will of themselves become the great sea of emancipation.[6]

However, not all Chan masters, let alone other Chinese Buddhists, shared Linji's radicalism, and many considered it dangerous in that it laid monastic discipline and meritorious works open to question. A reaction developed and found expression in, for example, a well-known Chan "case," the meeting of Baizhang and the fox. Baizhang was one of the Chan patriarchs, famous in particular for having introduced a strict Rule in Chan monasteries. Once, while preaching, he noticed an unknown old man who had come to listen to him. He asked him where he was from. The old man eventually confessed that he was really a fox (in Chinese and Japanese folklore, foxes are spiritual beings capable of metamorphosis) and that he had once been a Buddhist master living on that very mountain. But because he had wrongly declared that an awakened man transcends the law of *karma*, he had to be reborn as a fox for five hundred existences. He begged Baizhang to explain his mistake and thereby deliver him from this fate. So Baizhang told him that an awakened man is in perfect harmony with the law of *karma*. At these words, the old man obtained awakening, thereby transcending his *karma* and escaping forever his destiny as a fox.

For ancient Buddhism, the law of codependent origination constituted not only an explanatory schema describing the production of phenomena, it also made it possible to track back from an effect to the cause and thus to eliminate conditioning and finally reach extinction. One can see how Buddhism uses reason in a two-way fashion: The very reason that is the product of *karma* and that bogs us down in *saṃsāra* also enables us to make our way back upstream and eventually break the thread. So it is a matter not of denying reason, but rather of getting it to make a kind of U-turn. In truth, opinions on this point are divided: Is it a matter of drying up the stream of consciousness or simply of tracking back up it and then descending freely through it like a fish in a rushing torrent? The image of the fish swimming upstream has won great popularity in Zen: It is said that there is one stretch of the stream where the fish are transformed into dragons when they pass through it. This is the image that gave its name to the Tenryūji monastery (the Monastery of the Heavenly Dragon) in Kyoto, where I once practiced Zen (without, however, managing to make the famous leap).

Buddhist Causality under Scrutiny

Four kinds of Buddhist causality may, somewhat schematically, be distinguished. The first is what is generally presented as the orthodox doctrine: the psychogenetic theory of codependent origination, with its twelve links that lead from ignorance to ceaseless transmigration. This is the model of the Wheel of Life—as represented by Tibetan *thaṅkas*. The second form of causality is founded upon the storehouse consciousness (*ālayavijñāna*). According to this theory, all actions are like seeds deposited in this storehouse consciousness, seeds that, sooner or later, will ripen. Our consciousness is thus a kind of huge, eternal nursery for seedlings, the surrounding world constitutes the vegetation that it produces, and our successive lives are its seasons. When studied in detail, this theory proves to be far more abstruse and technical than the above metaphors suggest.

The third form of causality is based upon the ultimate reality, in its "thusness," which was "thus" before ever being given a name. Another metaphor for it is that of the immanence of a Buddha nature in every being (even the inanimate). The entire universe thus becomes a potential Buddha, and all that comes about is simply a manifestation of that Buddha nature. Nature is the "womb" of the *tathāgata* (another word for Buddha). This ultimate reality presents two aspects, which Chinese Buddhists call its "essence" and its "function": In its essence, it is indeterminate, absolute; in its function, it is the source of all phenomena. All that can be said of its ultimate aspect is what William James said of the absolute according to Plotinus: "The stagnant felicity of its perfection affects me as little as I affect it." But that absolute aspect is closely linked with its relative aspect, which, for its part, is the source of all my affects, affections, and disaffections.

The fourth canonical form of causality is founded upon the *dharmadhātu* (the "plane of essences" or "element of elements": both translations are possible). Here, we find ourselves back with the two aspects—the one absolute, the other relative—of ultimate reality. The *dharmadhātu* thus means both a universal or absolute principle and the constituted, relative universe. But unlike the preceding theory, which referred all causality to its absolute source in, as it were, a vertical fashion, here it is the causality of the "relative" plane of essences that is explained according to a horizontal model. Codependent origination is no longer perceived in a diachronic manner, as it was according to the first model, which took into consideration several lives of an individual, but instead in a synchronic fashion, which reveals the interdependence of all things at every moment. This is the famous "all is one," which is summed up in somewhat cavalier fashion by the Japanese saying: When a horse sneezes in Kyūshu (the southernmost island of the Japanese archipelago), a cow develops a cold in Hokkaidō (the northernmost island). All things are intimately interpenetrating, separated by not the slightest obstacle; they come to be and disappear all together. Every existence can be understood only in a holistic, ecological way, through the totality of its environment.

So everything that happens bears the stamp of ultimate reality and is somehow rendered sacred. But where that does leave ethics? What can be said in reply to those who object that such a concept legitimates all dictatorships and is fundamentally ideological? The Mahāyānist position calls to mind the somewhat ambiguous position adopted by Zhuangzi in his critique of Confucian ethics. Zhuangzi even sets the "too human"—therefore decadent—virtue of Confucius in opposition to the case of a tyrant who possesses the *dao* (for the *dao* is amoral, it treats men as "straw dogs," and there is even a *dao*, or "way," for tyrants, thieves, and assassins).

However, Chinese Buddhists such as Guifeng Zongmi (780–841) reckoned that the Buddhist theory of causality, in its original form at least, constituted an advance on the traditional Chinese notion of a "spontaneity" founded upon perfect harmony with the *dao*—precisely because it preserved the importance of morality and a measure of rationality in human destiny. On this point Buddhism remains a philosophy that recognizes a measure of free will. But if all action presupposes a form of illusion and implies retribution, hence some kind of suffering, when action cannot be avoided, it is important only to take it in full knowledge of what one is doing. This does not mean that we should do nothing; rather, when we take action, we should create as few ripples as possible on the surface of consciousness (both our own and that of others).

It was the importance of morality that prompted a Japanese Zen master such as Dōgen, who at first flirted with the various causal theories that were fashionable in his day, eventually to return to the causality of early Buddhism. In his quest for both the base and the summit, it turns out that the base *is* the summit (a fine example of nondualism). However, this theory of *karma* was to produce perverse effects, in particular at the social level, in that it provided a philosophy or justification for social discrimination. It was not on ethical grounds that the Japanese Buddhists of the Edo period abandoned the Mahāyāna theories of karmic causality (based on the Buddha nature or ultimate reality) and returned to Hīnayānist causality and the notion of an "intermediary being," a kind of psychic entity that serves as a bridge between two existences. What was but one of the twelve links in "codependent origination" (the third, *vijñāna* or discriminating consciousness) had already been interpreted in Mahāyāna in a more embryological fashion as describing the entry of consciousness into the womb. It took but a step to move from that position to one where, in practice, one abandoned the dogma of an absence of self and came to suppose that the same individual is reincarnated from one life to another. A further step was taken when one came to believe that the social shortcomings of an individual accompany him throughout all his rebirths. This created a curious vicious circle that explained not only why one had become an outcast in this life as a result of one's misdeeds in the past, but also why one would remain an outcast in future lives, no matter what one did to improve oneself: It was all because of the harmful "impregnations" that were linked with one's present status. The theory of *karma*, which had once justified hopes that an individual's life could improve in the long term, came to trap one particular social group, fixing it forever in its discriminatory group status. This question continues to be of burning interest in Japan, where until recently Buddhist temples were still automatically noting the status of outcasts (*burakumin*) in funerary inscriptions, thereby condemning such individuals to infamy in perpetuity.

The Absence of Self (*Anātman*)

The notion of the absence of self is probably the one that distinguishes Buddhism most clearly from other philosophical and religious doctrines. It is also the notion that is the hardest to grasp, so strongly does it stand in opposition to our own deepest convictions. How can one explain and interpret such a notion from a Western point of view? This is not just a Buddhist version of the demonstration produced by Pascal. It is true that, like Pascal, the Indian master Nāgasena proves to his interlocutor, Milinda (i.e., Menander) (who, as if by chance, happens to be a Greek) that the self is nowhere to be found, for it can be located in none of the physical or mental components of the individual. The Buddhist monk is as radically convinced of that absence as is Valéry who, if we are to believe him, contemplated his own face and properties "as a cow gazes at a train." But the Buddhist position then becomes even more radical: Whatever says or thinks "I" is not a subject (*pace* Descartes). The self as we usually conceive of it is an illusion, the product of a fundamental ignorance and of a whole series of causes and effects: the causality of *karma.* The whole edifice of ontology, the belief in being and in substance, collapses. At the heart of beings and things there is no longer that spark of ultimate reality, the *ātman,* which for Hindus constitutes the individual's share of the absolute, a trace of the ultimate principle or Brahman in the innermost depths of oneself. Behind all emotional and psychic states, all thoughts and actions, there is no immutable, federating and unifying principle to be found, nothing that could be called "self." There is thought, but no thinker. The notion of an agent, a presence at work behind actions, is simply an error produced by language. A similar idea is to be found in Nietzsche, who regarded belief in a subject as a simple error due to grammar.

The Buddhist concept of the absence of self (*anātman*) implies a radical rejection of the Hindu concept of self. The Indian renouncers' acquisition of a self was prepared for by the moralization of *karma,* the transition from cosmological concepts to moral ones—a transition that coincided with the switch from Brahmanism to Hinduism. The equation between the *ātman* and the Brahman provided a renouncer with a kind of lever on the invisible: By discovering the *ātman* within himself, he managed to short-circuit the cycle of births and deaths and achieve direct union with the Brahman. Although the early Buddhists also aimed to escape from the cycle of births and deaths, they opted for the opposite strategy and denied all reality to the Brahman/*ātman* pair.

Just as no permanent psychic entity exists beneath the flow of consciousness—no "substance" or spiritual essence—likewise, no permanent physical entity exists. Not only does the body change, it is also intrinsically empty: like the trunk of a banana tree, a bubble of foam, or an illusion. The body and the mind, in whose existence we have so firmly believed since Descartes, turn out to be errors of our misled senses. All that exist are series of impersonal psychic or physical entities—or at least these exist in early Buddhism. In Mahāyāna, though, even those series dissolve, revealing their intrinsic emptiness. The body becomes somehow transparent, yet by the same token extremely opaque to any ordinary mind.

Everything is fundamentally empty, extinguished, *nirvāṇa*-like—even the tempest raging within me or outside me. The whirl of emotions, the trees' branches twisting in a storm: It is all nothing but wind, emptiness, only a semblance of movement. In reality all is calm, at peace. There is nothing and no one behind this: no subject, no subjective meaning. Where we see beings dragged into the infernal cycle of births and deaths, there exists nothing but serene and limpid space where pure quiescence reigns. But it has to be seen to be believed, or believed to be seen. And once it is seen, there is no longer anything to see or anyone to see it. *Nirvāṇa* rejects voyeurs, just as the ocean rejects corpses. This vision of deliverance seems, to say the least, hard to reconcile with other Buddhist notions, in particular those of *karma* and transmigration.

To explain the apparent paradox of transmigration where there is nobody to transmigrate, the Indian sage Nāgasena resorts to the following parable: A man who had betrothed himself to a little girl and paid the marriage price to her father had to depart on a journey. The child grew up, and her father decided to marry her to another man in return for a new marriage price. The traveler returned and claimed the young woman from her husband. "I did not marry your betrothed," the latter said. "The little girl was one thing, the woman is another." As judged by common sense, he was clearly mistaken: A woman is certainly no longer a little girl, but that is not to say that she is "other."" Nāgasena explains that the same goes for the self from one existence to the next. However, although that reply seems to explain the paradox of continuity within discontinuity, it does not explain the paradox of the absence of self in the present life.

How should we interpret the Buddhist *anātman*, this passionate rejection of the self? Merleau-Ponty declares: "Subjectivity is one of those thoughts from which there is no turning back, even, indeed especially if one has passed beyond them."[7] In other words, negation of the self—whether spoken, thought, or enacted—at the same time affirms it: It can oppose it only by assuming it. We are therefore led to interpret it with a grain of salt: What is said is perhaps not quite what happens when one says it, for once again the performative magic of language is at work. To say that the self does not exist is not so much an observation, but rather wishful thinking, or even a pious wish (and until such time as that wish is realized, a pious lie).

Furthermore, the value of individuality, and hence also of its negation, does not mean the same in a traditional, strongly hierarchical society as it does in a society such as our own, which is democratic and individualistic. The earliest Buddhists were renouncers, individuals who, precisely because they had renounced the world, that is to say, society, found themselves in an altogether unprecedented situation, a position that was eminently individual. A renouncer, unlike the "men in the world" whom he has left behind and who are defined only by their involvement in the network of social relations, is an individual "outside the world," cut off from all social links. But that individuality, which we take for granted, was by no means self-evident in the Indian context of the time; and it was possibly because the Buddhist renouncer was better placed than anyone before him had been to feel the weight of this new situation that he wished to set down the "burden" of the self—by quite simply denying its existence.[8]

The notion of a self (*ātman*) or a person (*puruṣa*) nevertheless remained in use at the conventional level of Buddhist practice. It was partly a matter of adapting to local customs. In Asia, as in the West, at a conventional level we find two major concepts of subjectivity: on the one hand subjectivity of a cosmological nature, the occupation of a well-defined place in the cosmos; on the other, a "transcendental" subjectivity, free in front of the cosmos, which it transcends. Those two concepts are reflected in the two faces of the supreme individual, the Buddha, who both "renounces" and "conquers" the world. So the dogma of the absence of self does not do justice to the doctrinal complexity of early Buddhism. By opposing orthodoxy and heresy, as it does, it brushes aside the entire spectrum of nuanced replies to the question of the subject. In early Buddhism we find a tendency known as *pudgalavāda*, "personalist," according to which there does exist a *pudgala* (a self, a person) that transmigrates from one existence to another and even survives in *nirvāṇa*. In contrast, Mādhyamika denies all reality to both the body and the mind. In between the two, Yogācāra attributes to the consciousness of an individual a permanent nature that endures beyond death and regards this as a necessary link between the various existences, the basis upon which retribution for actions rests.

The Buddhist negation of the self that we have been considering so far is what might be called a philosophical negation. Among the early Buddhists, with their tendency toward realism, it was a matter of an absence that was demonstrated, as in Pascal, by a logical analysis: When one takes stock, mentally or discursively, of the whole collection of elements that constitute the organism, there is not one that can be found that can be called the self; there is no ghost in the machine, only what we might nowa-days call "hardware," along with "software." These components, for their part, do possess a certain reality. In Mahāhyāna Buddhism, in contrast, the Mādhyamika tradition preaches the illusory character of all things: The machine itself is empty, merely an illusory synthesis of ceaseless flows. Yet in day-to-day reality, Buddhists do recognize the existence of a conventional self, the "secondary self" that we share with four billion other people, mistakenly believing it to be our own real self. In a letter to André Lebey dated June 1908, Valéry wrote: "I have no soul, it is true, but it is 'as if' I had."

Furthermore, we also find in Mahāyāna a tendency that, even as it rejects the conventional self as illusory, nevertheless asserts the existence of a superior Self, which has to be discovered behind appearances. This Self is masked and plays its part so well in the masquerade that the mask has adhered to the skin. So what we must do is "strip bare the old man" in order to rediscover the real man within ourselves, the Buddha who we all are and have always been. The distinction between this notion of a Buddha nature immanent within each one of us and ancient Indian concepts of the *ātman* is not always clear, and some opponents of this theory hasten to denounce it as a heresy. It nevertheless constitutes a deep vein of East Asian Buddhism, in particular of currents such as Chan and Zen.

Linji said one day to his disciples: "Here in this lump of red flesh there is a True Man with no rank. Constantly he goes in and out the gates of your face. If there are any of you who don't know this for a fact, then look! Look!"

At that time there was a monk who came forward and asked, "What is he like—the True Man with no rank?"

The Master got down from his chair, seized hold of the monk, and said, "Speak! Speak!"

The monk was about to say something, whereupon the Master let go of him, shoved him away, and said, "True Man with no rank—what a shitty ass-wiper!"

The Master then returned to his quarters.[9]

Linji was heir to a tradition the motto of which was: "To see one's own nature and become a Buddha." The only way to do this was to be a man "without affairs," no rank. In fact, someone very disorienting.

Whoever comes to me seeking something, I immediately come out to size him up, but he doesn't recognize me. Then I put on various different robes. The student forms an understanding on that basis and begins to be drawn into my words.

Hopeless, this blind baldhead without any eyes! He concentrates on the robe I'm wearing, noting whether it is blue, yellow, red, or white. If I strip off the robe and enter a clean pure environment, the student takes one look and is filled with delight and longing. If I throw that away, too, the student becomes muddled in mind, racing around wildly in a distracted manner, exclaiming that now I have no robe at all! Then I turn to him and say, "Do you know the person who wears this robe of mine?" Suddenly he turns his head, and then he knows me at last.[10]

Linji's "True Man with no rank" also calls to mind Robert Musil's "man without qualities" and Valéry's totally detached "pure self." Linji said, "Be your own master, wherever you are, and you will immediately be true." To which Valéry adds, "In short, you place yourself as it were at the center, at the Place de l'Opéra of the universe—a mental, sensitive, one."[11] At any rate, Linji's "essentialism" is relative. In his own personal version of the tetralemma, he sometimes leaves out both man (the subject) and things (the object). For him, as for Musil, it seems that "subjectivity turns its back on our inner being just as much as objectivity does." In an often-cited passage, another major Zen figure, Dōgen, also tackles the question of the subject:

To learn the Buddha Way is to learn one's own self. To learn one's self is to forget one's self. To forget one's self is to be confirmed by all dharmas. To be confirmed by all dharmas is to effect the casting off of one's own body and mind and the bodies and minds of others as well. All traces of enlightenment [then] disappear, and this traceless enlightenment is continued on and on endlessly.[12]

To undermine the "essentialist" concept of the self that prevailed in his day, Dōgen resorts to the following comparison:

When a person goes off in a boat and looks back to see the shoreline, he mistakenly thinks the shore is moving. If he keeps his eyes closely on his boat, he realizes it is the boat that is advancing. In like manner, when a person [tries to] discern and affirm the myriad dharmas with a confused conception of [his own] body and mind, he mistakenly thinks his own mind and his own nature are permanent. If he makes all his daily deeds intimately his own and returns within himself, the reason that the myriad dharmas are without self will become clear to him.[13]

Stripped of all intrinsic value, the self constantly changes: so it is empty. On the other hand, apparent changes in our environment mask their fundamental immobility, their "thusness." Whereas Linji praises the man with no rank, Dōgen asserts the superiority of the "True Man *with* rank."

The Buddhist definition of the absence of self, its concept of personality as a series of physiopsychic aggregates, the comparison of consciousness to an onion, the successive layers of which conceal no hard kernel, and of the body to a mirage are all reminiscent of the deconstruction of the apparent personal unity of the corporeal subject as found in certain postmodernist thinkers such as Gilles Deleuze and Félix Guattari. These writers consider the self and the body to be a reductive illusion. According to them, there is in reality nothing but a multitude of energetic or driving vectors, "flows of intensity" or "desiring machines," that are in perpetual movement. The illusory sense of a deep-seated self, a kernel of the absolute that underlies organic and psychic phenomena, is in truth produced and operates at a purely skin-deep level. Could not the following passage, taken from *Anti-Oedipus*, have been penned by a Buddhist?"

It is at work everywhere, functioning smoothly at times, at other times in fits and starts. It breathes, it heats, it eats. It shits and fucks. What a mistake to have called it *the* id! Everywhere *it* is machines—real ones, not figurative ones: machines driving other machines, machines being driven by other machines, with all the necessary couplings and connections.[14]

There is yet another way to deny or relativize the conventional self in favor of a more complex form of subjectivity. This approach is not always formulated explicitly in philosophical treatises, but is excellently expressed through ritual. In the wake of the Marxist analysis of the fetishism of merchandise, there have been many descriptions of the way in which man projects himself into objects and is thereby alienated. In Buddhism, too, we find a theory of projection, which shows man how to "re-collect" himself and disinvest himself of the world of objects. Meanwhile, it is mistaken to regard the Buddhist cult of icons simply as a form of fetishism or idolatry, for this cult brings to bear what, borrowing Michel Foucault's expression, we might call the "pensée du dehors." Buddhism has invested ritual with a collection of thoughts on the "objective" dissemination of being. We are in objects, but no longer know it. This is a reflection on mediation: Man attains to certain energies, either within himself or in the cosmos, through the mediation of objects. That is an illusion, both literally and in the Freudian sense, you may say. But it is an illusion that is sometimes just as effective as psychoanalysis, if not more so.

This ritualistic approach also implies thought about what constitutes the body itself. As we have seen, the "disenchantment of the world" does not mean forgetting all the fables, but refusing to believe that our "self" can be situated anywhere but in our body. From this point of view, too, the advantage of Buddhism lies in its "twofold truth": On the one hand (in the case of Linji, for example), it rids the self of its rags, revealing the "naked man"; on the other (in the sphere of ritual), it engineers a dissemination of the self in portraits, icons, relics, and so on. The self outdoors—in a way, this concept stems from the dogma of the absence of a central self. The monotheism of that central self is replaced not by the atheism of the absence of self, but rather by the polytheism of the multiplicity of self, or even the pantheism of the omnipresence of self.

It is also important briefly to note the ideological "twofold truth" of a notion such as that of no-self, in other words, the fact that, like any philosophical notion, it can become the subject of a recuperation. For example, it was in the name of the Buddhist *anātman* that the theorists of Japanese imperialism preached abnegation to their troops during the war in the Pacific. The supreme sacrifice of the individual was in this way justified by the centrifugal movement that was supposed to drive the Japanese to seek their truth outside themselves, in the person of the emperor, which was identified with ultimate reality, the brazier in which all differences, all individualities became fused.

The Doctrine of Emptiness (*Śūnyata*)

In the first place there is a relative emptiness, the kind to which the first noble truth stated by the Buddha refers: Things have no lasting reality; everything in this world is evanescent, being produced by changing causes and conditions. That is particularly true of this body to which we are so attached. As Nāgārjuna says, "We consider emptiness to be codependent origination; it is pure designation and is, exclusively, the Middle Way. Since there is nothing that comes about without conditions, there is nothing that is not empty."[15]

But there is also an absolute emptiness. From the point of view of ultimate truth, things do not stem from codependent origination—"a law that loosens its grip on us the minute we understand it." According to Nāgārjuna, the Middle Way is that of emptiness midway between the two poles of our dualizing concepts, for every concept is a false concept.

Nāgārjuna extends his critique to the four noble truths of the early Buddhist doctrine, relegating all four to the status of conventional truth.

An identical critique of the four noble truths is to be found in the *Hṛdaya sūtra* or *Heart Sūtra*. This extremely short text from the tradition of the Perfection of Wisdom is probably the most popular of all *sūtras*, and is still recited every day in all East Asian countries by the monks and laymen of the various Buddhist schools. It is even to be found inscribed on tea cups, handkerchiefs, and ties. It is said to record the words of the bodhisattva Avalokiteśvara, one of the mythical figures of Mahāyāna, and distances itself clearly from the doctrine of Hīnayāna. It negates the content of all the traditional rubrics of the latter: the five physical and psychical aggregates that constitute an individual and all the sense organs are declared to be "empty." And this text goes still further: Even suffering, and in consequence the extinction of suffering (*nirvāṇa*), are emptied of reality. It ends paradoxically, with a *mantra*, a magic formula that seems out of place in this context: *Gate, gate, paragate, parasaṃgate, bodhi svāha* (the meaning of which, if meaning there be, is as follows: "Gone, gone, gone beyond, completely gone beyond: awakening!). But in truth, the entire *Heart Sūtra*, despite its highly "philosophical" tone, is used chiefly as an extremely effective *mantra*, capable of saving those who recite it even if they do not understand its meaning.

The notion of the Middle Way, which in early texts simply designated abstention from the extremes of hedonism (the pleasures of the flesh) and asceticism (the mortification of the flesh), soon took on a more philosophical meaning and came to designate the perilous path that passed between the Charybdis of eternalism and the Scylla of nihilism, existence and nonexistence. The tradition of the Perfection of Wisdom rejects all extremes, such as permanence and impermanence, form and the informal, the visible and the invisible, aversion and attraction, impurity and purity, the worldly and the supraworldly domains, ignorance and the end of ignorance, old age and death and their cessation. This ultimate wisdom (*prajñā*), known as "the mother of all Buddhas," even ascribes no reality to the Buddha and his awakening.

Buddhist emptiness is not hidden within fullness, like holes in a Gruyère cheese. It is the source of the phenomenal world—it is, in fact, nothing but that world (the Gruyère cheese itself, with or without holes). According to the *Heart Sūtra*, "emptiness is form (or matter), form (or matter) is emptiness." Emptiness does not stop when fullness begins: Fullness and emptiness are like the two sides of a Möbius strip, the recto of which is indistinguishable from the verso. The Chan master Shenxiu (606–706) said: "Do you hear the sound of the bell that is tolling? Does that sound exist during or before the tolling of the bell? . . . Does it exist only inside the monastery, or does it also reach the worlds in all ten directions?" He also said: "The body disappears, its shadow does not."[16] Dōgen, similarly, declared: "What one hears when one knocks at emptiness is a mysterious, endless sound that resounds both before and after the strike of the knocker."

The Buddhist "Pas de Deux"

As has repeatedly been pointed out, Buddhism is a thought of mediation that implies passing beyond any form of dualism, and the Buddhist notion of the two truths rejects the principle of the excluded middle. The locus classicus of the two truths is to be found in Nāgārjuna's *Madhyamakakārikā*:

The teaching of the doctrine [promulgated] by the Buddhas rests upon two truths: conventional truth and ultimate truth.

Those who cannot see the difference between those two truths cannot discern the profound reality in the teaching of the Buddha.

The ultimate meaning can be taught only by starting off from conventional truth. And it is only by understanding the ultimate meaning that one accedes to *nirvāṇa*.[17]

Reality eludes all philosophical doctrines. So there is no need to decide between materialism and idealism or to accept the dilemma of the hammer and the anvil. It is a matter of not forcing some superior truth upon the interlocutor, but on the contrary, of calling into question any truth that claims to be superior. "Ultimate truth" itself is constantly called into question (and at the same time confirmed) by the underlying existence of another truth, by the fact that it is neither the sole truth nor simple.

However, the twofold truth can give rise to errors of classification. The following anecdote, from the *Collection of Sand and Pebbles* by the Japanese monk Mujū Ichien (1226–1312) provides an amusing illustration of some of those errors. In the absence of his disciples, a priest brought salt from a salt merchant, paying him a prohibitive price. When his disciples

told him that he had been cheated, he set about thinking of a way to resolve the situation. The next day, when a man selling wood came to the
temple, he ordered him to unload his wood, then refused to pay him on
the grounds that he had cheated him on the previous day. His disciples in-
tervened, explaining that the man selling wood was not the same man as
the one who had sold him the salt. The priest replied that they had understood nothing: "To say that a seller of salt is a seller of salt and a seller of
wood is a seller of wood befits the spirit of the Particular Teaching. But in
the Perfect Doctrine, it is said that a seller of wood is as good as a seller of
salt and a seller of salt is as good as a seller of wood." Rather than argue
about it, the disciples took the merchant aside and paid him for the wood.
Mujū comments as follows:

That scholar truly possesses double vision. In Buddhist Law, one is familiar with
the doctrine of the two truths, the one absolute, the other profane. As absolute
truth expresses the principle of the universality of emptiness, in that truth there is
no distinction between oneself and others. . . . As for profane truth, this does distinguish the ordinary state from an illuminated state and differentiates illusion
from awakening without destroying the phenomenal aspect of everything. . . .

Our scholar misunderstood the notion of the Undifferentiated. If he is speaking of
phenomenal identity in the light of the absolute, then how can he show the identity *only* between salt vendor and lumber dealer? The man, those who lived with
him, and his retainers are all identical in this sense. Since everything in the Ten
Worlds is one aspect without differentiation, who is it that deceives and who is de-
ceived? But if, in the light of the phenomenal truth, we consider the phenomenal
aspect of things, then the salt vendor and the lumber dealer are separate beings.
Why should he suppress this side of it? Needless to say, his views were biased.[18]

To argue that "all is one, one is all" in order to claim that all is in order, all is for the best in the best of worlds—even massacres of innocents
(and, in that case, also the condemnation of crimes against humanity)—is
to get it wrong. It is to claim to speak in the name of the absolute when
one is still at the relative level, thereby transforming a deep and fruitful intuition into a justificatory ideology (as did some Japanese monks, who invoked the theory of the identity of awakening and the passions in order to
legitimate their own homosexual desires).

The ultimate truth of Mahāyāna also lends itself to an elitist interpretation, and the theory of the two truths supports social division (by permitting theoretical ultimate equality and de facto discrimination to coex-
ist). The transition to the notion of a universal Buddha nature ought to

have allowed legal equality to emerge. But the emergence of that idea was hampered by the notion of the two truths: In the empirical world, organized on the model of a hierarchy, it was to be expected that inequality would continue—at least among ignorant people. Sages, for their part, know how to recognize one another, whatever their social rank.

Sudden or Gradual

The "subitism" controversy, which divided Chan in the eighth century, did not really center upon the question of whether awakening is sudden or not: The sudden nature of the experience was not in question. Rather, it was concerned with whether awakening can result from pious works and contemplative techniques. Whereas the "gradual" school emphasized the usefulness of certain practices, the "sudden" school sweepingly rejected them. The two positions are clearly opposed in an anecdote about a poetry competition in which the alleged founders of both schools, Shenxiu (who died in 706) and Huineng (who died in 713) took part. According to Shenxiu's verse, "The body is the tree of awakening,/The mind is like a clear mirror./Take care always to polish it,/So that no dust gathers there." Huineng's retort was as follows: "There is no tree of awakening/Nor any clear mirror./Fundamentally, nothing exists./So where could dust gather?"

We are told that this didactic poem of Huineng won him the title of sixth Chan patriarch. Unfortunately, both poems are apocryphal and clearly represent the point of view of Huineng's disciples. According to this point of view, no practices at all are necessary, since everything is empty, so logically it led to a dead end: If all beings are intrinsically awakened, seated meditation and pious works are equally useless, and the Chan school itself, with its patriarchs, becomes pointless. In practice, however, this theoretical radicalism was very soon tempered.

The sudden and the gradual seem to suggest two types of experience that are incommensurable. No end or resolution to the disagreement between them is possible. Councils take place, but any form of reconciliation seems excluded. In what does this disagreement consist, if indeed it can even be expressed? From the "sudden" point of view, all initiation is illusory: All progress must, quite literally, take place in emptiness and must consequently be null and void, has never happened and never will. From the "gradual" point of view, it is, on the contrary, the "sudden" fiat ("Let there be light, and there was enlightenment!") that renders all progress, all awakening impossible and leads to an illusory resolution. Nevertheless, the disagreement is not entirely sterile, for it mobilizes thought, literally sets it in motion. To the question of which of the two views, the sudden or the gradual, is the best in both theory and practice, there can be no simple or unilateral answer. A twofold response is required. The sudden/gradual paradigm establishes a paradoxical structure, a two-way thinking that opens onto a double truth.

On Sudden Awakening and Its Implications

Followers of the way, if you want to get the kind of understanding that accords with the *Dharma*, never be misled by others. Whether you're facing inward or facing outward, whatever you meet up with, just kill it! If you meet a buddha, kill the buddha. If you meet a patriarch, kill the patriarch. If you meet an *arhat*, kill the *arhat*. If you meet your parents, kill your parents. If you meet your kinfolk, kill your kinfolk. Then for the first time you will gain emancipation, will not be entangled with things, will pass freely anywhere you wish to go.
　　—Linji Yixuan

It is no doubt wrong to speak of a sudden "perspective." The sudden is, rather, the vanishing point that makes the perspective possible. The word "sudden" refers to a truly upsetting experience, a mental catastrophe, an eruption of the "totally other" into the individual consciousness. So this essentially metaphysical discourse preserves within it or on its margins the possibility of an overflow. In the last analysis, the sudden does not stand in opposition to the gradual; rather, it is what subverts the opposition between the sudden and the gradual. It is an intuition that is evanescent, fleeting, abrupt, and total. It cannot be the programmed outcome of an empirical progress. Even if it is preceded by practice of a gradual nature, it is not in the manner in which an effect is preceded by its cause. What is involved is one of those paradoxical states that are resistant to all attempts to produce them (including seated meditation and *kōan*). To define awakening as a state to be achieved is still to allow oneself to be misled by ordinary language. Accordingly, the Chan texts constantly set us on our guard against any such interpretation. Awakening is considered to be totally unpredictable, unthinkable, beyond all expectation. It is perfectly "aporetic" in the sense that there is no path (*poros*) that can lead to it.

The term "subitism" thus designates two diametrically opposed approaches. The first, in that it encourages the devotee to "see his own nature," remains a metaphysics of presence, whereas the second strives to subvert all desire for presence, any idea of truth. According to the *Sūtra of Perfect Awakening*, an apocryphal Chan text widespread in the eighth century, "Given that consciousness is an illusion, one must detach oneself from it. Given that this detachment is an illusion, one must detach oneself from it, too. Given that that detachment from detachment is an illusion, one must detach oneself from this. At this point there is nothing from which one must detach oneself and all illusions have vanished."[19] At about the same time, the Chan master Shenhui was saying, "Whatever one ascends fearfully [that is to say gradually] . . . can only be an ugly hummock of accumulated earth. . . . If one has to resort to successive upward steps, one will never reach the goal and will establish the 'gradual' principle. . . . To understand without recourse to the gradual, spontaneously, that is the meaning of the sudden nature."[20] Thirteen centuries on, Wittgenstein produced a remarkable echo to Shenhui: "If the place I wish to reach could only be attained by climbing a ladder, I would give up the idea of reaching it. For where I really want to go is where I should, in truth, be. Anything that can only be reached by using a ladder does not interest me."[21] The total and definitive nature of awakening is underlined by Stephen Jourdain in a short work entitled, precisely, *Awakening*:

Priests, plumbers, politicians, sharp, lively minds, thick ones, cultivated people, uneducated people, men of probity, cheats—all of them are asleep, all equally oblivious, all convinced they are awake, all without consciousness in exactly the same way. This metaphysical slumber has no gradations, no nuances, is always on the same level, where one belongs either altogether or not at all.

How to make them understand that they are asleep? They would be prepared to agree to the idea that the degree to which they are conscious of themselves is in no way ultimate and that, quantitatively, their grasp of self could certainly be improved—just as the dawn can become brighter, more intense. But how to get them to believe—or simply to consider the hypothesis—that here, precisely, the day has not yet dawned? That the real question is whether the light that is familiar to them has anything to do with daytime? . . .

For the metaphor of daylight to be rigorous, the day would have to begin all of a sudden, with no dawn, no forewarning; it would have to burst forth, to blaze, to be there suddenly, totally, perfect, with the hands of your world watch pointing to midday.

But just as Molière's Monsieur Jourdain (who has nothing at all to do with the above-mentioned author) produced prose without knowing it, people are constantly weaving the prose of the world through their thoughts without realizing that they are doing so—and it is precisely the perpetual hum of their consciousness that sends them to sleep: "How to make them understand that even in the state of exemplary vigilance that is constituted by a customary self-awareness, they are ASLEEP!?" But alas, even the artificial device of capital letters, the typographical equivalent of a warning shot across the bows similar to a volley of words or blows from a man such as Linji, fails to shake the reader out of his/her torpor. Occasionally, however, such details do have the effect of certain particularly aberrant anomalies in dreams, anomalies that force the dreamer to recognize that what is going on is impossible, so he/she must be dreaming. That is probably how the "crazy" words and behavior of Chan masters should be understood. They play the role of an alarm clock, the only true sense of which, whatever the semantic content, is quite simply "DRRIINGG. . . ." What would we say of philosophers who, like the tea party guests in *Alice in Wonderland*, strived to discover "the hermeneutics of the Dring"? Yet that is exactly what most of those who practice Zen Buddhism do.

In Praise of the In-Between and of Transition

After that slow unfolding of the meaning of "subitism," let us turn suddenly to the gradual. There is a double truth in gradualism, for the term has two distinct referents. In the first place it designates a fundamental intuition, an implicit epistemology and anthropology, a coherent concept of the world and of awakening—in other words, a "structuring structure" that is not just a classificatory category, but also a guiding schema open to empirical multiplicity. But the term "gradualism" also designates a reified concept, an explicit "structured structure"—a doctrine that has served above all as a foil to the rival doctrine of "subitism." It is hard to speak objectively of gradualism, because one is more or less consciously influenced by a whole tradition that regards it simply as a concession to the weaknesses of ordinary practitioners or else (but it comes to the same thing) as a position outmatched by subitism. As has been noted above, subitism and gradualism make their appearance on the sectarian scene only because of reductionist definitions. However, gradualism was never effectively refuted by subitism, and it cannot be reduced to a mere deviation from or a preliminary phase of subitism.

Beyond the caricature of gradualism presented by subitists, there is a gradualism of a more fundamental nature. According to Nāgārjuna's *Madhyamakākārikā*: "All is as it seems, nothing is as it seems. That is the progressive teaching of the Buddhas." As Guy Bugault points out, this means that "the teaching of the Buddhas, even when gradual and discursive, is too subtle to be blocked by disjunctive filters."[22] In its more anthropological aspects, this gradualism reflects a vision of the world, a concept of reality and the sacred that is somewhat reminiscent of that described by Henri Hubert and Marcel Mauss in their study of sacrifice. According to them, the sacred space is structured, and ritual may be seen as a progression through that sacred space, moving from the outermost edge of the precinct inward to the holy of holies. This is also the structure of a *maṇḍala*, the visual device that, in the esoteric tradition, constitutes a means of access to awakening. Within this sacred space, any leap, any break in continuity, would provoke a loss of equilibrium that could be fatal. This concept of the sacred constitutes a fundamental element of archaic religious thought. In this context, gradual awakening can be seen as a process of discovering the ontological structures of reality and/or the anthropological structures of the imaginary.

Such gradualism is probably one of the dominant features of Chinese thought, whether religious or literate. It could be objected that this type of "natural" gradualism—understood as submission to the order of things and to the rhythms of nature, participation in the flow of life and respect for the multiplicity of reality—is in fact quite close to sudden "quietism," which reckons that everything has already been accomplished, so all efforts are superfluous. However, it differs from this in that it expresses the realization that nature does not make leaps. Sudden awakening severs the Gordian knot, rejecting the traditional game of knot tying and untying. Gradualism, for its part, enters into that game.

Because of its elitism and its apparent rejection of all soteriological methods, subitism laid itself open to a gradualist critique that developed within the very heart of the Chan school. In a letter to his brother Yun'yan Tansheng, the Chan master Daowu Yuanzhi (769–853) contrasted the teaching of their respective masters, Baizhang and Shitou, comparing the former to an ironmonger's store and the latter to a shop selling pure gold, and urged Yun'yan to leave "Baizhang's ironmonger's." Commenting upon this passage, Yangshan Huiji underlined the importance of mediations: "The ironmonger sells all kinds of things, ranging from mice droppings to pure gold. The seller of pure gold cannot supply the demands of those who want mice droppings." A similar argument is to be found in the Zen master Dokuan Dokugo: "When people of low ability hear talk of sudden awakening, it is like when small plants receive a heavy shower of rain: They are flattened and cannot grow." Whereas subitism seems to deny all value to mediation, gradualism endeavors to think through the in-between, the interminable journey upon which we are engaged. Unlike partisans of the sudden leap, it considers that the journey itself is not without significance, indeed is essential.

Twofold Truth

A form of truth, not a coherent and central truth, but a truth that is lateral
and divided.
　　　　—Thomas de Quincey

The history of Buddhism, like that of so many movements of
thought, seems to be governed by what Bergson, in *The Two Sources of
Morality and Religion*, suggested calling the "law of dichotomy," a law
"which apparently brings about a realization, by a mere splitting, of tendencies which began by being two views, so to speak, of one and the same
tendency."[1] As a result, "a tendency on which two different views are possible can only put forth its maximum, in quantity and quality, if it materi-
alizes these two possibilities into moving realities, each one of which leaps
forward and monopolizes the available space, while the other is on the
watch increasingly for its own turn to come."[2] At times, Bergson seems to
regard that "original tendency" as a synthesis or compromise, a projection
onto a median and intermediary level of two preexisting tendencies that
stem from two opposed sources. So is it a matter of one single source that
separates into two tendencies or of a dual source that is expressed by temporary syntheses that soon fall apart, only to reform further downstream?
The alternative is rather like the riddle of the chicken and the egg—where,
depending on the point of view, each can be either the cause or the effect
of the other. Another image that may serve to illustrate the Buddhist double truth is that of Wittgenstein's duck-rabbit, for this can be seen now as
a duck, now as a rabbit, with the beak of the duck becoming the ears of the
rabbit, or vice versa. The Dutch artist M. C. Escher has specialized in these
types of recursive images. In Chinese symbolism, the famous symbols *yin*
and *yang*, which, as is well known, represent the alternating phases or prin-

ciples of reality, offer a similar kind of example: At the very heart of the red part (*yang*), a tiny white circle can be seen (*yin*), and vice versa. But, it may be asked, are two truths better than one? What happens to our idea of truth when it splits into two, becoming a kind of recursive pattern—one in which form and content are equivalent?

Nearly all histories of philosophy tend to reduce the complexity of the historical development of this discipline to a ceaseless reinscription of the primordial duel of two traditions—duality in two senses: that of a grammatical *duo*, something in between a singular and a plural, and that of a battle (a *duellum*). The two traditions are represented by, for example, Parmenides and Heraclitus, Plato and Aristotle, or similar tandems. Every philosopher is represented as belonging at some point (if not throughout his life) to the current of either one or the other tradition. Thus, Bergson, writing *The Creative Mind,* saw himself as the distant heir to Heraclitus, the Greek philosopher famous for having declared that one never bathes twice in the same river, who, like Hegel later on, placed contradiction at the very heart of things.

Reality and Its Double

Buddhism is sometimes described as a grasp upon reality (a "grasp" made possible by the realization that there is, precisely, nothing to grasp). Let us, in passing, note the apparent paradox of a *reflection* that aims to understand the way in which thought itself, by engendering all kinds of false notions such as those of good and evil, covers over reality with a tissue of dualist representations that denies us all direct perception. In particular, dualist thought creates an ideal world, which seems to us more true, and encourages us to reject the world of the senses and empirical multiplicity.

Ever since Greek idealism, as expressed in Plato's myth of the cave, European thought has constantly assumed the existence of a double register of being: reality and appearance, essence and existence, the in-itself and the for-itself, and so on. There is a profound difference between the two mutually exclusive visions of the world represented by idealism and materialism. Yet in both Buddhist and Western thought, the two approaches co-exist throughout history. Epistemologically, there are probably no more reasons for choosing or for rejecting either in favor of the other. If the idealist loses hold of the prey by reaching for the shadow—figuratively speaking, of course, since reality is, precisely, in no way a prey—the realist, for his part, loses the shadow while reaching for the prey and—what is more—it is his own shadow, an essential part of himself. One day, the Daoist philosopher Zhuangzi noticed a strange magpie in a forest of chestnut trees. Instead of flying off when approached, the magpie remained intent on its prey, a praying mantis that, for its part, being about to pounce on a grasshopper, was oblivious of all else. For a moment, Zhuangzi, fascinated, paused to watch them, then realized that he, too, was just a link in the predatory chain. He returned home, much disturbed. When a disciple asked what the trouble was, he replied: "In clinging to outward form I have forgotten my own body. Staring at muddy water, I have been misled in taking it for a clear pool."[3] As for reality, it lies, as it were, in between those two kinds of water. Or, to change the metaphor, Buddhism hacks a middle way, rejecting on the one hand realism, on the other idealism (or nihilism, depending on the circumstances), "just as the ploughshare hollows out a furrow, enclosing it between two ridges of earth."[4]

From the Double to the Single, and Vice Versa

In a whole series of works, the philosopher Clément Rosset sets out to reject the logic of double truth, which, in his view, underlies all idealisms. Implicitly his critique may be applied to scientific thought, insofar as the latter presupposes the splitting of reality into the sensible and the intelligible. He suggests that this duality is the characteristic feature of metaphysics, "which is founded upon an, as it were, instinctive rejection of the immediate, which is suspected of somehow being the other of another reality." For an idealist, reality "begins only at the second take, which constitutes the truth of human life, a life that bears the stamp of duality."[5] For Rosset, in contrast, reality exists totally and can have no shadow or double. The "sudden" advent of reality, as he describes it, is somewhat reminiscent of Chan Buddhism. That sudden, unmediated perception is the opposite of ordinary, gradual perception, which requires both time and distance.

Despite its apparent immediacy, in most cases, reality is already transfigured by perception, thought, language, and belief. Reality for a botanist in the countryside is not the same as for a peasant or for a poet. Even in the case of mystical experience, "presence" in reality is never a "given," but is always constructed, and it implies a variety of degrees of depth, ranging from maximum reality to minimum reality—even if all those degrees are equally valid in absolute reality.

To be sure, the ideal can serve as a convenient refuge from the assaults of a prosaic reality and can provide a derisory alibi against the "reality principle." For instance, toward the end of his life, Hegel allegedly told an illegitimate son of his who had come to ask for recognition: "I know that I had something to do with your birth, but then I was living in the accidental; now I am living in the essential." But if idealism is often a form of escapism, the same can be said of many human activities that conceal reality from us while seeming to probe it more deeply. And if books were just a means of escaping from reality? Why write, if not to create a double to survive one, even if only for a short while, until the work is pulped? Such is the paradox of erudite scholars who in many cases prefer to try to understand a distant time or place rather than their present fellow men. Understanding "the other" comes to be used as an alibi justifying the scholar's rejection of everyday reality. Depending on one's mood, one can either regard this as a mild form of folly or, on the contrary, a refusal to allow oneself to be trapped in an ethnocentric tautology. Maybe this detour is the only way to accede to reality, but maybe it is simply a flight forward, a way to lose oneself.

The metaphysical endeavor, par excellence, is said to involve "setting immediacy aside, relating it to another world that holds the key to it, both from the point of view of its meaning and from that of its reality."[6] To this one may counter that belief in the immediacy of reality (the "reality of reality") involves a measure of naïveté. Particularly in the case of Chan/Zen discourse, which is probably the best-known example of an apologia for reality, recourse to the "rhetoric of immediacy" is by no means immediate and exempt from ulterior motives; in practice, it functions as an authoritarian argument, a way of laying claim to some privilege or prerogative where the truth is concerned. To strive for immediacy is not enough to achieve it. On the contrary, immediacy is one of those paradoxical states that one loses by seeking to attain them.[7]

The very least that can be said is that immediacy, transparency, immanence, or presence to being are certainly not among the things that are the most equally distributed in this world. In China, the land allegedly blessed by immanence, for every Zhuangzi and the handful of immortals who, we are told, concentrate wholly upon the *dao* and fuse with nature, there are whole legions of epigones for whom naturalness is nothing but an ideal and an alibi or an ideological posture. The partisans of Daoist naturalism, like the partisans of Christian mysticism, mostly speak from a lack or an absence. Praise for reality is often the mark of a metaphysics of presence. As for those who reject all metaphysics and confine themselves to what stands to reason (and perception), they incline to a Manichean view that excludes as heretical or even diabolical all forms of spirituality and every kind of transcendence that sets out to turn us away from the concrete and from sacrosanct immanence.

Idealism and Materialism

Religion, as a kind of utopia, is as likely to encourage escapism, rejection of the social reality, as it is a spirit of resistance, a refusal to be "held captive." It is sometimes an opium of the masses, manipulated by the dominant ideology, sometimes a tactic used to oppose that ideology, to elude it, supplant it, trick it, block it by creating heterotopias: "You think I am there, but I am already somewhere else." Hence the threat, or at least the nuisance that certain forms of "wild" religiosity represent for authoritarian regimes.

The fact that a religious notion may constitute a response to certain psychological needs may, as Freud notes, cast some doubt upon it, but does not suffice to prove it to be false. There are some illusions that are illusory only because they also serve a psychological function. For example, can it be said that the beauty of reality as sensed by a poet or an artist is illusory because it answers an aesthetic need? If so, the "cruelty of reality," far from equating with the "reality principle," could equally well simply serve to satisfy the needs of a masochist. Besides, can beliefs, some of which go back thousands of years and claim to stem from wisdom and experience, really be dismissed simply as lies, ramblings, or narcissistic flights of fancy? Something does take place in those religious experiences—even if we do not know quite what. The fact that we ourselves are unable to "communicate with being" (or may think we are) does not give us the right to prejudge the experiences of others, even if in every culture (even Himalayan ones), one undeniably does find elements of politics and ideology and constraint and illusion.

Those who denounce the certainties of belief do so on the basis of a different belief, also claimed to be infallible—a belief in material reality. They tend to confuse a critical sense with a belief in materialism, when the whole problem lies in retaining the former without being overwhelmed by the latter. To assert that religious idealism implies fanaticism, the Inquisition, and the wars of religion, as many so often do, is rather like maintaining that materialism implies trafficking in human organs by depriving the individual of any kind of transcendence and reducing human life to the interplay of supply and demand. It may be quite true that an excessively clear-cut separation between the ideal and the real can be problematic, but it cannot be denied that, to date, all attempts to fight against poverty and injustice have been in the name of some kind of idealism. It may be objected that the distinction between the ideal and reality does not necessarily imply any transcendence and that idealism can somehow be deployed horizontally, on a purely human level. But we know how difficult, even impossible, it is in this day and age to found morality without any kind of transcendent basis. According to Clément Rosset, even the claim to universalism of the Kantian moral imperative is somehow inadmissible inasmuch as it manifests a disturbing tendency to proselytism or even fanaticism. But that is not to imply that cynicism is the only remaining possibility, as the principle of the excluded middle would have it.

Reality sometimes gains from being duplicated (with or without transcendence), but it is just as likely to lose when that "duplicity," or rather "duplication," hardens into Manicheanism. So the problem lies not in the duplication itself, but in the use that is made of it. It is important always to be aware of the double register, at once logical and existential, of truth. What is true on the logical level may turn out to be false, or even dire, on the existential level, and vice versa. Besides, one cannot but admit that since reality presents itself to us in a veiled guise, illusion is itself a part of reality. The depth that thought adds to reality is not pure nonbeing, but constitutes a fundamental element of it. The distinction between what is sensually perceptible and what is intelligible, or between the material and the spiritual, is part and parcel of our Western apprehension of reality, even if in other cultures, such as those of China and Japan, it seems less relevant (although it is never totally absent). We may regret that splitting of reality, but simply to plump for one of the two terms, in our case materialism, does not make it possible to get around it, but simply exacerbates it. As Marcel Gauchet notes: "The real question is not that of being, but that of the internal constraints forcing us to present the question in this way. Why is there this structural division presenting all reality in two antagonistic aspects?"[8]

Impenitent Reality

Everything is indeed as it seems, nothing is as it seems. At once as it seems and not
as it seems. Neither the one nor the other.
  —Nāgārjuna

Reality is by nature a vague and evasive object precisely because it is
not an object. Like the *dao* or the wind in the trees, it is known chiefly by
its effects. What is it that we call reality or the real, anyway? As Clément
Rosset sees it, it is "all that exists according to the principle of identity that
states that A is A." Here, we are seemingly poles apart from Buddhist
thought, yet Buddhist thought, too, describes itself as equating with reality—but a reality no longer limited by the principle of identity. To put that
in more concrete terms, the word "real" seems to take on two different
meanings for Rosset. In the first place, minimally, it designates what Freud
called the "reality principle"—the realization that things are not what I, in
my primary or secondary narcissism, would like them to be. In this sense,
Rosset has perfectly good grounds for asserting that we must force ourselves to look at things squarely and see them for what they are. That may
be a truism, but in practice, how many of us are capable of seeing that the
emperor is naked, let alone of actually saying so?

But "real" designates reality not only as it is ordinarily perceptible
through the senses, but also as it is sometimes revealed in the midst of particularly intense experiences, some of which stem from a "wild mysticism."
Such experiences may be spontaneous or may be triggered by aids such as
alcohol, LSD, or mescaline. How can we account for an experience that
Henri Michaux describes as follows: "fifty different, simultaneous, contradictory onomatopoeias that change every half-second"?[9] Compared with
such an experience, our everyday reality seems a pale thing. But the reality
that reveals itself so unexpectedly, the "oceanic feeling" that Freud took to
be a remnant or a return of narcissism, soon gives way to a monotonous,
dull reality, devoid of joy, haunted by an absence, and impoverished because it is not transmuted by a vision. The victory of the "reality principle"
produces reality in all its cruelty, a chronic feeling of dereliction alternating
with fleeting moments of grace. Thus, it is in lived experience and the
memory of it in the mind of the subject that reality splits into two of its
own accord.

For most of us, existence seems to stem from a single register. Despite its complexity, suggested by elusive intuitions in the presence of certain be-ings and things, dreams promptly forgotten and doors all too soon slammed on their essential secret, existence seems sadly one-dimensional. From time to time, when for one reason or another our fascination with objective reality weakens, it may happen that we experience the feeling of a different dimension, a different kind of perception, another possible re-lation to reality. Occasionally that realization proves to be a lasting one and changes the subject's psychic life through and through. Such was the expe-rience of some Chan followers who obtained awakening unexpectedly by seeing the blossoms of a plum tree, hearing the sound of a rushing stream or of a pebble knocked against a bamboo, or even by leaning against a wall that was not there. Stephen Jourdain describes an experience of this kind in his *Eveil* (Awakening):

The supreme act of morality through which a mind, defying the hypnotic urge that impels it downstream of itself and there scatters it, instead turns upstream to-ward the source, projects the light of consciousness upon the diamantine present in which personal creation is achieved, taking by surprise the point of pure actual-ity in which the real subject really operates: all this in order to denounce the orig-inal projected travesty of human endeavor, the illusory, fraudulent nature of so-called reality in which this creature of a creature seeks to constitute itself and the dangerous, mortal joke of objective quality in which it manages to clothe itself.

Jourdain draws a clear distinction between the two modalities of re-ality evoked above:

I turned outward and contemplated the world (I say the world, not the subjective ersatz, the derisory imitation that the so-called waking state apprehends). I con-templated the splendor of the street or the station platform, which the creatures of my mind had earlier abandoned, stripped bare; I considered the Superfluous.

The multiplicity of reality, or rather (but is it not the same thing?) of our perception of it, is evoked metaphorically by the Zen master Dōgen:

For example, boarding a boat and sailing out to the midst of a mountainless sea, we look around and see no other aspect but the circle of the sea. Yet this great ocean is not circular, nor is it four-sided. Its remaining virtue is inexhaustible. It is like a palatial dwelling. It is like a necklace of precious jewels. Yet it appears for the moment to the range of our eyes simply as the circle of the sea. It is just the same with all things. The dusty world and [the Buddha Way] beyond it assume many aspects, but we can see and understand them only to the extent our eye is culti-vated through practice. To understand the [true] nature of all things, we must know that in addition to apparent circularity or angularity, the remaining virtue of the mountains and seas is great and inexhaustible, and there are worlds in [all] the four directions. We must know that this is not only so all around us, it is the same both with us right here and within a single drop of water.[10]

Should One Trust Appearances?

The gap between the two aspects of reality is often expressed as an ontological distinction between reality and the world of appearances. That opposition has a long history. As Heidegger points out, in early Greek thought, "to be" meant "to appear," so appearing was not regarded as something accidental. It was only later, in particular with Plato, that appearance was declared to be deceptive and lost its ontological status, being leveled downward in the same movement that raised being to new metaphysical heights. At the same stroke, what was purely apparent down here in this world was definitively divorced from the real being that lay somewhere else. In the gap between the two, the Christian doctrine later found its niche. Not until the Kantian revolution did the phenomenon recover its value as apparition.

At the polar extreme from Greek thought, in classical China, Zhuangzi was already questioning the opposition between reality and appearance: According to him, what is real is what exists simply by being there. The same goes for knowledge, nontruth, and dreams, all of which exist just as much as so-called true knowledge and so-called reality. Illusion and reality are both, equally, part of life; they possess the same reality of existence (dreams make one happy or sad) and also the same unreality, the same contrived nature.[11]

Even in the nineteenth century, the age of positivist reason, not everybody subscribed to the apology of ordinary realism. In his *Devil's Dictionary*, Ambrose Bierce, himself an atheist and rationalist spirit, defined realism as "the art of depicting nature as it is seen by toads. The charm suffusing a landscape painted by a mole, or a story written by a measuring-worm": what Zhuangzi would call the world as seen by a frog at the bottom of a well.

Get rid of the real and it comes rushing back. But is it the same reality, or already its double? In reality, the French proverb says: Get rid of the natural. . . . But which is it that is the more natural in this instance: the reality, or the appearance (given that each *is* one side of the real)? Reality is layered, so is at the very least twofold. It is all a matter of levels. Someone blinded by details is often said to be unable to see the forest for the trees. Another way of putting that, using a more active metaphor, might be: "He is unable to see the ant hill for the ants." Which is the more real, the ants or the ant hill? The behavior of the ants is determined by the needs of the ant hill, but the laws that govern those needs are of a higher complexity than the laws that determine each ant. We are here faced with two distinct, yet interdependent levels of reality, neither of which can be reduced entirely to the other. It is the relation between the two, their "codependent origination," as the Buddhists put it, that constitutes their ultimate reality.

While taking a walk, I sat down on a bench and became absorbed in contemplating the trees swaying gently this way and that in a shimmer of colors. Reality brushed against me. A ripple in the mirror of reality told me it was as yet but a reflection in the mirror of a pond. But why are we more entranced by reflections (whether of trees in the countryside, Impressionist water lilies, or Buddhist lotus flowers) in the crystalline clarity of still water than we are by the objects that are the source or pretext for those reflections? What is their true cause: the tree itself, or the pool? Is the reflection a reflection of the tree, or of the pool itself? Or both? Or neither? We are back with the Buddhist tetralemma ...

Could it be that religions and other forms of idealism, as desires for a different reality, a splitting of reality, simply constitute modes of escapism, denials of the singularly real, a deliberate plunge into illusion? As we have seen, for Freud, illusion always results from psychic conflicts that originate in childhood. Although in *Totem and Taboo* Freud considers the primitive horde's murder of the father to be a historical fact, essentially, Freudian theory is ahistorical. Yet how could we understand religious illusion so easily today had not a certain historical evolution prepared us for it? Thanks to Nietzsche, with his genealogy of morality, and also to a number of other genealogists, we find ourselves better positioned to understand the sociogenesis of our categories of thought. But if illusion is historically determined, then truth and reality must equally be so. Paradoxically enough, in both European and Asian cultures, immediacy itself has a long history.

"Reality," "immediacy," "thusness": all these terms are curiously abstract, already cut off from concrete experience, from that shimmering of things, the je ne sais quoi that Chan masters claim to be "as lively as a fish in water." To be sure, the abstract, too, is, after all, part of reality; all the same, I prefer the "sound of water" made by the frog in Matsuo Bashō's haiku:

Into the old pool
Leaped a frog.
The sound of water.

However, as soon as the haiku itself became a literary genre, thanks, precisely, to Bashō and his disciples, who produced "moments of truth" at a quasi-industrial rate, the situation was reversed. Like the banana tree (*bashō*, in Japanese) in the hermitage garden after which Bashō was named, the haiku now began to strike a hollow note. Today, that hermitage is a much visited tourist haunt where a new banana tree has been specially planted. Reality now has an answering machine to screen its calls, although just occasionally it does still respond to those who can discern deep silence at the heart of the cacophony of the tourists.

A Two-Edged Truth

Like Janus, the two-faced Roman god who presides over the month of January and looks toward both the past and the future, the Buddha, whose awakening is traditionally dated to December 8, is the guardian of the new year, where the new and the old worlds meet. In esoteric Buddhism, two-headed representations abound, and these were interpreted as symbols of the twofold truth. Sometimes one even comes across deities who illustrate that same principle by forming "the beast with two backs," deities such as Kangiten (the "Deva of Bliss"), an elephant-headed god of obstacles who has the power to bind and to unbind.

The essential "duplicity" of the Buddhist doctrine stems in particular from the fact that it can be taken either at the first level (as a live, oral tradition) or at the second level (as a written tradition ruled not by the spirit, but by the letter). The problem arises from the fact that Buddhism first became accessible to us not as pure experience (for this is always mediated, even when it is claimed to be "direct"), but through a written tradition constantly reinscribed within new contexts. Even if it originated orally, it consists primarily in a text that can be submitted to various hermeneutic procedures, all of which imply a distance. Even its "immediacy" is "a reality effect," a result of its textuality. Clearly, this situation is not peculiar to

Buddhism, but Buddhism is perhaps the only doctrine that has sought to analyze it strictly. It is in the light of this that we should understand oppositions such as Mahāyāna/Hīnayāna, sudden/gradual, esotericism/exotericism, along with their respective dialectical resolutions or irreducible tensions, as the case may be.

This double thought appears to be a remedy to counter "simple" duality (for all things are doubly double). It also provides an antidote to peremptory certainties. Polarity has played a particularly crucial role in the development of Mahāyāna. Around it, texts such as the *Lotus Sūtra* and the *Vimalakīrti Sūtra* were developed. There is also a twofold truth to immediacy, as is taught in, for example, the Chan school. Paradigms such as sudden/gradual may be interpreted as the Chinese versions of the twofold truth. One particular feature of early Chan is the double structure of practice, which corresponds to these two aspects, the sudden and the gradual. For example, Daoxin, the fourth patriarch (580–651) lists a whole series of spiritual exercises that he later rejects in the name of "spontaneity." It is necessary to learn all these techniques—gradual expedients belonging to the realm of conventional truth, which will eventually be abandoned—in order suddenly to accede to ultimate truth. Similarly, in the classic parable, a raft (Buddhist doctrine) is useful to cross a river, but becomes unnecessary once one reaches the other shore (awakening or *nirvāṇa*). The crossing itself has an importance of its own, the journey is somehow part and parcel of the point of arrival. That is something that tends to be forgotten by those who are in too much of a hurry and who think that they will reach their goal more quickly by taking shortcuts. Daoxin and the other masters of early Chan remained attached to the Mādhyamika line of thought, according to which one can reach ultimate truth only by way of conventional truth. Later however, the partisans of radical subitism came to think that ultimate truth implies a pure and simple rejection of conventional truth. They no longer regarded the latter as a mediatory truth or even a half-truth, but considered it a particularly harmful error. In this they may have been mistaken. The Middle Way underlines the paradoxical nature of reality: It is a complex truth that cannot be reduced to any single formulation or any single term—however ultimate it may be.

According to the *Treatise of Bodhidharma*, one of the earliest Chan texts, "an ordinary man takes the conventional for the ultimate; a sage can discern the conventional within the ultimate." This seems to mean that discourse relating to the absolute still belongs to the relative, whereas relative discourse can also express the absolute. Without dwelling upon Chan Buddhism's distinct taste for paradoxical formulas, we should note the dialectical value of the reversal: Starting from a static opposition between conventional truth and absolute truth—an opposition that is valid only at the conventional level—the text deconstructs that hierarchy by showing that, at the higher level, the truth that was initially perceived as "ultimate" turns out to be altogether "conventional." One might leave it at that and simply say that, in that it belongs to the realm of language, all truth is necessarily relative. But going beyond ultimate truth is achieved in the name of the same requirements that were temporarily reified in the concept of ultimate truth. Once launched, the dialectical movement cannot easily be halted. So it forces us to be open to doubt and to envisage the hypothesis that to insist upon transcendence might, after all, be a subtle way of remaining attached to conventional truth.

In the form in which it was borrowed from Mādhyamika, the concept of two truths plays a strategic role in Chan discourse. The twofold truth may be conceived as an attempt to come to terms with the fact that, in our everyday reality, we constantly pass to and fro between incompatible systems. But as a rhetorical tactic, it makes it possible to reconcile the relative and the absolute quite easily, to cash in on both sides. For that reason, some people may regard it as a double falsity, a kind of ventriloquism in that, as Maurice Merleau-Ponty remarked, "given that what is true *in principle* is never true *in fact*, and vice versa . . . the one condemns the other, but offers a reprieve, allowing it to remain operational within its own order."[12] A critique such as this should have had a destabilizing effect upon the Buddhist concept of truth. But, whereas in Western philosophy a double truth tends to become a half-truth, the opposite seems to have been the case in East Asian Buddhism (except in certain radical tendencies of Chan Buddhism).

In Western thought, the logical structure of the twofold truth is not altogether absent, but constitutes something of an exception, whereas in Buddhist thought, it dominates. Western (including Christian) thought is to some extent "diabolical" (from *diabolos*, "double"): Fundamentally Manichean, it insists on splitting reality into truth and error, good and evil, and considers equal contraries and the rejection of the principle of the excluded middle to be, precisely, quasi-diabolical. By doubling the diabolical and making every simple opposition twofold, Buddhist thought multiplies the layers of reality and the perspectives from which one can view the "thousand plateaus" of reality. It is true that Buddhism has also favored a return to the singular, a commitment to the concrete, an ecstatic presence to reality. Without denying that experience, we should, however, be aware that it can easily lead to a quasi-Parmenidean metaphysics of identity. And conversely, the negation of all immediacy may provide a footing for a positivist ideology. Buddhism repeats and includes the two movements—both dissemination and presence, both mediation and immediacy—in an open-ended dialectics, thereby insofar as possible avoiding bogging them down in a fixed truth. It could perhaps be defined as an oblique or tangential strategy.

The twofold truth might be summed up by one of Epictetus's sayings: "Everything has two handles: one by which you can carry it, the other by which you cannot."[13] Monsieur Teste, Valéry's alter ego or double, also declared: "The bottom of our mind is paved with crossroads." But to my mind, this notion is best expressed by D. H. Lawrence: "If you are walking westward . . . you forfeit the northern and eastward and southern directions. If you admit a unison, you forfeit all the possibilities of chaos." That is not to say that you should remain rooted to the spot, like Buridan's ass, stuck halfway between a bucket of water and a bale of straw, but rather that in order to orient itself, thought should reach out for all four cardinal points (the four points of the tetralemma?) And to do that, it must be aware of the dangers that await it at each.

The twofold truth, seen as a recursive mode of argument, also calls to mind a story told by Georges Didi-Huberman. A son asks his father, "Why does the tightrope dancer not fall?" "Because he has a balancing pole to hold!" "But why doesn't the balancing pole not fall?" "Oh, you silly boy, because the man is holding it!"[14] There is no way round this vicious pseudocircle, so the best thing to do is enter it and circulate correctly within it, as Heidegger advised in the case of the hermeneutic circle. This movement also puts me in mind of the "stone, paper, scissors" game. In this ancient game, still very popular in Japan, where it is known as *jankenpo*, the two players count to three, then make a symbolic gesture: An open hand symbolizes paper, a half-opened hand with the index and middle fingers extended symbolizes scissors, and a closed fist symbolizes a stone. Paper is stronger than stone, because it can wrap it; the scissors are stronger than paper, because they can cut it; and stone is stronger than scissors, because it can nick them.

The tension between the two truths is irreducible. Yet one must pass by way of the one in order to reach the other. The one cannot be understood without the other, but neither can they be reconciled in a facile synthesis. Buddhism has invariably albeit not always successfully striven to avoid becoming set into an orthodoxy or even an orthopraxy. The doctrine of the two truths has been helpful in this respect, for it has deterred all attempts to attribute a definitive meaning to the Buddha's words and to worship them as a fixed expression of the "ultimate truth" or to credit any "definitive" commentary with the status of an intangible deciphering of a "revelation." To be sure, Buddhism has not always managed to avoid either the temptation to systematize or the contrary temptation to assert that only pure experience, or only living words, nondiscursive speech, has any value. As Tom Tillemans notes, Tibetan Buddhism, particularly after Tsongkhapa (1357–1419), "managed to transform the tetralemma into a kind of modal logic in which, classically, the laws of double negation, of the excluded middle, and of contradiction all function,"[15] thereby blunting the cutting edge of the twofold truth. The same evolution can be detected in Chinese Mādhyamika. In Chan, in contrast, the balance turned out to be unstable: In particular, the most subitist tendency reinterpreted the notion of two truths in a unilateral fashion, giving precedence to the point of view of ultimate reality. The kōans of Chan, for example, abound in attempts to express "the truth of ultimate order." Chan's apparent fascination with concrete reality makes no difference: This is a reality transfigured by awakening and accordingly perceived from the point of view of ultimate truth; its physical relativity is transformed into metaphysical truth. In this way, the quest for transcendence leads to a radical immanence, and the soteriological structure that was developed as an expedient becomes an end in itself. Around the eighth century it is thus possible to detect a switch from the notion of twofold truth as a mediation between two "equi-vocal" practices to the dichotomous and exclusive positions expressed in debates such as the controversy over sudden and gradual awakening. Even when a hierarchical twofold truth maintains the complementarity of the two levels, it is often only in a form of "militant syncretism"—a way of having the last word. There is no longer any sustained hesitation, or indeed any lasting irresolution between the two levels. Chan tends to reduce one level to

the other (which is either absolute or immanent), at the same stroke re-
pressing any agonistic tension between them. In this way, a shift is made
from a twofold or two-edged truth to two contradictory truths, one of
which is, in the last analysis, reduced to the other: in short, a shift from
ambivalence to contradiction and thence to reduction.

According to Buddhist orthodoxy, the polarity of thought is nothing
but an illusion. But passing beyond that involves more than simply returning to unity, for the opposition between those two possibilities still implies a duality. It is only from within duality itself, deconstructing it by
means of the notion of twofold truth and mobilizing it in such a way that
it can no longer rest upon itself, clinging to the strength of its position,
that one can proceed beyond it. If some forms of Buddhism—which does
not necessarily mean the orthodox—having moved beyond the dilemma,
then endeavor to move beyond the tetralemma, it is certainly not in order
to establish themselves in an immutable position, some kind of absolute
synthesis that would bring all oscillation to an end.

So the twofold truth is not just a Buddhist concept that I am trying to import into Western philosophical discourse. Rather, it constitutes
the tension that manifests itself between true discourse and "the discourse of truth," the latter itself being no more than a form of ideology
that has to be discovered behind grand ideals. Yet the paradigm of the
twofold truth also provides an extremely convenient hermeneutic device,
a way of eluding all conflicting interpretations, all risk of schisms, and
eventually a way of producing with impunity pseudosyntheses that
negate all dilemmas. How can we avoid the somewhat facile circularity
of a twofold truth that is always in danger of remaining bogged down at
the third level of the tetralemma ("at once A and B")? How can we move
on to the next level, and then beyond it, in some way that is not purely
logical and speculative?

The notion of twofold truth asserts ontological duality only the better to deny it, using formulas such as "nirvāṇa *is saṃsāra*," "passions *are*
awakening," and so on. But the reverse is equally true: By denying duality,
Buddhist discourse already accepted it and contributed to maintaining it.
In other words, it is quite possible that its effects are the contrary of what
they claim to be. For example, the paradoxical assertion that the ordinary
passions themselves constitute awakening leads to a kind of apology for the
world of the senses that differs hardly at all from materialism or even from

hedonism. Moreover, identification of the two levels of reality leads to their mutual contamination: It implies both that phenomena are absolute and also (and this is something that is usually forgotten) that the absolute itself is somehow "phenomenal"—that is to say, historically and culturally determined. As you can see, Hegel invented nothing.

External Thought

Buddhism is not just a philosophy coupled with a religion (or vice versa), it is also a psychology (or rather a psychosomatic therapy). And it is furthermore a teaching that is mythological and "ritological." The twofold truth opens Buddhism up to the various modalities of otherness: local cults, dreams and the imaginary, ritual, and, finally, sexuality (mediated in particular by compassion, a sublimated form of passion).

Forms of Buddhist Sexuality

For me, the Buddhist message as regards sexual matters evokes couplets from a song made popular by Marie Dubas in the period between the two world wars. Some are in the Hīnayānist mode: "Calm this clamorous desire / For it's enough to scare the birds away"; others in the Mahāyānist or even Tantrist mode: "Best have done with it at once / For it's enough to scare the birds away."

Those couplets reproduce the schema of the twofold truth. Traditional morality, which belongs to the realm of conventional truth, must be transcended—if necessary, transgressed—in order to accede to ultimate truth. Only those who awaken to the reality of desire and manage to transmute it can attain to that ultimate truth. The same idea finds expression in numerous paradigmatic stories, such as the one about the two monks, Prasannendriya and Agramati. Right up to the day of his death, Agramati observed an intransigent ideal of purity, but on account of his false views, he nevertheless ended up in hell. In contrast, his companion, Prasannendriya, notorious for his constant breaches of morality, obtained awakening because he had managed to realize the principle of nonduality.

In Tantrism, in particular, sexuality, once dominated, is used as a source of spiritual energy. Buddhism did not stop thinking with the advent of Tantrism; on the contrary, but it now did so differently—ritually—with the body, as well as the mind. Tantric doctrine, with its theory of the possibility of "becoming a buddha in this very body," draws the ultimate consequences from the principle of nonduality, identifying the passions with awakening at the level of absolute truth. The energy of the passions becomes the catalyst of awakening. The complementarity of concentration (*samādhi*) and wisdom (*prajñā*) and of other, similar couples is represented symbolically, but is also activated ritually, through the union of the masculine principle (*vajra*, diamond or thunderbolt, the male sex) and the feminine principle (lotus, the female sex organ). The same symbolism reappears in Chinese and Japanese Tantrism—although the sexual practices to which it referred have long since been relegated to the back burner. The Tantric notion of the transmutation of desires through the ritualization of the sexual act seems to stem from the notion of the "revolving of the support," the revolution of consciousness that constituted one of the themes of the "idealist" school (Yogācāra). It involves "not rejecting or fleeing from phenomena, the body, and the passions, but transmuting them through this 'revolving' or 'metamorphosis,' as it were, simply by converting a negative sign into a positive one."[1] "Simply" is easily said, however; and plenty have come a cropper in the process. Let us at least remember that Buddhism's attitude toward sexuality has been nuanced and ambivalent, with sexuality regarded now as an obstacle, now as a path leading toward awakening.

On Buddhism as a Therapy

In opposition to those who classify Buddhism either as a philosophy or as a religion, some people insist that it is above all a psychosomatic therapy. Its therapeutic value has, undeniably, always been one of the essential components of Buddhism. As has often been noted, Indian Buddhism makes great use of medical metaphors, and the list of the four "noble truths" is sometimes assimilated to a medical diagnosis. Not only may Buddhism have been influenced by Indian medical thought, but furthermore its monks and nuns have played an important role as doctors of both bodies and souls, despite the fact that in principle they denied the existence of the latter. Given that Buddhist dogma denies the existence of any individual spirit, it is somewhat paradoxical to speak of the "spirituality" of Buddhism. But in practice, the notion of spirit, in the various senses of the term, came to play a major role in Mahāyāna, especially in China and Japan. Essentially, Buddhism is a school of thought—albeit a rather unusual one, since it ultimately leads to nonthought. Its motto could be: To reach the invisible through the visible, to reach nonthought through thinking. Western philosophy, in contrast, seeks to achieve precisely the reverse, that is, to reduce the invisible to the visible and to convert the unknown into the known and nonthought into thought.

Even if its monks are not always known for their integrity, Buddhism regards itself as an integrating practice. But this psychic integration involves a disintegration of ordinary perceptions. The performative practice of Buddhist yoga stands in opposition to the analytical approach of Buddhist philosophy (for example, its detailed examination of the constituents of consciousness, as recommended by the Abhidharma scholasticism). This type of practice involves a systematic attempt to modify the various states of consciousness by means of meditation, "lucid dreaming," ritual possession, and so on. Intoxicating products are in principle forbidden. But it is worth noting in passing that the word "toxic" comes from *toxon*, "poison-tipped arrow," and this evokes the parable of the doctor-Buddha. In this parable, ordinary consciousness is described as intoxicated, clouded, hampered by the obstacles of the passions and worldly knowledge. It is therefore a matter of altering one's relation to oneself, to one's body, and to the world. This modification calls for a prior disordering of the structures of consciousness. But this process is not without hazards. Woe to those who, with insufficient preparation, try to batter through the doors of the unconscious—particularly by chemical means. The voluntarist nature of the Buddhist way of proceeding nevertheless stands in contrast to the more natural approach of traditional Chinese thought as formulated in the *Yijing* (The Book of Changes). That is particularly true of Chan and Zen. But while the forced march (or rather sitting) of the *sesshin*, the intensive sessions of Zen meditation, is set within a definite, ritualized framework, with those practicing it carefully controlled, it is, after all, a matter of realizing that the door is, and always has been, wide open.

According to Dōgen, meditation consists in "dropping off body and mind." The meditator is not dealing solely with the unstable association of a body and a soul, as in classical metaphysics. Rather, as Freud suggests, he/she has to cope with closely linked, inextricable thoughts both pure and impure. The hybrid animal that man is can have no totally pure intentions. The ego is not simply one element of psychism: It perfumes (or befouls) the very air that one breathes. Even the purest of ideals is immediately corrupted by the miasmas that rise from underlying thoughts and can retain a semblance of purity only if these are constantly repressed or sublimated. Only the nonthought of Chan has a chance of avoiding this mental dilemma constituted by the fact that, as Jacques Prévert put it (untranslatably): "Le mental ment, monumentalement."

In *Rameau's Nephew*, Diderot manages to convey the constant shifting of ordinary thought, which Buddhists compare to a monkey leaping from branch to branch:

I let my mind rove wantonly, give it free rein to follow any idea, wise or mad, that may come uppermost; I chase it as do our young libertines along Foy's Walk, when they are on the track of a courtesan whose mien is giddy and face smiling, whose nose turns up. The youth drops one and picks up another, pursuing all and clinging to none: My ideas are my trollops.[2]

Whether wise or crazy, thoughts are simply trollops, seductresses, and the *philosophe*, rather than condemn the world's oldest profession as a puritan would, simply observes the movements of his mind, taking care to remain aloof from them.

Freud was well aware of this complexity of thought. In *The Interpretation of Dreams*, he notes: "We often have to deal with thoughts from different centres. . . . Some are foreground thoughts, others background thoughts."[3] Left to oneself, one apprehends only conscious thought, the top layer in the basket, so to speak. Ordinary consciousness perceives only the thoughts in the foreground, meanwhile—without knowing it—being influenced by other, background ones. It is those influences that psychoanalysis and Buddhist meditation, each in its own way, seek to recover (or re-collect), precisely in order to free oneself from them and to get a grip on oneself.

The fundamental element in this endeavor is possibly mindfulness, awareness of both oneself and everything else. It is a matter of forestalling forgetfulness of being—of remaining aware that our thought constantly sinks into forgetfulness. In a sense, we are all Alzheimer patients in remission. The apparent continuity of the flow of consciousness masks this fact, which we sense only each morning upon awaking, when we forget the intense dreams through which we have just lived. Awakening results from a constant struggle against the amnesia by which we are threatened: It is above all an anamnesis. As both Freud and Nietzsche saw, that forgetting is an active forgetting, in league with our ordinary consciousness (and what the Buddhists personify as Māra, their name for the spells cast by the world of the senses, spells that tie us to illusion and bear us, bound hand and foot, to death).

On one point, Buddhism and psychoanalysis seem to converge: the idea that conscious thought is only the tip of the iceberg. The floating attention of psychoanalysis, which makes it possible to bring thought associations to the surface, thereby revealing the unconscious, irresistibly puts one in mind of the Buddhist *smṛti*, a term that evokes attention paid to the process of thought, and anamnesis. Buddhism could perhaps be described as mastery over underlying thoughts and Buddhist practice as an archaeology of the self, a spiritual kind of spelunking, a return to some private Magdalenian stratum or to the "green paradise" of childhood (or prechildhood). It has been said that India, through Hindu and Buddhist Yoga, discovered the unconscious long before psychoanalysis did. But is the same thing involved in both cases? Freud discovered (or rediscovered) the unconscious, but this was a "scientific" unconscious, and his new science of dreams or of the unconscious denies all credit to tradition, to the sacred, to *philosophia perennis*. Freud did not go so far as the notion of a "collective unconscious," as his disciple and rival Carl Gustav Jung was to, followed by all those who uphold the idea of *homo religiosus*. Nevertheless, he did consider the unconscious to be a universal and atemporal reality. He never entertained the possibility that it might reflect a particular epistemological, historically determined situation. Yet if that unconscious, far from being a "given," instead resulted from some epistemological happening (for example, the "Greek miracle," that first separation between reason and the irrational, which became a source of repression), it would turn out to be simply a Western phenomenon.

What do other cultures have to say in this respect? Do not they, too, have an unconscious, whether individual or collective? By denying them such characteristics, would not one be in danger of slipping back into the old debate on "primitive mentality" and attributing rational thought solely to the West? To do so would be to forget that Lévi-Strauss has already passed that way and shown that "savage thought" is another form of logic (a mytho-logic). The fact remains that the dividing line between the conscious and the unconscious, or between dream and reality, varies from one culture to another. It might well be thought that the same applies to the structure of the non-Western unconscious (which it would perhaps be better to express in the plural form), so the latter is not necessarily structured, as ours is, by the Oedipus complex (always supposing that that is really the case where we are concerned). Japanese psychoanalysts, for example, have discovered, or rather invented, an "Ajase complex," said to be specific to the Japanese culture. Ajase (Ajātaśatru in Sanskrit) is the Indian king, a contemporary of the Buddha, who not only starved his father to death, but also tried to kill his mother. The Buddhist tradition fastened in particular upon the latter point, and the "Ajase complex," which came to Freud's attention as early as 1931, was subsequently presented as a counterpart to the Oedipus complex.

Buddhist practice would thus appear to be a plunge into the deep waters of the psyche. But, according to Chan, this stage may in practice simply constitute a lure, a stumbling block on the path to awakening, True Chan practice is defined as nonthinking, a way to progress beyond images and imagination. As Linji says: "Why do I tell you this? Because you followers of the Way seem to be incapable of stopping this mind that goes rushing around everywhere looking for something. So you get caught up in those idle devices of the men of old."[4]

Nonthinking renders the mind as clear and limpid as a mirror. That metaphor, which recurs frequently in Chan texts, comes straight from Zhuangzi: "Water that is still gives back a clear image of beard and eyebrows; reposing in the water level, it offers a measure to the great carpenter. And if water in stillness possesses such clarity, how much more must pure spirit. The sage's mind in stillness is the mirror of Heaven and earth, the glass of the ten thousand things."[5]

One of the six traditional supranormal powers derived from the practice of meditation is knowledge of the thoughts of others (a telepathic ability to receive mental images). As is well known, Chan asserts the possibility of a mind-to-mind transmission. Yet it seems to have downplayed telepathic phenomena. The superiority of nonthinking over all forms of reflective or imaginative thought is illustrated by the following anecdote, for which the distant source is again Zhuangzi and which appears in a number of Chan variants. A Chan master was put to the test by a monk from India or central Asia who claimed to be able to read his thoughts. At first he did indeed manage to guess what the Chan master was thinking, up until the moment when the latter plunged into the depths of nonthought, leaving the monk stranded, shamefaced, and embarrassed. When you seek a Chan master, in the end, it turns out that he cannot be found.

Upon his return from the Japanese "empire of signs," Roland Barthes wrote as follows: "How can we *imagine* a verb which is simultaneously without subject, without attribute, and yet transitive, such as for instance an act of knowledge without knowing subject and without known object? Yet it is the imagination which is required of us faced with the Hindu *dhyāna*, origin of the Chinese *chan* and the Japanese *zen*, which we cannot translate by *meditation* without restoring to it both subject and god: drive them out, they return, and it is our language they ride on."[6] In Chan and Zen, *dhyāna* (the term that, in Sino-Japanese transcription, gives its name to this school) is recommended only as an expedient for beginners and cannot lay claim to any exclusivity. Although some people tend to regard it as the "royal road" where practice is concerned, it may constitute a stumbling block. That is the message conveyed by the following story. Mazu Daoyi was sitting in *dhyāna*. His master, Nanyue Huairang, asked him why he was doing this. Mazu replied that he was hoping thereby to become a Buddha. Huairang then picked up a fragment of tile and began to polish it. When Mazu, in surprise, asked him the reason for his action, he replied that he was hoping that, by polishing this piece of tile, he would turn it into a mirror. Mazu pointed out the obvious impossibility of this, only to hear the following retort: "And how could anyone become a Buddha by practicing seated *dhyāna*?" Huairang was drawing attention to the dualist illusion according to which practice could be a means to an end (awakening). Chan Buddhism thus came to denounce the eponymous practice of *dhyāna*, considering it to be too quietist. As usual, the most violent critique came from Linji:

There are a bunch of blind baldheads who, having stuffed themselves with rice, sit doing Chan-type meditation practice, trying to arrest the flow of thoughts and stop them from arising, hating clamor, demanding silence—but these aren't Buddhist ways! . . . They sit by the wall in meditation, pressing their tongues against the roof of their mouths, absolutely still, never moving, supposing this to be the *Dharma* of the buddhas taught by the patriarchs. What a mistake![7]

In accordance with the Mahāyāna dynamic, after advocating the practice of sitting still in order to recollect, then of "sitting and forgetting" (all distinctions), one came to advocate "forgetting to sit," or even "forgetting to forget." But we should not be misled by Linji's diatribe: He himself no doubt spent much of his time seated in *dhyāna* and in the name of conventional truth continued to assert what he denied in the name of ultimate truth. In Chan/Zen, the denunciation of "contemplative techniques" was to lead to the paradoxical situation of those very techniques being practiced increasingly assiduously the more they were decried.

Paradoxical States: Dreaming, Visions, Awakening

Buddhism does not establish the same opposition between dreaming and reality as Western thought does, or the same epistemological distinction between dreams and visions, or the same relation between visions and madness. In a famous moral tale, Zhuangzi sets the tone: "Once Zhuang Zhou dreamt he was a butterfly, a butterfly flitting and fluttering around, happy with himself and doing as he pleased. He didn't know he was Zhuang Zhou. Suddenly he woke up and there he was, solid and unmistakable Zhuang Zhou. But he didn't know if he was Zhuang Zhou who had dreamt he was a butterfly, or a butterfly dreaming he was Zhuang Zhou. Between Zhunag Zhou and a butterfly there must be *some* distinction! This is called the Transformation of Things."[8] In another passage, Zhuangzi recounts a conversation between Changwuzi and a disciple of his. When the disciple asks him about one of Confucius's sayings, Changwuzi replies:

He who dreams of drinking wine may weep when morning comes; he who dreams of weeping may in the morning go off to hunt. While he is dreaming he does not know it is a dream, and in his dream he may even try to interpret a dream. Only after he wakes does he know it was a dream. And someday there will be a great awakening when we know that this is all a great dream. Yet the stupid believe they are awake, busily and brightly assuming they understand things, calling this man ruler, that one herdsman—how dense! Confucius and you are both dreaming! And when I say you are dreaming, I am dreaming too.[9]

Similar intuitions are to be found in the West—among the Romantics, for example or, closer to us, in Henri Michaux. But by and large they are exceptional, whereas in East Asia such cultural perceptions are quite common. Michaux recounts one of his dreams as follows:

I dreamed that I was sleeping. Naturally, I was not fooled by that, since I knew I was awake, up until the moment when, as I fell asleep, I remembered that I had just awoken from a sleep in which I dreamed that I was sleeping. Naturally I was not fooled by this until the moment when, losing all confidence, I began to gnaw at my fingers in rage, wondering, despite the growing pain, whether I was really gnawing my fingers or was just dreaming that I was gnawing my fingers in frustration at not knowing whether I was awake or asleep and dreaming that I was in despair at not knowing if I was sleeping or just . . . and wondering whether ..."[10]

This dream seems to turn sour because the dreamer is unable to let himself go, caught as he is in this "double interplay of mastery and dispossession." The human mind is particularly twisted, as is shown by certain attempts to note down dreams. It sometimes happens that one dreams in a dream, then wakes up (still in the dream) and notes down the dream—all in attempt to remain asleep. Freud said that dreams are the guardians of sleep, but he never—not even in a dream—imagined, as Buddhists do, that one can also awaken in a dream.

For a Buddhist, there is no marked difference between a dream obtained during sleep and a vision obtained in a waking state—or, to be more precise, during meditation, in a state of *samādhi* or concentration, which is often described as "being neither asleep nor awake." This way of distinguishing between sleeping and waking, so unlike ours, sometimes makes it impossible to tell whether one is dealing with visions or with dreams. The dividing line between the visible and the invisible is no longer drawn where it seems obvious to us. When the Zen master Keizan Jōkin (1268–1325) spent the night on the site of the monastery that he was planning to build and, in a dream, beheld a wonderful monastery, then later discovered in external reality a number of the elements that he had seen in his dream, he experienced a fusion of the real and the imaginary that confirmed his determination to carry out his plan. In this instance, it was the dream that was perceived as the highest expression of reality. So to dream one's life is not better than to live it, since it is, precisely, to live it, and it can be lived fully only by dreaming it. Dreaming is not a "second life," since it merges with the waking state: It is a part of this life, the only true one.[11]

Visions and dreams become instruments that make it possible to dismantle the rigid categories that we impose upon reality and to reveal the perpetual flux of possibilities amid which the Buddha lives. In a text entitled "Muchū setsumu" (Telling a dream within a dream), Dōgen asserts that dreams are as real as objective reality: "Since the wonderful Dharma of all the Buddhas is only transmitted from Buddha to Buddha, all the dharmas of dream and waking are ultimate reality. In waking as in the dream are found the initial thought of awakening, the practice, awakening and *nirvāṇa*. Both dreaming and waking are ultimately real, neither is superior or inferior."[12]

Buddhists, like Western writers ever since Homer, have always distinguished between "true" dreams and misleading ones. Whereas some dreams, founded upon illusion, increase ignorance and suffering, others constitute an eruption of reality into consciousness. Dreams of ascension, for example, instead of being merely of a sexual nature, as Freud thinks, are believed by Buddhists truly to lead to a place or a state of extreme purity from which one can accede to ultimate awakening.

The Freudian interpretation tends to reduce dreaming to an unconscious monologue. The ancients knew that there are different kinds of dreams, some of which imply either vertical communication with higher spheres or horizontal communication with other human beings. In Buddhism, as in Christianity, revelations are often mediated by dreams or visions. Spinoza thought that nobody had ever received any revelation of God without the aid of the imagination. Closer to our own times, Roland Barthes remarked, "Dreaming allows for, supports, releases, brings to light an extreme delicacy of moral, sometimes even metaphysical sentiments, the subtlest sense of human relations, refined differences, a learning of the highest civilization, in short a *conscious* logic, articulated with extraordinary finesse, which only an intense waking labor would be able to achieve."[13]

However, it is worth noting that, for Freud, dreams know nothing of the principle of contradiction: "The way in which dreams treat the category of contraries and contradictories is highly remarkable. It is simply disregarded. 'No' seems not to exist so far as dreams are concerned. They show a particular preference for combining contraries into a unity or for representing them as one and the same thing."[14] It is precisely because dreams always have several or indeed many meanings that "as with Chinese script, the correct interpretation can only be arrived at on each occasion from the context."[15] All the same, a key to the understanding of dreams is still possible for Freud. For instance, steep paths, ladders, and stairs are symbolic representations of the sexual act. Similarly, "In men's dreams a necktie often appears as a symbol for the penis. No doubt this is not only because neckties are long, dependent objects and peculiar to men, but also because they can be chosen according to taste—a liberty which, in the case of the object symbolized, is forbidden by Nature."[16] But Freud resists the temptation to reduce everything to a psychoanalytical meaning and makes room in his theories for the unknown. To some extent, this constitutes an admission on his part that a higher dimension always exists, the twofold truth of dreams, as it were: "There is often a passage in even the most thoroughly interpreted dream which has to be left obscure; this is because we become aware during the work of interpretation that at that point there is a tangle of dream-thoughts which cannot be unraveled and which moreover adds nothing to our knowledge of the content of the dream. This is the dream's navel, the spot where it reaches down into the unknown."[17]

That twofold truth might be as follows: Dreams are symbolical and can be explained by hermeneutics (the Freudian approach), but they are also performative and may lead to awakening, in particular through the practice of lucid dreaming. The latter approach has been carried quite far, above all in Tibetan Buddhism. The Tibetan practice of *milam* (literally, "dreaming"), a veritable "yoga of dreaming," the purpose of which is consciously to modify the content of the dream, was one of the "six teachings" of Nāropa (twelfth century), the five others being: the production of inner warmth, recognition of the illusory nature of the body, perception of the clear light, the theory of an intermediate state (*bardo*), and the practice of thought transmission. Echoes of such a dream practice are also detectable in Japanese Buddhism.

Chan, on the other hand, has tended (in theory at least) to devalue the importance of dreams and the imagination and likewise that of all other forms of mediation between illusory consciousness and awakening. It could be said that, as it spread among Chinese literati circles, this doctrine lost its sway over the Middle Kingdom, the intermediary space of mediation and of the imaginary. Conversely, however, as it spread in popular circles, it became reinvested by the powers of the imaginary. That is how it was that, although ejected from the official discourse of the Chan school, dreams returned through the hidden door of ritual to haunt the Chan imaginary, not just through incubation, a technique based on an anxious expectation of oneiric signs supposed to foster a spiritual rather than a physical cure—calling to mind the technique used in ancient Greece in Asclepius's sanctuary—but also through a practice of dreams, or rather, a practice *within* dreams. As in Greece, the images of dreams were "animated" in the sense that, like icons, they were considered to reveal a presence and to channel a "power." It was above all in dreams that apparitions of Buddhas and gods occurred. Dreaming to some extent constituted a ritual area in which the invisible took on shape, providing the framework for a veritable hierophany. The mental space of dreaming duplicated the physical space of the temple; the dream image of the god duplicated the icon.

Lucid dreaming is not unknown in the West, but only recently has it become the object of a systematic study. One precursor in this field was a nineteenth-century sinologist, Hervey de Saint-Denys (who died in 1892). Freud knew of his works, but chose to ignore them and wrote as follows: "The Marquis d'Hervey de Saint-Denys . . . claimed to have acquired the power of accelerating the course of his dreams just as he pleased, and of giving them any direction he chose. It seems as though in his case the wish to sleep had given place to another preconscious wish, namely to observe his dreams and enjoy them."[18]

Just as philosophy denies the possibility of metaphysical "experience," it also denies the reality of the dream experience (or rather, certain philosophers speaking in its name do so), on the grounds that anything that can be told about one's dream must be merely a secondary or even a primary elaboration. Nevertheless, experiments with lucid dreaming appear to confirm that subjects are able to communicate consciously with the external world even from within their dreams. So the problem lies not so much with the experience itself, but rather with rational thought's strange reluctance to envisage its possibility.

Freud reduces all psychic life to more or less deferred reactions to external events. That is why he denies dreaming the power of communication with anyone but oneself (with the exception of the psychoanalyst to whom one recounts the dream). Yet there are within us plenty of things other than ourselves, and it is a shame to deny ourselves the possibility of discovering them—a possibility that many cultures regard as self-evident. In principle, we no longer believe in ghosts. Neither does Freud, even if from time to time he drops his guard and reverts to a "primitive mentality" for which he later apologizes. But in his moments of ordinary lucidity, he denies that ghosts can really haunt our dreams. All that he can see at work there are our own ambivalent feelings with regard to the dead. Let us assume that those dreams are projections of our unconscious, acting on its own. That unconscious is so uncanny or strangely familiar, at once so close to our innermost secrets yet so far from all that we are to ourselves that, as a result, the difference between this other one within me, who is more me than I myself am, and other subjectivities of the external world becomes less pertinent. But that makes the enigma all the greater: How can one be so very much a stranger to oneself? As Saint Augustine already had remarked, "Qui in me seminavit hoc bellum?"—Who sowed this war within me? Does the fact of naming that unknown *me* make it less alien? The forces that rule our unconscious are very real, and simply demythologizing them makes very little difference. What advantage is gained by explaining the ghost of Hamlet's father as an illusion resulting from some psychic projection, rather than regarding him as a real ghost? In either case, the real cause is unreachable and does not disappear simply because it is known. The unconscious remains ungraspable: It towers above us as spirits do and dogs our steps as closely. The chimeras of the unconscious are no less ferocious than those of fable. Both can lead to madness.

The Buddhist discovery, somewhere in between reason and madness, of the deepest depths and utmost heights of consciousness (or, if you like, the unconscious and the superconscious) is perhaps the equivalent of a practice of "controlled madness," the aim of which is to become mad without losing one's head, without sinking into silence and terror. This practice, which is quite common in Buddhist cultures, is somewhat exceptional in ours, no doubt for lack of a lifeline (or, as the French put it, *garde-fou*). Like a madman, an awakened individual is someone who has passed "through the looking glass." But is it the same looking glass in all cases?

Symbols, Myths, Rituals

Let us begin this discussion of the potentially fruitful nature of symbols in Buddhism with a fine passage from Paul Claudel's *Conversations dans le Loir-et-Cher*. It records a dialogue between Saint-Maurice, an aviator, and Grégoire, an antiques dealer by profession. At one point the conversation leads to a description (quasi-Plotinian and very Orientalist in character) of the transition from the One to the many according to East Asian Buddhism. Grégoire produces the following explanation:

Look! It all begins with a crystal ball held by all eight fingers and two thumbs, which meditators warm with their own hearts as if it were another, luminous, heart. It is analogous to the scepter or those wooden tablets that ancient statues of mandarins hold in order to focus their eyes and attention. Then that empty and unchanging water gradually becomes tinged with a little color and, as its density increases, becomes opaque. It is like the jade that celadon was to imitate a little later. Eventually, between those creative fingers, this pure matter, a sample of the original element, assumes all kinds of shapes, some simple, some complex, a mixture of beings, the entire range of the bronzes, agates, and porcelains that we admire in the New York museum. Like those lapis lazuli things carved from compacted azure. The smooth swelling or pure bloom constituted by a white Song vase is a supreme exhalation from the depths of the lotus, the sacred globe that opens up, a receptacle for a soul flowering and proffering its nothingness.

In short, what Westerners take to be some trinket is a kind of talisman or material aid that enables the Asian soul to settle back upon itself: It operates as a rosary clasped between one's fingers; a jewel that confers immobility. There must be some Sanskrit or Tibetan term for it.[19]

Claudel's pearl metaphor is certainly a gem (a pearly reflection that evokes the light of the rising sun). It is, however, but a pale Orientalist imitation of the *cintāmaṇi*, or "wish-fulfilling jewel," a figure of major importance in Tantric symbolism and Japanese mythology. The very same luminous jewel adorns the tail of the Japanese fox, the mythological animal that represents the god of rice and fertility, Inari, but is also an emanation of the solar goddess Amaterasu, herself a manifestation of the cosmic Buddha Dainichi (in Sanskrit, Vairocana, "Great Sun").

The "gradual" progress from the One to the many, as described by Claudel, may be set in opposition to the "sudden" metaphor of the pearl used by the Chan master Zongmi. He compares the human spirit to a bright, transparent pearl that can reflect all colors perfectly. He uses the example of the color black reflected in the bright pearl to illustrate the relation between ignorance and knowledge. When black is reflected in the pearl, it becomes totally black. A simple mind will take it to be a black pearl and will refuse to believe that in truth it is a bright pearl. Even if he eventually admits that the latter is the case, he will think that the pearl is smeared with black and must be polished if it is to reveal its brightness. Another person will think that it is the blackness, or some other color, that defines a bright pearl, so every time she sees colored pearls, she takes them to be bright ones; indeed, such a person would not recognize a bright pearl if shown one, since the colors to which she is accustomed are nowhere to be found. A third person, having heard it said that the colors reflected in the pearl are false and that the pearl is basically colorless, will deduce that it is void of all substance and so does not exist.

Stringing his pearl metaphor together in this way, Zongmi has in mind the concepts and spiritual practices of the various currents of Chan of his day. According to him, all that is necessary is to recognize that the pearl (the mind) is essentially luminous and that the colors reflected in it (the passions) are illusory. Thereafter, whatever the aspect of the pearl, you will no longer believe that it is black (in other words, that the mind is ruled by the passions); you will avoid seeking it where there are no colors (an error stemming from a belief that the mind is distinct from the passions); and you will avoid asserting that neither light nor darkness exists, or even any pearl (a point of view based on an ontological emptiness, which sweepingly denies the existence of the mind and likewise of everything else).

Myth Forgotten

What is the place of myth in Buddhism? Those determined to hold solely to a philosophical and agnostic doctrine claim that it is insignificant. In some ways, early Buddhism certainly constituted a demythologization, as the doctrinal evolution of Buddhist scholasticism testifies. The very legend of the Buddha incorporates a demythologizing tendency, as can be seen from the episode of Buddha's temptation by the Buddhist devil, Māra. Buddha undergoes three trials: He has first to face Māra's armies, next to resist seduction by Māra's daughters, and finally to respond to the challenge of Māra himself, who accuses him of usurpation. For a clearer understanding of this demythologizing aspect within the myth itself, it is helpful to turn to Greece and briefly consider the myth of Oedipus, which presents certain analogies with that of the Buddha. I will follow the analysis produced by Jean-Joseph Goux, which shifts the emphasis placed on parricide and incest (by the now dominant Freudian interpretation) to the episode of Oedipus's encounter with the Sphinx (or rather the Sphinge).[20]

The trial faced by Oedipus consists in confronting a female monster whose nature is composite, like that of chimeras. The three parts of the monster symbolize the three Indo-European functions distinguished by Georges Dumézil (wisdom and sovereignty, war, and sensuality and fecundity). The psychological and mythological interpretation of the Indo-European legends related to the myth of Oedipus suggests that, when the young man confronts such a monster, it is not his father that he tries to kill, but rather the maternal forces that block his progress toward the woman destined for him. Oedipus, who avoids committing this murder, then finds himself married to his own mother.

In myth, matricide is the murder that severs the umbilical cord and makes it possible to accede to a wife. For many Buddhist monks, that matricide remains unresolved, and if it is accomplished (symbolically, of course), it is so as to obtain ultimate deliverance. The father is strangely absent from all this and, strictly speaking, his murder is "insignificant"— even if Linji does speak metaphorically of "killing both father and mother" in order to clear all obstacles from the path leading to awakening. In Japanese Buddhism, the figure of the goddess Benzaiten, at once a dragon mother and a seductress, plays a role of capital importance. She is also the daughter of the dragon king, who gives her magic pearl (*cintāmaṇi*), the symbol of awakening, to the Buddha. Of course it is rather dangerous to be too easily persuaded by a psychoanalytical interpretation (whether Freudian or Jungian) of the reptilian deities (*nāga*) in Buddhism, but much Buddhist hagiography can certainly be read as a family romance. In legends relating to the daughters of the dragon king, for example, many features call to mind the French legend of Melusine, the snake woman from the which the Lusignan family was descended (the name "Melusine" is sometimes interpreted as "mother of the Lusignans"). Similar legends can be found in European folklore.

Too little attention has been paid to the fact that the three fundamental passions defined by the Buddha (desire, ignorance, hatred) correspond, albeit arranged in a different order, to the three functions of the Indo-European ideology: ignorance is the contrary of wisdom (the first function), hatred is linked with war (the second function), and desire is linked with sensuality (and so with the third function).[21] Similarly, like Oedipus's response to the Sphinx, the Buddha's response to Māra in the temptation episode covers the three functions (caresses, blows, and questions, in the case of the Sphinx). However, whereas initiation implies the qualities and perils that correspond to those three functions, Oedipus sidesteps the first two. In the case of the Buddha, resistance to temptation thus fits into the trifunctional schema—being one of the three phases of initiation. So it truly is a matter of a royal investiture as a preliminary to (and duplicate of) awakening. The Buddha is still inscribed in the trifunctional ideology (even if he transcends it), whereas Oedipus, for his part, sidesteps it.

A philosopher manifests all the presumption of one who relies on his own wisdom; he lacks the modesty of a disciple. But contrary to what has frequently been believed since Freud, the myth of Oedipus cannot be reduced to the version given by Sophocles in *Oedipus Rex*. Therein lies the supreme irony of the myth's final episode as Sophocles presents it in *Oedipus at Colonus*: This figure, who has been entirely self-reliant and has sent the seer Tiresias packing back to his oracles, eventually himself becomes a seer. Oedipus, like Socrates, thus seems the very epitome of the autonomous philosopher who (at least initially) refuses to abide by tradition and cuts the Gordian Knot. The same determination to be independent is detectable among certain Chan thinkers: Their sole goal is to be their own masters. Yet it may well be thought that, had the Sphinx been a Chan master, Oedipus would have failed in his reply and furthermore would have received a hail of blows. He was too quick to assume that he had solved the riddle, when all he had done was drain it of its sense (or rather of its apparent non-sense). Nietzsche, for his part, points out "the necessity of counter-Alexanders who will retie the Gordian knot of Greek culture."[22] Philosophy is thus, in its very nature, profanatory. All the same, Socrates does obey his *daimon*, which is not solely the voice of reason (even in the metaphysical sense). In his case, is it a matter of autonomy or of heteronomy?

Descartes, for his part, stands on his own two feet, unsupported by crutches. But according to Merleau-Ponty, a philosopher progresses limpingly. In Chinese mythology, limping seems to characterize the divine "step of Yu," the gait of the civilizing hero, a hybrid being who advances haltingly, on a zigzag course. Descartes, however, walks straight. He has cleared a tabula rasa, severed the famous knot, and liquidated his Greek past (or so he thinks). Oedipus, Descartes, and others such as the "historical" Buddha and the Chan master Linji have nothing to do with the mediation of symbols, myth, and ritual—in other words, with tradition. They reject all divine and social transcendence, placing their entire faith in themselves.

What is the systematic (and therefore artificial) doubt of Descartes, or even the ritualized "great doubt" of a Zen practitioner, in comparison to an initiatory death, passing beyond the limit as in initiation, a true encounter with the Sphinx or dragon? A philosopher seems to be one who refuses to take that ultimate (or primary) risk, who is satisfied with less and remains imprisoned in the world of words (with a few unfortunate exceptions, Nietzsche and a few others, who never recovered or remained dumbfounded by the experience). A philosopher does not go all the way; he turns back at the cave's entrance, contenting himself with exchanging a few words with the guard posted at the threshold. So perhaps Oedipus was the first philosopher, the first to refuse initiation. But even after two millennia under a philosophical regime, the need for initiation remains—as is attested by the vogue for psychoanalysis.

Philosophical thought, like Chan subitism (the exception that proves the Buddhist rule) rejects all mediation between myth and logic. It has forgotten the blind spot, or rather the immense zone of shadow created by its vision, the blindness that opened up the space that it illuminates. Instead of sticking to reality, it recreates an impoverished world that it can dominate. Even when it does happen to call itself into question, it does so for the most part within the same familiar ritual framework.

By rejecting the gods and ritual, Oedipus and philosophy cut themselves off from access to the profound psychic source. By submitting to the gods and to rituals, archaic religion cut itself off from access to reason. On this point too, Buddhism seeks a middle way—not in between faith and intelligence, which is the Christian, overly individualistic version of the problem, but between initiation and reason.

Missed Opportunities

Not only did Oedipus fail in, or rather avoid his initiation, but he was fooled by the Sphinx, a power of darkness—just as, in the last analysis, Descartes was perhaps fooled by the evil genius that he thought he was invoking playfully, without really believing in it. But is it not said that the great skill of the Devil lies in encouraging the belief that he does not exist? In the case of the Buddha's victory over Māra, not to mention Christ's in the face of Satan, the temptation did not, after all, amount to all that much. Similarly, in its obvious humanism, the Sphinx's riddle (What is it that has four legs in the morning, two at midday, and three in the evening?) seems childish. The Devil, if he exists, must have other tricks up his sleeve, and certainly more than three strings to his bow, three questions to answer, three temptations to overcome. In the Buddha's case, can we even speak of temptation, given that at no point does he seem to have lost his self-control? There is really nothing at stake in this game; the test is hardly testing: He who is being tested never gets close to madness, never experiences the great doubt. Winning without danger, he triumphs without glory. He questions neither himself nor his world, which accounts for a certain arrogance on his part. But in this way maybe he misses the essential point; compared with his Indian predecessors, the rationalist Buddha of the four noble truths is, basically, merely a thinker of no great originality. In reducing evil to ignorance, he neglects the demonic aspect of man and, in so doing, produces the unconscious, a return of the repressed. Tantric Buddhism is neither more nor less than that return of the repressed. Buddhist thought is divided by a movement similar to what, through Oedipus and his successors, separates myth from philosophy in Greece.

Buddhism cannot be reduced to the "historical" Buddha and his doctrine, both products of a demythologization. A purely rational Buddhism would be a Buddhism without a shadow, condemned to remain theoretical or, if put into practice, to create repression. All later Buddhist thought has sought to escape from that overly simplistic vision. Perhaps, in contrast to the "Greek miracle," this is the "Buddhist miracle," the emergence of a thought that, in the last analysis, was able to overcome the temptation of dichotomy and to preserve initiation while, at the same time managing, from time to time, to sever the Gordian knot and the paralyzing bonds of tradition.

Despite certain setbacks, myth continued to spread in the shadow cast by the Buddhist *stūpa*. Alongside legends in which the *nāga* and other reptilian or chthonic deities, gods of the earth, the trees, and the ponds, were happy to convert to the new doctrine, there are plenty of stories in which Buddha and his disciples have to display cunning or violence in order to get the better of local gods and subject these to their will. In all Asian cultures, the more or less forced integration of local cults into Buddhism found one of its principal ideological justifications in the theory of the two truths. According to this model, local cults represent now pure error, now a first step in the direction of conventional truth, and in the latter case can be retained as they are. All that is needed is to interpret them in accordance with a particular grid in order to give them their Buddhist meaning. The gods of popular religion either convert to Buddhism or turn out basically to be simply particular manifestations of Buddhas. Such integration has been pushed the furthest in Japan, where it resulted in a two-faced ideology such as Ryōbu Shintō (Shintō based on the two sections of the *maṇḍala*), which is Shintō in name only and really a product derived from Buddhism. The *Shasekishū* (Collection of sand and pebbles) thus contains a passage on Ise Shrine, the most sacred of all the Shinto precincts, according to which the Inner Sanctuary symbolizes the Buddha Dainichi of the Womb *maṇḍala* while the Outer Sanctuary represents the Buddha Dainichi of the Vajra *maṇḍala*.[23] This text, written by a Zen master, furthermore and for good measure associates the two sanctuaries with the Chinese cosmological principles of *yin* and *yang*, the masculine and the feminine.

Paradoxically, this resurgence of the gods at the heart of esoteric or Tantric Buddhism was to encourage the rise of a new and allegedly national religion, Shintō, which—circumstances abetting—rose to rival Buddhism, which, as a result, came to be labeled a foreign religion. During the Meiji Restoration (1868–71), this even led to a particularly virulent repression of Buddhism. However, in recovering its full mythological dimension, medieval Japanese Buddhism had not simply brought about a regression to popular superstition, as has been claimed. On the contrary, it carried Buddhist thought forward, mining a vein that had become almost exhausted in certain schools of philosophical Buddhism while at the same time bringing into operation the same principle of twofold truth that characterized philosophical Buddhism. In this way, it rediscovered affects that, from another angle, associated it with a depth psychology.

This evolution was also encouraged by a ritualization of Buddhist practice. Such returns of myth and ritual may provide access to ultimate truth. According to Tantric Buddhism, by dint of passing through images and forms, one eventually arrives at an absence of images and forms, emptiness. But this involves a real passage through them, not just an intellectual overview: This initiation cannot be eluded by merely critical intelligence or insight, as certain Buddhist currents claim.

Ritual Perspectives

Ritual has had a bad press in the West, at least it has ever since Luther. As is well known, Luther denounced, among other things, the liturgical excesses of the Catholic Mass. The history of religions has taken over that "Protestant" view, tending to undervalue the ritual aspects of the religions studied and to favor their purely doctrinal aspects. In this respect it has also been influenced by psychoanalysis. Freud associated fixations and obsession with details with the kind of distortion that turns little things into items of the greatest importance, a tendency that neurosis and religious ritual share in common. Such features of ritual undeniably exist, but they clearly represent no more than one aspect of the situation. Anthropology, on the other hand, has sought to restore value to the propensity for ritual. In his study of prayer, Marcel Mauss wrote:

[Whereas], for philosophers and theologians, ritual is a conventional language through which the interplay of images and internal feelings can be expressed, albeit imperfectly, for us, it becomes reality itself. For it contains all that is active and alive in prayer: It holds in reserve all the meaning that has been put into words and contains the seed of all that may be deduced from it, even by means of new syntheses: The practices and social beliefs that are condensed there are heavy with the past and the present and pregnant with the future.[24]

Buddhist practice is centered on the body: not only in meditation, to which it tends all too often to be reduced, but also in ritual. Without ritual, Buddhist thought itself loses its reality, its specificity. To seize upon its arcane elements, logic is not enough; some form of ordination is needed. The postulate according to which truth should be equally accessible to all, by virtue of the principle that good sense is the best shared thing in the whole world, is not applicable in Buddhist lands. Here, a critical mind certainly preserves its importance, but faith also has a role to play, as does ritual. As we have seen, even the arguments of a logician such as Nāgārjuna need to be reset in this religious context, without which they would be no more than "children's games with empty shells." As a result of refusing to take account of the ritual element, people have come to study Buddhism as an entity on its own, independent of its intellectual and cultural context. That is an altogether artificial separation and masks all that Buddhist ritual, and likewise the metaphysics that stems from it, owe to, for instance, Vedic tradition and Hinduism.

Unlike Tantrism, Chan/Zen is often characterized by its antiritualism. But to do so is to fail to see all that is fundamentally ritualistic in the very antiritualism that is ritually invoked by the Western apologists of "libertarian" Zen. Seated meditation, from which Zen derives its name, is first and foremost a ritual imitation of the posture adopted by the Buddha. The *kōan* also play an important role in this ritual process. Attention has often been drawn to the importance, in Chan maieutics, of the sometimes violent confrontations between masters and their disciples. But it is also important to stress the fact that, with the institutionalization of Chan, these "encounters" themselves became carefully orchestrated rituals. In medieval Japan, particularly in the literary Zen of the "five mountains" (*gozan*), the *kōan* became the objects of bookish study, while in other monasteries, they were learned by heart and became the objects of a veritable fetishism. Finances permitting, one could purchase ready-made replies to the principal *kōan*. The initiation that a master conferred upon his disciples in the course of private lessons came to consist essentially in the revelation of stereotyped responses to the classic *kōan*. This makes one wonder whether the sole purpose of the *kōan* really was to bring about an awakening. Zen monks resorted to the hieratic style of the *kōan* in order to justify a variety of monastic arts and rites, ranging from initiation to funeral rites. Such a use of *kōan* went hand in hand with the sacralization of monastic life, and this in its turn evolved into a series of liturgical sequences whose physical and technical aspects and, above all, secret meaning the monks were required to master. Although such practices never supplanted those of meditation and the traditional *kōan*, they did duplicate them and, in doing so, profoundly modified their meaning.

An analysis of icons, *stūpa*, and other ritual Buddhist artifacts suggests the inadequacy of the narrowly functionalist view that regards an image simply as an *aide-mémoire* and justifies it on the grounds of the happy psychological effects it is held to exert upon the pious. But does that mean that one should remain at the phenomenological level, venturing to do no more than emphasize the "ideology of presence" that underpins the cult of images? Is there not a danger of setting too high a value upon that ideology (in the sense of a system of ideas) and of attributing too great a coherence to it? The first thing to do is to show that such a system exists. Even if it is never fully actualized, even partial actualizations of it are revealing. Having established the virtual existence of the system, two reservations need to be made: On the one hand, the ideology is constantly brought into question by what, in the system, opens on to otherness. On the other, one should not allow the immanent, innocent meaning of these symbols to mask their social and political function or their ideological character (in the Marxist sense).

However, a sociological or ideological objectivization all too often tends to dismiss the "lived experience," the phenomenological interpretation of the subject, as purely illusory. That disenchanted approach is summed up by Marcel Mauss when, in the conclusion to his study on *mana*, the magic force inherent in beings and things, he declares: "Without a doubt, it is always a matter of society paying itself in the false currency of its dream."[25] That "always" is too strong: "Often" would be better, but even so, an assumption is a far cry from certainty. A religious person, citing the words of Saint Paul or Laozi on the paradoxical nature of truth, would be quick to object that the supernatural may manifest itself precisely in the context of cheap superstition, for it, unlike an "objective" observer, is not limited by the categories of verisimilitude and implausibility. Without a doubt, as long as it clings to the positions of positivist rationalism, the "broader reason" that Mauss called for appears to be incapable of penetrating the "irrationality" of magic.

Clearly, ritual is a matter of "you could say that" (in both senses of the expression: as a performative act, "let us say that ..." and also as an impression, "it seems that ..."). If so, is the believer's relation to an icon based simply on incomprehension, confusion between the true and the false, or on semicomprehension, midway between real comprehension and ignorance? Can one, in the latter case, still speak of "real comprehension," albeit in a different mode? And what about the "false currency" of dreams? What if the use value of that currency, like that of fiduciary money, depended upon an initial act of faith? What if, as in the Baudelairian anecdote told by Jacques Derrida,[26] the counterfeit money was reserved for the "poor," that is to say, for anthropologists and other types of "dissociated" beings?

Language, Poetry, Literature

Discursive language, bogged down in abstract concepts, cannot explain reality. That, in brief, was what Linji, in his forceful way, tried to teach his disciples. One day he received from Governor Wang a request to expound the Chan doctrine. He responded to this request, as he was bound to, but not without manifesting his reluctance:

"Today, having found it impossible to refuse, I have complied with people's wishes and stepped up to the lecture seat. If I were to discuss the great concern of Buddhism from the point of view of a follower of the sect of the Chan patriarchs, then I could not even open my mouth, and you would have no place to plant your feet.

But today I have been urged to speak by the Constant Attendant, so why should I hide the principles of our sect? Perhaps there are some valiant generals here who would like to draw up their ranks and unfurl their banners. Let them prove to the group what they can do!"

A monk asked, "What is the basic meaning of Buddhism?"

The master gave a shout.

The monk bowed low.

The Master said, "This fine monk is the kind who's worth talking to!"

Someone asked, "Master, whose style of song do you sing? Whose school of teaching do you carry on?"

The Master said, "When I was at Huangbo's place, I asked a question three times and three times I got hit."

The monk started to say something. The Master gave a shout and then struck the monk, saying, "You don't drive a nail into the empty sky!"

The Master resumed, saying, "This religious gathering today is held for the sake of the one great concern of Buddhism. Are there any others who want to ask questions? Come forward quickly and ask them!"

"But even if you open your mouths, what you say will have nothing to do with that concern. Why do I say this? Because Śākyamuni said, did he not, that 'The *Dharma* is separate from words and writings, and is not involved with direct or indirect causes.'"

"It's because you don't have enough faith that today you find yourself tied up in knots. I'm afraid you will trouble the Constant Attendant and the other officials and keep them from realizing their Buddha nature. It's best for me to withdraw."[27]

Linji had made his point, but not without speaking at some length, thereby demonstrating what the Chan masters called "a grandmother's kindness." Puhua, a contemporary of Linji and in some respects his rival, was more radical in his refusal to speak. When questioned, he resorted to a kind of glossolalia, a form of language that echoes the words of his interlocutor. "One day Puhua was in front of the monks' eating hall eating raw vegetables. The Master saw him and said, 'Exactly like a donkey!' Puhua brayed like a donkey. The Master said, 'This thief!' Puhua said, 'Thief, thief!' and walked away."[28]

In a critical comment on Freud, Émile Benveniste remarks that all language operates through dichotomy and the excluded middle.[29] The Buddhist realization is therefore obtained in spite of language, through procedures that are closer to those of dreaming and of rhetoric than to those of ordinary language. A war is waged against the "weight of words," using strategies to deconstruct the linguistic veil by which things are shrouded and to express—in a paradoxically linguistic fashion—the register of ultimate truth that lies beyond words. Buddhist thought calls into question a number of fundamental Western assumptions regarding language and representation. Signs can be arbitrary—as Ferdinand de Saussure, the founder of structural linguistics, believes—only if one imagines things as existing as such, beyond language. It is an idea that prevails in certain currents of Buddhism, but is called into question in others, which underline the adequacy of language to reality. Tantric Buddhism, in particular, uses "true words" that at first sight are pure signifiers, but that also claim to constitute inexhaustible reserves of the signified: Such are the incantatory and mnemotechnic formulas known as *mantra* and *dhāraṇī*. They are to be found everywhere, even in a school as antimagic as Chan/Zen. What is more, even the *kōan* of Zen themselves often come to serve as mantras.

As Nietzsche correctly perceived, language is metaphorical essentially, not accidentally. So rhetoric is not a derived or parasitic phenomenon, but rather one of the paradigmatic forms of discourse. In consequence, literature tells us as much about truth as does philosophical discourse, which, for its part, is by no means free of the languors of language. The notion of twofold truth lends itself quite well to an approach to reality that is at once literary and philosophical and furthermore makes it possible to pass beyond both those approaches.

Commentators reflecting upon Laozi's famous saying "He who knows does not speak; he who speaks does not know" have often underlined how paradoxical it was to produce a work of some five thousand words (the *Daode jing*) in order to explain this. But Laozi was no fool, nor were his Daoist and Buddhist successors. So perhaps something more complex than mere inadvertency on their part is involved—evidence of a need that enlightens us as to the profound and paradoxical nature of reality. How can the unsayable be said? That is a challenge that Buddhist masters try to face, in particular in poems written just before their deaths. Thus Sengzhao (374–414), sentenced to commit suicide by the sovereign of the later Qin, wrote as follows:

The four great elements have no master;
The five aggregates are fundamentally empty.
When my head approaches the naked blade, it will be like be-
    heading the wind of springtime.[30]

That poem may be compared to another, composed by the Chan master
Wuxue Zuyuan (1226–1286), who was due to be executed as a spy by the
Mongols:

In the whole universe, there is no longer a place where I can
    plant my solitary bamboo;
I am glad, for man is empty, like everything else.
I salute you, three-foot-long sword of the great Yuan Mongols!
What you seek to behead in your lightening reflection is the
    wind of springtime.[31]

Wuxue's sangfroid saved his life, and he emigrated to Japan, where he
became a Zen patriarch. Another Chinese patriarch, Dongshan Liangjie
(807–869) left the following poem:

If, out of so many apprentices, as numerous as the grains of sand
    in the Ganges, not one has achieved awakening,
The fault lies with those who sought it through the language of
    others.
If one wishes to obtain forgetfulness of the sensible forms, all
    traces erased,
One must ardently strive to walk in the void.[32]

The same idea reappears in a poem by Dongshan's disciple, Guangren (837–909):

My path lies beyond the blue-tinged spaces,
Like a wandering white cloud with no fixed place.
There was once in this world a tree without roots,
Whose yellowing leaves blow back on the wind.[33]

Lastly, here is a poem by Xutong Zhiyu ("Stupid through wisdom,"
1185–1269):

At the age of eighty-five,
I know neither Buddha nor patriarchs. . . .
And off I go, swinging my arms,
All traces cut off, in the great void![34]

But sometimes even a poem is de trop. A number of Chan masters condemned this custom of producing "last words." Some expressed their criticism in—precisely—their very last poem (noblesse oblige, after all). But for those who reject all mastery and want nothing to do with any kind of spiritual nobility, there are other ways to queen the pawn of other players. To adapt one of Wittgenstein's metaphors, it is rather as if one is playing a different language game, moving one's queen according to the rules of chess when one's opponent thinks he is playing checkers. Obviously enough, the game soon stalls in an impasse—a paradoxical kind of checkmate that remains hidden:

One day Puhua went around the streets of the town begging people to give him a one-piece robe. But although people offered him one, he refused all their offers.

The Master sent the director of temple business out to buy a coffin. When Puhua returned to the temple, the Master said, "I've prepared this one-piece robe for you!"

Puhua shouldered the coffin and went off with it. He threaded his way through the streets of the town, calling out, "Linji has prepared a one-piece robe for me! I am going to the east gate to take leave of the world!"

The townspeople trooped after him, eager to see what would happen. Puhua said, "'I'm not going to do it today. But tomorrow I'll go to the south gate and take leave of the world."

He did this for three days, till no one believed him any more. Then on the fourth day, when no one was following or watching him, he went alone outside the city wall, lay down in the coffin, and asked a passerby to nail on the lid.

In no time, word spread abroad, and the townspeople came scrambling. But when they opened the coffin, they found that all trace of his body had vanished. They could just catch the echo of his hand bell sounding sharp and clear in the sky before it faded away.[35]

In the non-Euclidian space of Chinese thought, a periphrasis is sometimes the shortest route to reach one's goal. But there is something pathetic about the turns taken by such peripatetic language, so some people, among them the layman Vimalakīrti, prefer silence. Not just any kind of silence, though: rather, a "thundering silence"—a *silentium loquens*, a reverberating, "telling silence" that strikes straight to the heart of things and beings. As Kumārājiva wrote: "Discussion through silence is the supreme discussion." Similarly, Candrakīrti, the "spokesman" of late Mādhyamika, declared that "the absolute is the silence of saints." But if it is sometimes hard to tell what speech means, how can one possibly tell what this silence means? There are many kinds of silence, as Father Dinouart shows in his *L'art de rester silencieux* (1771). And there are, furthermore, a number of different metalinguistic ways of communicating. As Gregory Bateson's falsely ingenuous remark has it: "The French can say something simply by desisting from their gesticulations."

"Whether you can speak or not," said the layman Pang, "there is no way out." Whether one remains silent or speaks, truth is performative. To tell the truth is to give a perfect and at times perfidious performance not necessarily appreciated by all and sundry. A famous example in Chan is the Buddha's way of transmitting the Law. As will be remembered, Śākyamuni silently showed his disciples a flower. Mahākāśyapa was the one who smiled, at which Śākyamuni, using speech, proceeded to pass on the Law that he had just transmitted to him silently, "from mind to mind." In his *Wumen guan* (The gateless pass) the Chan master Wumen Huikai (1183–1260) produced the following critique:

Yellow-faced Gautama, behaving as though there was nobody near him, forced good people into slavery and, hanging up a sheep's head, sold dog meat instead. . . . But if everyone had smiled at that moment, how could he have transmitted the treasure of the Eye of the true Law, and if Mahākāśyapa had not smiled, how could he have transmitted the treasure of the Eye of the true Law? If he declares that the Eye of the true Law has been transmitted, this old fool seeks to mislead those loitering there. But if he says it has not been transmitted, why did he approve of Mahākāśyapa and him alone?[36]

Faced with the apparent dilemma between silence and speech (for even ordinary silence is still a *lemma*, a kind of argument), there are many ways of getting around the excluded middle. One means is what some have called the twilight language (in Sanskrit, *saṃdhā-bhāṣya*) of Tantric Buddhism. The semantic field of this expression covers the terms *saṃdha* ("intention, deliberate talk"—in other words, "intentional" language), *saṃdhi* ("fusion," a synthesis of contraries), and *saUNDERDOTmdhya* (the twilight of morning and evening, the two moments when day and night meet, which are particularly prized in Brahmanic ritual). Take the case of *mahāsukha*, the "great bliss" or supreme delight said to be produced by the union of *upāya* (skillful means) and *prajñā* (wisdom): The expression may be understood either in the sense of the sexual union of the practitioner with his ritual partner or else in the psychological sense of a combination of wisdom and expedients. An "intentional" interpretation must operate simultaneously in both registers, but in practice, certain schools of Buddhism place the emphasis on the sexual/ritual interpretation (this came to be known as "left-handed" Tantrism). However, a true practitioner of Tantrism ought to be ambidextrous, even if the left-handed way presents a number of literally "sinister" aspects. According to Jean Varenne, "the particular feature of twilight language is, precisely, to bring about the conjunction (*saṃdhyā*) of the two possible interpretations with a very specific intention (*saṃdhā*)."[37]

As we have seen, Sino-Japanese Buddhism developed at the confluence of Indian Buddhism and Chinese thought. You could say that Buddhism inoculated Chinese thought with a sufficient dose of transcendence to prevent it from becoming bogged down in immanence and that, in return, it received sufficient immanence to avoid the Indian temptation of transcendental idealism. The Indian Buddhist epistemological break that defines the transcendent absolute as ineffable is thus counterbalanced by the "transcendent immanence" of Chinese thought, in which there is no break in continuity between the *dao*, human speech, and the human world. According to this conception, human speech "flows straight from the source"; it derives from the absolute—albeit without postulating any revelation, as the "religions of the Book" do. This being so, mystical knowledge takes two forms, as the *Daode jing* already declared: Through non-knowledge and silence, it is possible to grasp the absolute in its essence (which is to have no essence); through intuitive knowledge or wisdom (*prajñā*) and through live speech (distinct from inert, discursive speech), it is possible to grasp it in its effects. Language cannot express the absolute, yet it cannot not express it, for they share an identical nature.

Chinese Buddhism inherits from Zhuangzi, but outstrips him dialectically. One of Zhuangzi's best-known metaphors is that of the fish trap and the rabbit snare: "The fish trap exists because of the fish; once you've gotten the fish, you can forget the trap. The rabbit snare exists because of the rabbit; once you've gotten the rabbit, you can forget the snare. Words exist because of meaning; once you've gotten the meaning, you can forget the words."[38] As Zhuanzi sees it, words point toward reality, but must be abandoned once reality is grasped. In similar fashion, Indian Buddhism speaks of the raft that makes it possible to cross the river of existence, but that must be abandoned once the other shore is reached. Many Chan texts used the metaphor of the finger that points to the moon to convey the idea that the finger (words, Buddhist teaching) is not the moon (reality, the absolute, awakening). However, in the realm of twofold truth, that is not the case. Here, the finger *is* the moon, and the moon is nothing but a finger. The Japanese poet-monk Ryōkan (1758–1831) writes as follows:

> It is thanks to the finger
> That you can point out the moon.
> It is thanks to the moon
> That you can understand the finger.
> The moon and the finger
> Are neither different nor identical.
> This parable serves simply
> To guide the practitioners toward awakening.
> Once you have seen things as they are,
> There is no more moon, no more finger.[39]

In Wittgenstein we find a similar passage: "When someone points to the sun, you do not say that he is pointing out both the sun and himself, just because it is he who is pointing the finger; yet by making that gesture, he may well attract attention to himself at the same time as to the sun."

So it is that speech constantly spills over beyond what it says. And perhaps that overspill is not, as analytical philosophers claim, an "aberration" that must be rectified—but rather an essential function of language. On the highway of words, there can be no traffic police. However, in order to get the most out of language and its overspills and to know how to stop short of going too far, you must precisely grasp its meaning and the constraints to which it is subject.

Words reveal reality to us, in particular the part of reality constituted by our deepest thoughts. The intuition is to be found in a number of Western philosophers that—to parody the proverb—whatever is stated clearly is conceived clearly and that utterance does not follow on after thought. Merleau-Ponty, for example, distinguishes two languages, "language that comes after the event, that is acquired and that disappears behind the meaning it carries—and language that comes forth at the moment of expression, the kind that actually allows me to slip from signs to meaning: the one is spoken language, the other speaking language."[40] Giving himself up to the pleasure of words, he tries to bridge the gap between philosophy and poetry:

Happy writers, speaking men . . . do not ask themselves, before speaking, whether speech is possible. . . . Contented, they place themselves in the shade of that great tree and continue their internal monologue aloud; their thought blossoms into speech; effortlessly they are understood; they become others as they say what is most intimately theirs. . . . They cross bridges made of snow without noticing how fragile they are; they exploit to the limit the incredible power to which every consciousness accedes if it believes itself to be coextensive with the truth, the power to convince others and enter into their retreats.[41]

Chan masters, for their part, sometimes seek to tear themselves away from language, sometimes abandon themselves to the flow of speech "like a ball tossed into a stream," in order, precisely, to discover their liberty amid the chains of thought and language. They either transgress established customs or, on the contrary, seem to delight in conforming with them. As Pascal would say, one should observe custom, "but always with an idea of one's own at the back of one's head"—or rather, with a kind of nonthought that is no longer the thoughtlessness of the common man, always thinking and striving.

Epilogue: After All ...

Now that we have (provisionally) come full circle, it is to be hoped that we will be more wary of falling into the trap set by the logic of the excluded middle and will think twice before accepting dilemmas such as those involving faith and reason, rationality and the irrational, philosophy and religion, intellect and intuition, logic and rhetoric, spirituality and materialism, East and West. Yet at the same time we should not lose all critical sense, either confusing everything in a vague syncretism or rejecting it all as a matter of principle, whether we find ourselves in a mystical darkness in which all cats are gray or amid the brilliance of an Enlightenment in which no cows are sacred.

Perhaps that is too much to ask, but by now we surely know that it is the only way to achieve the bare minimum necessary. Let us replace the stiff language of ideologies by our own. As a Chan master would say, my tongue is boneless, moving freely in all directions. That was precisely how language originated. Having already introduced a few Buddhist words into my own personal dictionary and my own internalized monologue, I am now trying to slip them into a dialogue, if not into *Webster's* and the *Oxford English Dictionary* (both of which, as it happens, already contain quite a few of them). To that end, I have underlined certain resemblances between two types of discourse, the one Western, the other Buddhist: the resemblances between the logic of Aristotle and that of Nāgārjuna, for example. In so doing, I no doubt appear to be attempting the very thing for which I have reproached others, that is to say, trying to attach islands to the continent, to annex certain Buddhist concepts to Western thought. But now it is not a matter of a simple annexation—at least I hope not. Rather, my purpose is to turn that continent into an archipelago by making it aware of its own driftings. Although the twofold truth of Buddhism seems in principle opposed to the single truth (or single truths) upon which Western culture is founded, it does not, on first acquaintance, seem unapproachable. Its Indo-European origins even bestow a familiar air upon it—which, however, is not to say that it can be absorbed into some Hegelian kind of synthesis. If we follow up its effects, we realize that it soon leads us into a terrain that is unknown to us (or that we have left fallow) and that at the same time it obliges us to rediscover certain truths that have been forgotten.

The present work amounts simply to a reconnaissance of that terrain, an initial foray into the islands of an archipelago that we too hastily took to be a continent, as did Columbus when he discovered the Antilles. In this archipelago, our thought may perhaps grow accustomed to doing the rounds (in both senses), as in the Polynesian *kula* rite, in which precious cowrie shells are exchanged between one shore and another. Let us pass from one island to another, feeling no nostalgia for any idealized Ithaca, for the true Ithaca is, precisely, an archipelago—neither island nor continent, or possibly both at once, or something else altogether.

There is clearly no last word to be had—yet one (if not two) always is. So let me leave that word to the grammarian Nicolas Beauzée who, in 1789, when on the point of death, is believed to have declared: "My dear friends, I go or am going, for both the one as well as the other is, or are, said."

Pronunciation of Sanskrit, Chinese, and Japanese Sounds

Sanskrit

u = oo
e = eh
ā = ah
ī = ee (as in "eel')
c = tch
j = dj
ḍ = d (guttural)
ś and ṣ = sh (Śākyamuni = Shakyamooni)
ṃ = m (nasal)
ṅ = ng
ñ = gn (as in "gnu")
ṛ = ri

Chinese

x = sh
zh = dj (Zhuang = Djooang)
z = ts (zi = tse)
q = tch (Qin = Tchin)
ian = ien

Japanese

u = oo
e = eh
ā = ah
ō = oh
ū = ooh
g = gu

Notes

PROLOGUE

   1. Mujū, *Sand and Pebbles*, 136.

CHAPTER I

   1. De La Vallée Poussin, *Bouddhisme*, xv.
   2. Droit, *The Cult of Nothingness*, 12–13.
   3. On this question, see Schwab, *The Oriental Renaissance*.
   4. Claudel, *Connaissance de l'Est*, 105.
   5. Merleau-Ponty, "L'Ouest et la philosophie," in *Éloge de la philosophie*, 162–63.
   6. Ibid., 166–67.
   7. Rorty, "Le cosmopolitanisme sans émancipation," 570.
   8. Lyotard, "Discussion," 581–82.
   9. Ibid., 582.
  10. Welbon, *The Buddhist Nirvāṇa*.
  11. On this question see Lopez, *Prisoners of Shangri-la*.

CHAPTER 2

   1. See Jullien, *Detour and Access*.
   2. See Lévi-Strauss, *The Savage Mind*.
   3. Valéry, *Lettres à quelques-uns*, 113.
   4. Bergson, *The Two Sources of Morality and Religion*, 259.
   5. Hegel, *The Philosophy of History*, 280.
   6. Montaigne, *Essays*, 856.
   7. Quignard, *Rhétorique spéculative*, 13, 17–18.
   8. Bonnefoy, *L'improbable*, 104.
   9. Deleuze and Guattari, *What Is Philosophy?*, 45.
  10. Ibid., 51, 91–92.
  11. Mauss, *Oeuvres*, 2:158–59.
  12. Descombes, *Philosophie par gros temps*, 144.
  13. Freud, "The Uncanny," 402.
  14. Bonnefoy, *L'improbable*, 14.

15. Wittgenstein, *The Blue and Brown Books*, 27.

16. Ibid., 17.

17. Ibid., 20.

18. Geertz, *Works and Lives*, 48.

19. Valéry, *Tel quel I*, 13.

20. Valéry, "Discours sur l'esthétique," in *Oeuvres I*, 1307.

21. Bugault, *L'Inde pense-t-elle?*, 248. My discussion of the principle of the excluded middle is indebted to this work.

22. Dewey, *The Theory of Inquiry*, 346.

23. Nietzsche, "Beyond Good and Evil," in *Basic Writings*, 217.

24. See Austin, *How to Do things with Words*.

25. Nietzsche, *The Will to Power*, 279.

26. De Man, *Allegories of Reading*, 124–25.

27. Borges, *Labyrinths*, 213.

28. Nietzsche, "Beyond Good and Evil," in *Basic Writings*, 205.

29. Ibid., 203

30. Ibid., 205.

31. Watson, trans, *The Complete Works of Chuang Tzu*, 288. For consistency and to avoid confusing those not familiar with Chinese, in extracts and epigraphs taken from translations that use the Wade-Giles system of romanization, I have silently changed the spellings to the pinyin system used in the rest of the work.

32. Foucault, "What is Enlightenment?" 304–7.

33. Descombes, *Philosophie par gros temps*, 139.

34. Foucault, "Structuralism and Poststructuralism," 443.

35. Horkheimer and Adorno, *Dialectic of Enlightenment*, 3–42.

36. Benveniste, *Indo-European Language and Society*, 323–24.

37. Marx, *Early Writings*, trans. Joseph O'Malley (Cambridge: Cambridge University Press, 1969), 83, cited in Goux, *Symbolic Economies*, 99.

38. Goux, *Symbolic Economies*, 5.

39. See Foucault, *Madness and Civilization*.

40. Goux, *Symbolic Economies*, 131–32.

41. Wittgenstein, *Remarks on Frazer's Golden Bough*, 3e.

42. Mus, *Barabuḍur*, 2:175.

CHAPTER 3

1. See in particular, Jullien, *Detour and Access*.

2. Robinet, "Une lecture de Zhuangzi," 111.

3. Jullien, "Naissance de l'imagination," 73–76.

4. Watson, trans., *The Complete Works of Chuang Tzu*, 57–58.

5. Ibid., 50–51.

6. Ibid., 97.

7. Yü, "Chung-feng Ming-pen," 433.

8. Ibid., 747.

9. Ibid., 974.

10. Ibid., 458–59.

11. Augusto Gilbert de Voisins, cited by Boothroyd and Détrie in *Le voyage en Chine*, 1053–54.

12. Segalen, *Lettres de Chine*, 201.

CHAPTER 4

1. Merleau-Ponty, *La prose du monde*, 129–30.

2. Derrida, "Faith and Knowledge," 4, 29–30.

3. Benveniste, *Indo-European Language and Society*, 516.

4. Ibid., 522.

5. Ibid., 454–55.

6. Ibid., 458.

7. See Malamoud, *Cooking the World*.

8. LaCapra, *Emile Durkheim*, 291.

9. Weber, *The Protestant Ethic*, 117.

10. Groethuysen, *Origines de l'esprit bourgeois en France*, 104.

11. Derrida, "Faith and Knowledge," 5.

12. Ibid., 2.

13. Ibid., 22.

14. Ibid., 17.

15. Borges, *Lubryrinths*, 119–26.

16. Michaux, *Misérable miracle*, 193.

17. Freud, *The Future of an Illusion*, 71.

18. Nietzsche, "Beyond Good and Evil," in *Basic Writings*, 260–61.

19. Freud, *Civilization and Its Discontents*, 11.

20. Ibid., 20.

21. Hulin, *La mystique sauvage*, 20.

22. Letter of July 24, 1929, cited in R. Dadoun, "Un vol d'Upanishads au-dessus de Sigmund Freud," *Nouvelle Revue de Psychanalyse* no. 22 (1980): 150–51.

23. See Dadoun, ibid., 151; and Hulin, *La mystique sauvage*, 32.

24. Akoun, *L'Occident*, 461.

CHAPTER 5

1. Benveniste, *Indo-European Language and Society*, 99.

2. *Mahāyānaviṃśka*, stanza 9, 10, in Silburn, *Aux sources du bouddhisme*, 175.

3. *Laṅkāvatāra*, stanza 4, in Silburn, *Aux sources du bouddhisme*, 222–25.

4. Ibid., 266.

5. *Mahāyānasūtralaṃkāra*, in Silburn, *Aux sources du bouddhisme*, 247.

6. See Faure, *Le Bouddhisme Ch'an en mal d'histoire*, 99.

7. Mus, *Barabuḍur*, 233.

8. The discussion that follows owes much to the study by Guy Bugault. See *L'Inde pense-t-elle?*, 247.

9. Watson, trans. *The Zen Teachings of Master Lin-chi*, 21–22.

10. See Stein, *Vie et chants de 'Brug-pa Kun-legs le yogin*, 393.

CHAPTER 6

1. Lamotte, *L'enseignement de Vimalakīrti*, 315.

2. Ibid., 192.

3. Faure, *La vision immédiate*, 115.

4. Lamotte, *L'enseignement de Vimalakīrti*, 291.

5. Watson, trans., *The Zen Teachings of Master Lin-chi*, 43.

6. Ibid., 31.

7. Merleau-Ponty, *Éloge de la philosophie*, 191.

8. On this point, see Dumont, *Homo Hierarchicus*.

9. Watson, trans., *The Zen Teachings of Master Lin-chi*, 13.

10. Ibid., 60.

11. Valéry, *Lettres à quelques-uns*, 174.

12. Dōgen, *Shōbōgenzō Genjō kōan*, 134–35.

13. Ibid., 135.

14. Deleuze and Guattari, *Anti-Oedipus*, 1.

15. Silburn, *Aux sources du bouddhisme*, 182.

16. See Faure, *Le Bouddhisme Ch'an en mal d'histoire*, 177.

17. See Silburn, *Aux sources du bouddhisme*, 179.

18. Mujū, *Sand and Pebbles*, 158.

19. See Silburn, *Aux sources du bouddhisme*.

20. Gernet, *Entretiens*, 53–54.

21. Wittgenstein, *Vermischte Bermerkungen*, 7

22. Bugault, *L'Inde pense-t-elle?*, 268.

CHAPTER 7

1. Bergson, *The Two Sources of Morality and Religion*, 316.

2. Ibid., 257.

3. Watson, trans., *The Complete Works of Chuang Tzu*, 26.

4. *Prasannapadā*, introduction, translated by J. May, cited in Bugault, *L'Inde pense-t-elle?*, 264.

5. Rosset, *Le réel et son double*, 60.

6. Ibid., 66.

7. On this question, see Faure, *The Rhetoric of Immediacy*, 53–78.

8. Gauchet, *The Disenchantment of the World*, 202.

9. Michaux, *Misérable miracle*, 20.

10. See Dōgen, *Shōbōgenzō Genjō kōan*, 137–38.

11. Robinet, "Une lecture de Zhuangzi," 113.

12. Merleau-Ponty, *Résumés de cours*, 124.

13. Epictetus, *Manual*, 43.

14. Didi-Huberman, *Devant l'image*, 132.

15. See Tillemans, "La logique bouddhique," 195.

CHAPTER 8

1. Stein, "Étude du monde chinois," 504.

2. Diderot, *Rameau's Nephew*, 255.

3. Freud, *The Interpretation of Dreams*, 335.

4. Watson, trans., *The Zen Teachings of Master Lin-chi*, 26.

5. Watson, trans., *The Complete Works of Chuang Tzu*, 142.

6. Barthes, *The Empire of Signs*, 7–8.

7. Watson, trans., *The Zen Teachings of Master Lin-chi*, 43, 57.

8. Watson, trans., *The Complete Works of Chuang Tzu*, 49.

9. Ibid., 47–48.

10. Cahier de l'Herne, *Henri Michaux*, Paris: Editions de l'Herne, 1966, 30–31.

11. On this question, see See Faure, *Visions of Power*, 114–43.

12. See Dōgen, *Shōbōgenzō*, and Faure, *Rhetoric*, 216–17.

13. Barthes, *The Pleasure of the Text*, 59–60.

14. Freud, *The Interpretation of Dreams*, 388.

15. Ibid., 353.

16. Ibid., 391.

17. Ibid., 564.

18. Ibid., 611.

19. Claudel, *Conversations*, 124–5.

20. Goux, *Oedipus Philosopher*.

21. Dumézil, *La courtisane et les seigneurs colorés*, 36–45.

22. Nietzsche, "Ecce Homo," in *Basic Writings*, 731.

23. Cf. *Sand and Pebbles*, 74.

24. Mauss, "La prière," in *Oeuvres*, 1:385.

25. Mauss, *Sociologie et anthropologie*, 119.

26. Derrida, *Given Time*, 84–107.

27. Watson, trans., *The Zen Teachings of Master Lin-chi*, 9–10.

28. Ibid., 87.

29. Benveniste, *Problems in General Linguistics*, 65–75.

30. Demiéville, *Poèmes chinois d'avant la mort*, 15.

31. Ibid., 90.

32. Ibid., 39–40.

33. Ibid., 44.

34. Ibid., 89.

35. Watson, trans., *The Zen Teachings of Master Lin-chi*, 102–3.

36. See Faure, *Chan Insights and Oversights*, 198.

37. See J. Varenne, *Le Tantrisme*, 178–79.
38. Watson, trans., *The Complete Works of Chuang Tzu*, 302.
39. See Abé and Naskel, *Great Fool*, 152.
40. Merleau-Ponty, *La prose du monde*, 17.
41. Ibid., 201–2.

Bibliography

Abé, Ryuichi, and Peter Naskel. *Great Fool: Great Master Ryōkan*. Honolulu: University of Hawai'i Press, 1996.

Akoun, André, ed. *L'Occident contemporain: mythes et traditions*. Turnhout, Belgium: Brepols, 1991.

Augé, Marc. *Génie du paganisme*. Paris: Gallimard, 1982.

———. *Pour une anthropologie des mondes contemporains*. Paris: Flammarion, 1997.

Austin, J. L. *How to Do Things with Words*. Cambridge, Mass.: Harvard University Press, 1962.

Barthélémy Saint-Hilaire, Jules, *Le Bouddha et sa religion*. Paris: Didier, 1860.

Barthes, Roland. *The Pleasure of the Text*. Trans. Richard Miller. New York: Noonday Press, 1975.

———. *The Empire of Signs*. Trans. Richard Howard. New York: Hill and Wang, 1982.

Bataille. Georges. *Oeuvres complètes*. Vol. 6. Paris: Gallimard, 1970.

Bellour, Raymond, ed. "Henri Michaux." In *Cahiers de l'Herne*. Paris: Editions de l'Herne, 1990.

Benveniste, Émile. *Problems in General Linguistics*. Trans. Mary Elizabeth Meek. Coral Gables: University of Miami Press, 1971.

———. *Indo-European Language and Society*. Trans. Elizabeth Palmer. Coral Gables: University of Miami Press, 1973.

Bergson, Henri. *The Two Sources of Morality and Religion*. Trans. R. Ashley Andra and Cloudsley Brereton. London: Macmillan, 1935.

———. *The Creative Mind*. Trans. Mabelle L. Andison. New York: Philosophical Library, 1946.

Bierce, Ambrose. *The Devil's Dictionary*. New York: Oxford University Press, 1999.

Bonnefoy, Yves. *L'improbable et autres essais*. 1980. Paris: Gallimard, 1992.

Boothroyd, Ninette, and Muriel Détrie. *Le voyage en Chine: Anthologie des voyageurs occidentaux du Moyen Age à la chute de l'empire chinois*. Paris: Robert Laffont, 1992.

Borges, Jorge Luis. *Labyrinths: Selected Stories and Other Writings.* Ed. Donald A. Yates and James E. Irby. New York: New Directions, 1964.

Boureau, Alain. *Le simple corps du roi.* Paris: Editions de Paris, 1988.

Bugault, Guy. *L'Inde pense-t-elle?* Paris: Presses Universitaires de France, 1994.

Cahiers de l'Herne: Henri Michaux. Paris: Editions de l'Herne, 1966.

Certeau, Michel de. *Histoire et psychanalyse entre science et fiction.* Paris: Gallimard, 1987.

Chenet, François, ed. "Nirvāṇa." In *Les Cahiers de l'Herne,* no. 63. Paris: Editions de l'Herne, 1993.

Claudel, Paul. *Connaissance de l'Est.* Paris: Gallimard, 1974.

———.*Conversations dans le Loir-et-Cher.* Paris: Gallimard, 1974.

Collins, Steven. *Selfless Persons: Imagery and Thought in* Theravāda *Buddhism.* Cambridge: Cambridge University Press, 1982.

Conche, Marcel. *Nietzsche et le bouddhisme.* Paris: Encre marine, 1997.

Curval, Philippe. *Regarde fiston s'il n'y a pas un extra-terrestre derrière la bouteille de vin.* Paris: Denoël, 1980.

Davidson, Donald. *Paradoxes de l'irrationalité.* Paris: Editions de l'Eclat, 1991.

Deleuze, Gilles, and Félix Guattari. *Anti-Oedipus: Capitalism and Schizophrenia.* Trans. Robert Hurley, Mark Seem, and Helen R. Lane. Minneapolis: University of Minnesota Press, 1983.

———. *A Thousand Plateaus: Capitalism and Schizophrenia.* Trans. Brian Massumi. Minneapolis: University of Minnesota Press, 1987..

———. *What Is Philosophy?* Trans. Hugh Tomlinson and Graham Burchill. New York: Columbia University Press, 1994.

De Man, Paul. *Allegories of Reading.* New Haven: Yale University Press, 1979.

Demiéville, Paul. *Le concile de Lhasa.* Paris: Presses Universitaires de France, 1952.

———. *Poèmes chinois d'avant la mort.* Trans. Jean-Pierre Diény. Paris: Asiathèque, 1984.

Derrida, Jacques. *Given Time: I. Counterfeit Money.* Trans Peggy Kamuf. Chicago: Univeristy of Chicago Press, 1992.

———.*Of Grammatology.* Trans. Gayatri Chakravorty Spirak. Baltimore: Johns Hopkins University Press, 1997.

———. "Faith and Knowledge: The Two Sources of 'Religion' at the Limits of Reason Alone." Trans. Samuel Weber. In *Religion,* ed. Jacques Derrida and Gianni Vattimo. Stanford: Stanford University Press, 1998.

Descombes, Vincent. *Philosophie par gros temps.* Paris: Editions de Minuit, 1989.

Dewey, John. *Logic: The Theory of Inquiry.* New York: Holt, 1938.

Diderot, Denis. *Rameau's Nephew.* Trans. Jacques Barzun. Chicago: University of Chicago Press, 1990.

Didi-Huberman, Georges. *Devant l'image.* Paris: Editions de Minuit, 1990.

Dōgen. *Shōbōgenzō*. In the Taishō edition of the Buddhist canon, ed. Takakusu Junjirō and Watanabe Kaigyoku. Tokyo: Taishō issaikyō kankōkai, 1924–1932. Vol. 82, 2582.

————. *Shōbōgenzō Genjō kōan*. Trans. Norman Waddell. *The Eastern Buddhist* 5, 2, 1972: 129–40.

Droit, Roger-Pol. *L'oubli de l'Inde: Une amnésie philosophique*. Paris: Presses Universitaires de France, 1989.

————. *The Cult of Nothingness: The Philosophers and the Buddha*. Trans. David Streight and Pamela Anderson. Chapel Hill: University of North Carolina Press, 2000.

Dumézil, Georges. *La courtisane et les seigneurs colorés: Esquisses de mythologie*. Paris: Gallimard, 1983.

Dumont, Louis. *Homo Hierarchicus: The Caste System and Its Implications*. Trans. Mark Sainsbury. Chicago: University of Chicago Press, 1970.

Durkheim, Émile. *The Elementary Forms of Religious Life*. Trans. K. E. Fields. New York: Free Press, 1995.

Duthuit, Georges. *Représentation et présence: Premiers écrits et travaux, 1923–1952*. Paris: Flammarion, 1974.

Elster, John. *Sour Grapes: Studies in the Subversion of Rationality*. Cambridge, Cambridge University Press, 1983.

Epictetus. *Epictetus: The Discourses as Reported by Arrian, the Manual, and Fragments*. Trans. W. A. Oldfather. 2 vols. Loeb Classical Library. New York: Putnam's Sons, 1926–28.

Farouki, Nayla. *La foi et la raison: Histoire d'un malentendu*. Paris: Flammarion, 1996.

Faure, Bernard. *La vision immédiate: Nature, éveil, et tradition selon le Sōbōgenzō*. Aix-en-Provence: Le Mail, 1987.

————. *Le Bouddhisme Ch'an en mal d'histoire: Genèse d'une tradition religieuse dans la Chine des T'ang*. Paris: École Française d'Extrême-Orient, 1989.

————. *The Rhetoric of Immediacy: a Cultural Critic of Chan/Zen Buddhism*, Princeton, Princeton University Press, 1991.

————. *Chan Insights and Oversights: An Epistemological Critique of the Chan Tradition*. Princeton: Princeton University Press, 1993.

————. *Visions of Power: Imagining Medieval Japanese Buddhism*. Princeton: Princeton University Press, 1996.

————. *The Red Thread: Buddhist Approaches to Sexuality*. Princeton: Princeton University Press, 1998.

————. *The Power of Denial: Buddhism, Purity, and Gender*. Princeton: Princeton University Press, 2003.

————, trans. *Le traité de Bodhidharma: Première anthologie du bouddhisme Ch'an.* Aix-en-Provence, Le Mail, 1986.

Ferry, Luc. *L'homme-dieu, Ou le sens de la vie.* Paris: Grasset, 1996.

Foucault, Michel. *Madness and Civilization.* Trans. Richard Howard. New York: Pantheon, 1965.

————. "Structuralism and Poststructuralism." In Michel Foucault, *Aesthetics, Method, and Epistemology,* ed. Paul Rabinow. New York: The New Press, 1994, 433–58.

————. "What is Enlightenment?" In Michel Foucault, *Ethics, Subjectivity, and Truth,* ed. Paul Rabinow. New York: The New Press, 1994, 303–19.

Freud, Sigmund. "The Uncanny." In *Collected Papers.* Vol. 4. Trans. and ed. Joan Rivière. New York: Basic Books, 1959, 368–407.

————. *Civilization and Its Discontents.* Trans. James Strachey. New York: W. W. Norton, 1961.

————. *The Future of an Illusion.* Trans. James Strachey. New York: W.W. Norton, 1961.

————. *Totem and Taboo.* London: Ark Paperbacks, 1983.

Gauchet, Marcel. *The Disenchantment of the World: A Political History of Religion.* Trans. Oscar Burge. Princeton: Princeton University Press, 1997.

Gernet, Jacques, trans. *Les entretiens du maître de dhyāna Chen-houei du Ho-tsö.* Paris: Adrien Maisonneuve, 1949. Reprint, Paris: École française d'Extrême-Orient, 1977.

Goux, Jean-Joseph. *Les iconoclastes.* Paris: Le Seuil, 1978.

————. *The Coiners of Language.* Trans Jennifer Curtiss Gage. Norman: University of Oklahoma Press, 1994.

————. *Symbolic Economies: After Marx and Freud.* Ithaca: Cornell University Press, 1990.

————. *Oedipus, Philosopher.* Trans Catherine Porter. Stanford: Stanford University press, 1993.

Groethuysen, Bernard. *Origines de l'esprit bourgeois en France.* 1927. Reed. Paris: Gallimard, 1977.

Hegel, G. W. H. *The Philosophy of History.* Great Books of the Western World. Chicago: Encyclopaedia Britannica, 1952.

Geertz, Clifford. *Works and Lives: The Anthropologist as Author.* Stanford: Stanford University Press, 1988.

Heidegger, Martin. *Introduction to Metaphysics.* Trans. Gregory Fried and Richard Polt. New Haven: Yale University Press, 2000.

Hofstadter, Douglas R. *Gödel, Escher, Bach: An Eternal Golden Braid.* New York: Vintage Books, 1989.

Horkheimer, Max, and Theodor W. Adorno. *The Dialectic of Enlightenment.* Trans. John Cumming. London: Verso, 1997.

Hulin, Michel. *La mystique sauvage: Aux antipodes de l'esprit.* Paris: Presses Universitaires de France, 1993.

Jankélévitch, Vladimir. *Le pur et l'impur.* 1960. Paris: Flammarion, 1990.

Jourdain, Stephen. *Éveil.* Paris: Le Temps qu'il fait, 1985.

Jullien, François. "Naissance de l'imagination: Essai de problématique au travers de la réflexion littéraire de la Chine et de l'Occident." *Extrême-Orient, Extrême-Occident* no. 7 (1986): 23–81.

———. *Detour and Access: Strategies of Meaning in China and Greece.* Trans. Sophie Hawkes. New York: Zone Books, 2000.

LaCapra, Dominick. *Emile Durkheim, Sociologist and Philosopher.* Ithaca: Cornell University Press, 1972.

La Vallée Poussin, Louis de. *Le dogme et la philosophie du bouddhisme.* Paris: Beauchesne, 1930.

Lacroix, Michel. *L'idéologie du New Age.* Paris: Flammarion, 1995.

Lamotte, Etienne, trans. *L'enseignement de Vimalakīrti (Vimalakīrtinirdeśa).* Paris: Peeters, 1987.

Leiris, Michel. *Langage tangage, Ou ce que les mots me disent.* Paris: Gallimard, 1995.

Lévi-Strauss, Claude. *The Savage Mind.* Chicago: University of Chicago Press, 1966.

———. *The Raw and the Cooked.* London: Pimplico, 1994.

Lopez, Donald S. *Prisoners of Shangri-La: Tibetan Buddhism and the West.* Chicago: University of Chicago Press, 1998.

Lyotard, Jean-François. "Discussion entre Jean-François Lyotard et Richard Rorty." In "La traversée de l'Atlantique." *Critique* no. 456 (1985).

Malamoud, Charles. *Cooking the World: Ritual and Thought in Ancient India.* Trans. David G. White. New York: Oxford University Press, 1996.

Mannoni, Octave. *Clefs pour l'imaginaire, Ou l'autre scène.* 1969. Paris: Le Seuil, 1985.

Mauss, Marcel. *Sociologie et anthropologie.* Paris: Presses Universitaires de France, 1950.

———. *Oeuvres.* 3 vols. Paris: Editions de Minuit, 1968.

Merleau-Ponty, Maurice. *Éloge de la philosophie et autres essais.* Gallimard, 1960.

———. *Résumés de cours.* Paris: Gallimard, 1968.

———. *Le visible et l'invisible.* Paris: Gallimard, 1968.

———. *La prose du monde.* Paris, Gallimard, 1969.

———. *In Praise of Philosophy and Other Essays.* Trans. John Wild and James Edie. Evanston, Ill.: Northwestern University Press, 1988.

Michaux, Henri. *Un barbare en Asie.* 1933. Paris: Gallimard, 1986.

———. *Misérable miracle: La mescaline.* Paris: Gallimard, 1991.

Montaigne, Michel de. *The Complete Essays of Montaigne.* Trans. Donald M. Frame. Stanford: Stanford University Press, 1958.

Mujū, *Sand and Pebbles (Shasekishū): The Tales of Mujū Ichien; A Voice for Pluralism in Kamakura Buddhism.* Trans. Robert E. Morrell. Albany: State University of New York Press, 1985.

Mus, Paul. *Barabuḍur.* Trans. Alexander W. Macdonald. New Delhi: Indira Gandhi National Center for the Arts, 1998.

Nathan, Tobie. *Psychanalyse païenne: Essais ethno-psychanalytiques.* Paris: Odile Jacob, 1995.

Nietzsche, Friedrich. *The Will to Power.* Trans R. J. Hollingdale. Ed. Walter Kaufmann. New York: Random House, 1967.

———. *Le livre du philosophe: Études théorétiques.* Paris: Flammarion, 1991.

———. *The Basic Writings of Nietzsche.* Trans. Walter Kaufmann. New York: Modern Library, 1992.

Quignard, Pascal. *Rhétorique spéculative.* Paris: Gallimard, 1997.

Rank, Otto. *Don Juan et le double.* 1932. Paris: Payot, 1997.

Renou, Louis, and Jean Filliozat. *L'Inde classique: Manuel des études indiennes.* 2 vols. Paris: École française d'Extrême-Orient, 1996.

Robinet, Isabelle. "Une lecture de Zhuangzi." *Études chinoises* 15, nos. 1–2, 1996.

Rorty, Richard, "Le cosmopolitanisme sans émancipation: En réponse à François Lyotard." *Critique* no. 456 (1985): 569–80.

Rosset, Clément. *Le principe de cruauté.* Paris: Editions de Minuit, 1988.

———. *Le réel et son double: Essai sur l'illusion.* Paris: Gallimard, 1993.

———. *Le démon de la tautologie.* Paris: Editions de Minuit. 1997.

Saint-Denys, Hervey de. *Les rêves et les moyens de les diriger.* 1867. Paris: Tchou, 1964.

Saul, John R. *Voltaire's Bastards: The Dictatorship of Reason in the West.* New York: The Free Press, 1992.

Schwab, Raymond. *The Oriental Renaissance: Europe's Rediscovery of India and the East, 1680–1888.* New York: Columbia University Press, 1987.

Segalen, Victor. *Lettres de Chine.* Collection 10–18. 1967. Paris: Union Générale d'Editions, 1993.

———. *Oeuvres complètes.* 2 vols. Paris: Laffont, 1995.

Silburn, Lilian, ed. *Aux sources du bouddhisme.* Paris: Fayard, 1997.

Stein, Rolf A. *Vie et chants de 'Brug-pa kun-legs le yogin.* Paris: Maisonneuve et Larose, 1972.

———. "Étude du monde chinois: Institutions et concepts." *Annuaire du Collège de France,* 1974.

Strickmann, Michel. *Mantras et mandarins: Le bouddhisme tantrique en Chine.* Paris: Gallimard, 1996.

Suzuki, Daisetz T. *Zen and Japanese Culture.* 1959. Princeton: Princeton University Press, 1970.

Takakusu Junjirō, *The Essentials of Buddhist Philosophy.* Ed. Wing-tsit Chan and Charles A. Moore. Honolulu: University of Hawai'i Press, 1947.

Tillemans, Tom J. F. "La logique bouddhique est-elle une logique non-classique ou déviante? Remarques sur le tétralemme (*catuṣkoti*)." *Les cahiers de philosophie* no. 14 (1992): 183–89.

Valéry, Paul. *Tel quel I.* Paris: Gallimard, 1941.

———. *Tel quel II.* Paris: Gallimard, 1943.

———. *Monsieur Teste.* Paris: Gallimard, 1978.

———. *Lettres à quelques-uns.* Paris: Gallimard, 1977.

———. "Discours sur l'esthétique." In *Oeuvres*, vol 1. Ed. Jean Hytier. Paris: Gallimard, 1957.

Varenne, Jean. *Le Tantrisme: Mythes, rites, métaphysique.* Paris: Albin Michel, 1997.

Vernant, Jean-Pierre. *Myth and Thought among the Greeks.* London: Routledge, Kegan Paul, 1983.

Watson, Burton, trans. *The Complete Works of Chuang Tzu.* New York: Columbia University Press, 1968.

———, trans. *The Lotus Sūtra.* New York: Columbia University Press, 1993.

———, trans. *The Zen Teachings of Master Lin-chi: A Translation of the Lin-chi lu.* New York: Columbia University Press, 1993.

Weber, Max. *The Protestant Ethic and the Spirit of Capitalism.* London: Routledge, 2001.

Welbon, Richard. *The Buddhist Nirvāṇa and Its Western Interpreters.* Chicago: University of Chicago Press, 1968.

Wittgenstein, Ludwig. *The Blue and Brown Books.* New York: Harper and Row, 1960.

———. *Vermischte Bemerkungen.* Ed. Georg Henrik von Wright, in cooperation with Keikki Nyman. Oxford: Blackwell, 1977.

———. *Remarks on Frazer's Golden Bough.* Trans. A. C. Miles. Atlantic Highlands, N.J.: Humanities Press International, 1979.

Yü, Chün-fang. "Chung-feng Ming-pen and Ch'an Buddhism in the Yüan." In *Yüan Thought: Chinese Thought and Religion under the Mongols*, ed. Hoklam Chan and William Theodore de Bary. New York: Columbia University Press, 1982, 419–47.

Index

Abhidharma, 89–90
Agramati, 142
Ajase (complex of), 147
Ajataśatru. *See* Ajase
alayavijñāna, 91, 106
anātman, 108ff. *See also* ātman
analytic philosophy, 32–33, 47
ātman, 89, 109, 111
Aristotle, 23, 94
Artaud (Antonin), 10
Asaṅga, 92
Avalokiteśvara, 12, 116

Baizhang, 105, 123
Barthélémy Saint-Hilaire (Jules), 3
Barthes (Roland), 148, 151
Bashō (Matsuo), 135
Bateson (Gregory), 169
Benveniste (Émile), 37–38, 44, 70–71,
    87, 166
Bergson (Maurice), 23, 74, 76–78,
    125–26
Bierce (Ambrose), 21, 69, 133; on Kant,
    26
Biyan lu, 54

Bodhidharma, 99. *See also Treatise of
    Bodhidharma*
Bonnefoy (Yves), 31
Borges (Jorge Luis), 39, 78
Brahmanism, 109. *See also* Hinduism
Budai (Jpn: Hotei), 67
Buddha: and Mahākāśyapa, 98; and
    Māra, 156–59; as philosopher, 159–60;
    Segalen on the, 61
Buddhism: and Daoism, 51; and Confu-
    cianism, 51; and the Internet, 16–17; as
    humanism, 13–14; Chinese, 49–51;
    Protestant, 15; Tantric, 13, 50, 161,
    169–70; Tibetan, 10–12
Buddhist art, 60–61
Bugault (Guy), 34–35
burakumin (outcasts), 108
Burnouf (Eugène), 3
Candrakīrti (eighth century), 67, 94–95,
    168. *See also* Mādhyamika
Catholicism, 14–15, 75
Chan (Zen), 54, 58–59, 97–98, 136, 148
Char (René), 89
China: and scientific thought, 33–34
Chinese thought, 52–56. *See also* Confu-
    cianism, Daoism, Chinese Buddhism

Christianity, 14–15, 65, 75–77
Cicero, 70
cintāmaṇi (wish-fulfilling jewel), 155
Claudel (Paul), 4, 85, 154–55
Co-dependent origination (skt. *pratītya-samutpāda*), 89, 107
cogito, 24–25. *See also* Descartes
Confucianism, 52–57
Confucius (Kongfuzi), 51, 53–54, 75, 96, 149
Cros (Charles), 88

Dainichi (skt. Mahāvairocana), 161
Dalai Lama, 10–12, 17
Daoism, 50–51
Daowu Yuanzhi (768–853), 123
Daoxin (580–651), 136
death poems, 166–67
Debussy (Claude), 61
Deleuze (Gilles) and Guattari (Félix), 27–28, 114
de Man (Paul), 39
Demiéville (Paul), 74
demythologization, 15
Derrida (Jacques), 70, 76–78, 164
Descartes (René), 22, 24–25, 41, 93, 158–59
Descombes (Vincent), 29, 33–34, 43, 45–46
Dewey (John), 35
dharma, 87
dharmadhātu, 106
dhyāna, 148
Diderot (Denis), 145
Didi-Huberman (Georges), 138
Dinouart (Father), 168
Dōgen (1200–1253), 102, 107–8, 113, 117, 132–33, 145, 151
Dongshan Liangjie (807–869), 167
Dorje Shugden, 11
disenchantment of the world, 28
Dokuan Dokugo, 124
dreams, 151–52

Droit (Roger-Pol), 2
Drugpa Künleg, 98
Dumézil (Georges), 156
Durkheim (Émile), 71, 73

Enlightenment, 41–44

Farouki (Nayla), 21, 28, 78–79
Favret-Saada (Jeanne), 29, 47
Feuerbach (Ludwig), 84
Flaubert (Gustave), 19
Foucault (Michel), 41–42, 45
Frazer (James), 46
Freud (Sigmund), 30, 42–43, 47, 81–85, 129, 134, 145–47, 151–53
Frontibus, 26

Gauchet (Marcel), 130, 74–75, 85
Geertz (Clifford), 23, 32
Gelugpa, 11
Goux (Jean-Joseph), 44, 156ff
Gozan (Five Mountains), 163
Gradualism, 122 ff. *See also* Subitism, Sudden and Gradual
Groethuysen (Bernard), 75
Guangren (837–909), 167
Guifeng Zongmi (780–841), 107, 155–56

Habermas (Jürgen), 45–47
Heart Sūtra. See Hṛdaya Sūtra
Hegel (G.W.F.), 4, 6–7, 18, 23, 128
Heidegger (Martin), 20, 133
Hīnayana, 86–88. *See also* Mahāyāna
Hinduism, 80, 109
Horkheimer (Max) and Adorno (Theodor W.), 38, 44
Hṛdaya Sūtra (*Heart Sūtra*), 116
Hubert (Henri) and Mauss (Marcel), 71, 123. *See also* Mauss
Hulin (Michel), 83
Huineng, 91–92, 95, 119
Hundun (Chaos), 58–59

immanence, 27, 129. *See also* transcendence

immediacy, 127–29

Inari, 155

intermediary being (skt. *antarabhāva*, Jpn. *chūu*), 108

Ionesco (Eugène), 32

James (William), 29–30, 106

Jansenists, 75

Jesuits, 75, 96

Jourdain (Stephen), 121–22, 132

Joyce (James), 24–25

Jullien (François), 52ff

Kangiten (Tantric deity), 135

Kant (Emmanuel), 25–26, 41–42, 47, 76–77, 130

karagokoro ("Chinese Mind"), 56

karma, 89, 103ff, 108

Kcizan Jōkin (1268–1325), 150

kōan (ch. *gong'an*, "case"), 54, 98–99, 105, 139, 162–63, 166

Kojiki, 56

kokugaku (National Learning), 56

Krishnamurti (Jiddu), 73

Kumārājiva, 168

LaCapra (Dominick), 73

Lamaism, 59. *See also* Tibetan Buddhism

Laozi, 50–51, 166

La Vallée Poussin (Louis de), 1

Lawrence (David Herbert), 138

Leibniz (W. G.), 56

Leiris (Michel), 21, 101

Lévi (sylvain), 71

Levinas (Emmanuel), 96

Lévi-Strauss (Claude), 28, 32, 46–47, 147

Linji Yixuan, 53, 55, 73, 97–99, 104–5, 112–13, 120, 147–49, 157, 164–65, 168

Locke (John), 44

Lyotard (Jean-François), 8

Mādhyamika, 94ff, 111–12

madness, 45–46

magic, 46–47. *See also* witchcraft

Mahākāśyapa, 98, 169

Mahāyāna (Great Vehicle), 13–14, 68, 88, 104, 112, 144

Malamoud (Charles), 72

Maṇḍalas (Two), 161

mantra, 166

Manzan Dōhaku (1636–1715), 59

Māra, 156–59

Marx (Karl), 5, 44–45

Mauss (Marcel), 28–29, 162, 164

Mazu Daoyi (709–788), 148

meditation, 25, 148–49

Merleau-Ponty (Maurice), 7, 64, 110, 137, 171–72

Michaux (Henri), 30, 79–80, 90, 131, 150

Middle Way, 66, 115–16, 136. *See also* Mādhyamika

Milinda, 108–9

monotheism, 74, 78–79

Montaigne (Michel de), 23

Mujū Ichien (1226–1312), 117–18

Mus (Paul), 28, 47, 66, 95

Musil (Robert), 113

mysticism, 79–85

myth, 24, 43, 74

Nāgārjuna, 67, 94–96, 101, 115–17, 123, 162. *See also* Mādhyamika

nāga (dragon), 157

Nāgasena, 108–10

Naitō Kōnan, 5

Nanyue Huairang (677–744), 148

Nāropa (1016–1120), 152

Neobuddhism, 6, 17

New Age, 16–17, 43

Nietzsche (Friedrich), 14, 23, 37–41, 44–45, 77–79, 82, 158

Nirvāṇa: 14, 90, 110; and *saṃsāra*, 79, 101–2; *is* saṃsāra, 140; principle, 14, 84

Oedipus, 81, 156–59
Onmyōdō (Way of the Yin and Yang), 50
Orientalism, 5–7, 65
Oriental Renaissance, 2
Ozeray (Michel-Jean-François), 3

Pascal (Blaise), 108, 111, 172
Plato, 133
polytheism, 24, 69, 79
Prasannendriya, 142
Presocratics, 23
Protestantism, 45, 74–75
psychoanalysis, 42–43. *See also* Freud
pudgala (self, person), 111
Pudgalavāda, 111
Puhua, 165

Quignard (Paul), 26–27

Rahula (Walpula), 13
religio, 70
Ricci (Matteo), 13, 75
Rinzai (Zen), 99. *See also* Linji Yixuan
Ritual, 71–72, 161ff
Robinet (Isabelle), 53, 56
Rolland (Romain), 82–84
Rorty (Richard), 7–8
Rosset (Clement), 127, 130–31
Rousseau, 19
Russel (Bertrand), 32
Ryōbu Shintō, 160–61
Ryōkan (1758–1831), 171

sacred and profane, 71
Saint-Denys (Hervé de), 153
Śākyamuni. *See* Buddha
samādhi, 150
saṃdha-bhāsya (intentional language), 169–70
Saul (John), 18
Saussure (Ferdinand de), 166
Schiller (Friedrich von), 83

Schopenhauer (Arthur), 4, 14
Segalen (Victor), 60–63
Sengzhao (378–414), 36, 166
sexuality (Buddhist), 143, 170
Shasekishū, 161. *See also* Mujū Ichien
Shenhui (684–758), 121
Shenxiu (606–706), 117, 119
Shintō, 160–61
smṛti, 146
Socrates, 22–23, 68, 70, 99
Sōtō (Zen), 99. *See also* Dōgen, Keizan Jōkin, Manzan Dōhaku
Spinoza, 151
stūpa, 58
subitism, 74. *See also* Sudden and Gradual
Sudden and Gradual, 119ff
Śunyatā (Emptiness), 115ff
Suzuki (Daisetsu), 4, 6

Takakusu (Junjirō), 86
Tantric Buddhism. *See* Buddhism
Tantrism, 59, 143. *See also* Tantric Buddhism
Tenryūji, 106
tetralemma, 86, 94, 139–40
Three Jewels, 65
Tillemans (Tom), 139
Tintin and Milou, 45
transcendence, 53–56, 130, 170
transcendental concepts, 28, 101ff
Treatise of Bodhidharma (Ch. *Damo lun*), 136–37
Tsongkhapa, 139
Truths (Two), 95, 118, *and passim*
Tibetan Buddhism. *See* Buddhism

Vajrayāna (Diamond Vehicle), 59, 87–88. *See also* Tantric Buddhism
Valéry (Paul), 21–22, 27, 31, 33–34, 109, 112, 138
Varenne (Jean), 130
Vedantism, 96

Vedic ritual, 71–72
Vijñānavāda, 91
Vimalakīrti, 68, 102, 168
Vimalakīrti Sūtra, 101
Vinaya, 16, 90
Voisins (Augusto Gilbert de), 62–63
Voltaire, 18–19, 77

Weber (Max), 28, 45, 74–75
witchcraft, 29, 47
Wittgenstein (Ludwig), 5, 22, 25–26,
    31–33, 46, 125, 171
World Parliament of Religions, 4
Wumen Huikai (1183–1260), 169
Wuxue Zuyuan (Jpn. Mugaku Sogen,
    1226–86), 167
Wuzong (Emperor), 51

Xutong (1185–1269), 167

Yangshan Huiji (ca. 814–891), 124
Yijing, 27, 56, 144
Yin-Yang, 50. *See also* Onmyōdō
Yogācāra, 91–92, 111, 143
Yun'yan Tansheng (781?–841), 123

Zen: 6, 16, 99–100, *see also* Chan, Rin-
    zai, Sōtō; gardens, 15
Zhen'yan (Jpn. Shingon), 50, 59
Zhongfen Mingben (1263–1323), 58–59
Zhuangzi, 47, 57–58, 96, 103, 107,
    127–28, 147–49, 170
Zongmi. *See* Guifeng Zongmi

Cultural Memory | *in the Present*

Bernard Faure, *Double Exposure: Cutting Across Buddhist and Western Discourses*

Alessia Ricciardi, *The Ends Of Mourning: Psychoanalysis, Literature, Film*

Alain Badiou, *Saint Paul: The Foundation of Universalism*

Gil Anidjar, *The Jew, The Arab: A History of the Enemy*

Jonathan Culler and Kevin Lamb, eds., *Just Being Difficult? Academic Writing in the Public Arena*

Jean-Luc Nancy, *A Finite Thinking*, edited by Simon Sparks

Theodor W. Adorno, *Can One Live after Auschwitz? A Philosophical Reader*, edited by Rolf Tiedemann

Patricia Pisters, *The Matrix of Visual Culture: Working with Deleuze in Film Theory*

Talal Asad, *Formations of the Secular: Christianity, Islam, Modernity*

Dorothea von Mücke, *The Rise of the Fantastic Tale*

Marc Redfield, *The Politics of Aesthetics: Nationalism, Gender, Romanticism*

Emmanuel Levinas, *On Escape*

Dan Zahavi, *Husserl's Phenomenology*

Rodolphe Gasché, *The Idea of Form: Rethinking Kant's Aesthetics*

Michael Naas, *Taking on the Tradition: Jacques Derrida and the Legacies of Deconstruction*

Herlinde Pauer-Studer, ed., *Constructions of Practical Reason: Interviews on Moral and Political Philosophy*

Jean-Luc Marion, *Being Given: Toward a Phenomenology of Givenness*

Theodor W. Adorno and Max Horkheimer, *Dialectic of Enlightenment*

Ian Balfour, *The Rhetoric of Romantic Prophecy*

Martin Stokhof, *World and Life as One: Ethics and Ontology in Wittgenstein's Early Thought*

Gianni Vattimo, *Nietzsche: An Introduction*

Jacques Derrida, *Negotiations: Interventions and Interviews, 1971–1998*, ed. Elizabeth Rottenberg

Brett Levinson, *The Ends of Literature: Post-transition and Neoliberalism in the Wake of the "Boom"*

Timothy J. Reiss, *Against Autonomy: Global Dialectics of Cultural Exchange*

Hent de Vries and Samuel Weber, eds., *Religion and Media*

Niklas Luhmann, *Theories of Distinction: Redescribing the Descriptions of Modernity*, ed. and introd. William Rasch

Johannes Fabian, *Anthropology with an Attitude: Critical Essays*

Michel Henry, *I Am the Truth: Toward a Philosophy of Christianity*

Gil Anidjar, *"Our Place in Al-Andalus": Kabbalah, Philosophy, Literature in Arab-Jewish Letters*

Hélène Cixous and Jacques Derrida, *Veils*

F. R. Ankersmit, *Historical Representation*

F. R. Ankersmit, *Political Representation*

Elissa Marder, *Dead Time: Temporal Disorders in the Wake of Modernity (Baudelaire and Flaubert)*

Reinhart Koselleck, *The Practice of Conceptual History: Timing History, Spacing Concepts*

Niklas Luhmann, *The Reality of the Mass Media*

Hubert Damisch, *A Childhood Memory by Piero della Francesca*

Hubert Damisch, *A Theory of /Cloud/: Toward a History of Painting*

Jean-Luc Nancy, *The Speculative Remark (One of Hegel's Bons Mots)*

Jean-François Lyotard, *Soundproof Room: Malraux's Anti-Aesthetics*

Jan Patočka, *Plato and Europe*

Hubert Damisch, *Skyline: The Narcissistic City*

Isabel Hoving, *In Praise of New Travelers: Reading Caribbean Migrant Women Writers*

Richard Rand, ed., *Futures: Of Derrida*

William Rasch, *Niklas Luhmann's Modernity: The Paradox of System Differentiation*

Jacques Derrida and Anne Dufourmantelle, *Of Hospitality*

Jean-François Lyotard, *The Confession of Augustine*

Kaja Silverman, *World Spectators*

Samuel Weber, *Institution and Interpretation: Expanded Edition*

Jeffrey S. Librett, *The Rhetoric of Cultural Dialogue: Jews and Germans in the Epoch of Emancipation*

Ulrich Baer, *Remnants of Song: Trauma and the Experience of Modernity in Charles Baudelaire and Paul Celan*

Samuel C. Wheeler III, *Deconstruction as Analytic Philosophy*

David S. Ferris, *Silent Urns: Romanticism, Hellenism, Modernity*

Rodolphe Gasché, *Of Minimal Things: Studies on the Notion of Relation*

Sarah Winter, *Freud and the Institution of Psychoanalytic Knowledge*

Samuel Weber, *The Legend of Freud: Expanded Edition*

Aris Fioretos, ed., *The Solid Letter: Readings of Friedrich Hölderlin*

J. Hillis Miller / Manuel Asensi, *Black Holes / J. Hillis Miller; or, Boustrophedonic Reading*

Miryam Sas, *Fault Lines: Cultural Memory and Japanese Surrealism*

Peter Schwenger, *Fantasm and Fiction: On Textual Envisioning*

Didier Maleuvre, *Museum Memories: History, Technology, Art*

Jacques Derrida, *Monolingualism of the Other; or, The Prosthesis of Origin*

Andrew Baruch Wachtel, *Making a Nation, Breaking a Nation: Literature and Cultural Politics in Yugoslavia*

Niklas Luhmann, *Love as Passion: The Codification of Intimacy*

Mieke Bal, ed., *The Practice of Cultural Analysis: Exposing Interdisciplinary Interpretation*

Jacques Derrida and Gianni Vattimo, eds., *Religion*